Mary Bratton, MS, LPCC, MA

From Surviving to Thriving
A Therapist's Guide to Stage II Recovery for Survivors of Childhood Abuse

Pre-publication
REVIEW . . .

"**D**rawing on the knowledge gained from her years of experience and from a practitioner's perspective, Mary Bratton tells what works for survivors of trauma. There are not enough adjectives to describe what Bratton has captured in this book. She takes a life-long debilitating disorder and unravels its intricacies in concise, succinct, and understandable language. She explicitly explains the impact of trauma and the normal reactions by the victims. She acknowledges that people do survive their childhood traumas through an array of brilliant and ingenious coping mechanisms but they never escape them. Bratton provides the reader with the key to open and go beyond the victim's debilitating locked door by discussing how to work with and provide treatment for an individual's traumatic experience. This guide to Stage II recovery is a must read for all, including survivors."

Phillip A. Whitner, PhD
Sr. Staff Counselor,
University Counseling Center,
The University of Toledo,
Ohio

From Surviving to Thriving
A Therapist's Guide
to Stage II Recovery for Survivors
of Childhood Abuse

THE HAWORTH MALTREATMENT & TRAUMA PRESS
Robert A. Geffner, PhD
Senior Editor

New, Recent, and Forthcoming Titles:

Sexual, Physical, and Emotional Abuse in Out-of-Home Care: Prevention Skills for At-Risk Children by Toni Cavanagh Johnson and Associates

Cedar House: A Model Child Abuse Treatment Program by Bobbi Kendig with Clara Lowry

Bridging Worlds: Understanding and Facilitating Adolescent Recovery from the Trauma of Abuse by Joycee Kennedy and Carol McCarthy

The Learning About Myself (LAMS) Program for At-Risk Parents: Learning from the Past—Changing the Future by Verna Rickard

The Learning About Myself (LAMS) Program for At-Risk Parents: Handbook for Group Participants by Verna Rickard

Treating Children with Sexually Abusive Behavior Problems: Guidelines for Child and Parent Intervention by Jan Ellen Burton, Lucinda A. Rasmussen, Julie Bradshaw, Barbara J. Christopherson, and Steven C. Huke

Bearing Witness: Violence and Collective Responsibility by Sandra L. Bloom and Michael Reichert

Sibling Abuse Trauma: Assessment and Intervention Strategies for Children, Families, and Adults by John V. Caffaro and Allison Conn-Caffaro

From Surviving to Thriving: A Therapist's Guide to Stage II Recovery for Survivors of Childhood Abuse by Mary Bratton

"I Never Told Anyone This Before": Managing the Initial Disclosure of Abuse Re-Collections by Janice A. Gasker

Breaking the Silence: Group Therapy for Childhood Sexual Abuse, A Practitioner's Manual by Judith A. Margolin

From Surviving to Thriving
A Therapist's Guide to Stage II Recovery for Survivors of Childhood Abuse

Mary Bratton, MS, LPCC, MAC

HMTP

The Haworth Maltreatment and Trauma Press
An Imprint of The Haworth Press, Inc.
New York • London

Published by

The Haworth Maltreatment and Trauma Press, Inc., an imprint of The Haworth Press, Inc., 10 Alice Street, Binghamton, NY 13904-1580

The Haworth Press, Inc., 10 Alice Street, Binghamton, NY 13904-1580

Cover design by Monica L. Seifert.

Library of Congress Cataloging-in-Publication Data

Bratton, Mary.
    From surviving to thriving : a therapist's guide to stage II recovery for survivors of childhood abuse / Mary Bratton.
      p. cm.
    Includes bibliographical references and index.
    ISBN 0-7890-0256-6 (alk. paper).
    1. Adult child sexual abuse victims—Psychology. 2. Adult child sexual abuse victims—Mental health. 3. Adult child sexual abuse victims—Rehabilitation. I. Title.
RC569.5.A28B73 1999
616.85'8223906—dc21
                                                                             98-39341
                                                                                                   CIP

This book is a tribute to all the people who have allowed me the privilege to be a partner on their journey to recovery. Underpinning and illustrating the content of the book are excerpts from the journal of one exceptionally strong and courageous young woman, who chooses to be called Jessica in these pages. Interspersed throughout the text are poems, writings, and artwork by other survivors. Because of legal considerations, none of them can take full credit for their contributions, and even first names have been altered. Here, unconnected to their creations and stories, I wish to acknowledge them for who they really are. With gratitude and admiration, this book is dedicated to my clients, who have gifted me with both their pain and their healing.

*With love to Murray, Riley, and Drew
for their encouragement, confidence, and support*

ABOUT THE AUTHOR

Mary Bratton, MS, LPCC, MAC, presently maintains a private psychotherapy practice at Harbor Behavioral Healthcare in Toledo, Ohio, where she specializes in treatment of adult survivors of childhood trauma and abuse. She also provides training and consultation services as Director of Intervention Resources. Before coming to Harbor Behavioral Healthcare, she gained ten years' experience as a family therapist and family interventionist at a major inpatient/outpatient chemical dependency treatment facility in Toledo. A member of the National Association of Alcohol and Drug Abuse Counselors (NAADAC), she is a frequent speaker at professional conferences and workshops, including the U.S. Journal Conference on Codependency and Adult Children in Cincinnati, Ohio; the Institute for Drug and Alcohol Studies in Evansville, Indiana; the Ohio Drug and Alcohol Studies Institute in Gambier and Columbus, Ohio; the All Ohio Counselors Conference in Columbus, Ohio; and the Child Sexual Abuse Treatment Institute in Toledo, Ohio. Most recently, she was keynote speaker at the Children in Crisis Conference in Highland, Indiana, and at the Indiana Foster Care and Adoption Association Training Institute in Indianapolis. The author of numerous journal articles on various aspects of family and survivor therapy, including publications in *The Counselor, Focus,* and *Changes,* she is also the author of *A Guide to Family Intervention* (Health Communications, Inc., 1987).

CONTENTS

Preface

This is a book about treatment for survivors of childhood abuse, about helping clients make the critical move from being a victim to being a survivor who triumphs and thrives. At a deeper level, it is a book about the ingenuity and indestructibility of the human spirit, about the brilliance of the child victim and the power of the adult survivor, about the predictable responses to both abuse and healing.

The book is based on the author's firm conviction, developed over years of clinical practice, that survivors of childhood abuse are profoundly normal and absolutely extraordinary. They are incredibly resilient and resourceful, not despite their childhood experiences, but because of them. The behavior patterns that are still troubling them are not evidence of pathology but proof of the brilliant children they were and the strong adults they have become.

The entire therapeutic agenda emphasizes what's right rather than what's wrong. The overriding themes are resolution and empowerment. The question is not "What's wrong with me?" The questions are "How did I get this way?" and "How do I need to change?"

All the strategies described quickly become self-initiating for the client, encouraging autonomy and speeding recovery. Offset summaries outline interventions and offer considerations for treatment planning. Workable and experiential exercises for each stage of healing facilitate reframing of self-experience, allow completion of interrupted, frozen trauma, and directly target areas of developmental loss. Exercises are accompanied by examples of client art and writing. The journaling of one survivor, Jessica, is interspersed throughout the text, and the progression of her recovery both echoes and illustrates the therapeutic journey.

The process is active, not passive. Trauma is experienced actively, and it must be actively unblocked and resolved. A variety of modalities are employed to engage even the most difficult client. Specific and sequential interventions are self-contained and adaptable to varied clinical styles and orientations. The techniques are not offered as replacements for existing skills. Rather, they are designed to be superimposed on already excellent skills to augment effectiveness and versatility. The author is a pragmatist when it comes to therapy, repeating what works and discarding what doesn't and, similar to so many other therapists, discovering some of the most effective interventions in moments of clinical desperation, when the client's need for relief outweighs conformity to the established routine. The highlighted client exercises and the therapeutic strategies are only suggestions. The therapist must judge if they apply.

At the time of this writing, the nature of traumatic memory and traumatic amnesia remains the subject of professional debate and controversy. Although the dynamics of traumatic memory dissociation and repression are addressed, none of the therapeutic strategies are exclusively directed toward retrieving repressed factual memory. The suggested techniques are based on accepted trauma treatment methodology (Briere, 1989, 1992; Foa, 1997; Kritsberg, 1993; Whitfield, 1995; Williams, 1994) and reflect the current state of knowledge in the field (Alpert, 1995; Brown, 1998; Brown and Pope, 1996).

The terms victim and survivor are both used in the text. The client is defined as victim only in the context of active abuse. More frequent references to the survivor, even in the prerecovery and early recovery stages, reinforce the healing process and the client's own responsibility for healing.

This book does not purport to be a work of research. The focus is practice, not theory. Pertinent areas of clinical investigation are summarized and referenced. In the interest of the busy therapist, sources are cited because they are readable and inclusive, not necessarily because they are primary. Core concepts are explained in language that can be used with the client in session. However, an underlying understanding and a working knowledge of the etiology and neurophysiology of trauma response (Everly, 1990, 1993; Everly and Lating, 1994; Kramer, 1993; Van der Kolk, 1985), the distorted cognitive system of the abuser (Marshall and Eccles, 1991; Marshall, Laws, and Barbaree, 1990, Sgroi and Bunk, 1988), the nature of traumatic memory (American Psychological Association,

1996; Carlson, 1996; Herman, 1992; Pope and Hudson, 1995; Terr, 1994; Van der Kolk and Fisler, 1995; Williams, 1992), and the dynamics of traumatic memory dissociation and repression (Herman, 1992; Terr, 1994; Van der Kolk and Fisler, 1995) advance assessment and intervention.

The book is meant to be a practical, hands-on desktop companion to inform and enrich the work of clinicians who want to move beyond Stage I debriefing and help survivors of childhood abuse achieve Stage II transformation in self-image and life patterns. It supports the therapist as partner and guide in the healing journey, serving as both model and measure for progress and success.

Mary Bratton

PART I:
THE FRAMEWORK FOR HEALING

Chapter 1

The Therapeutic Agenda

Childhood abuse is trauma, the pure physical trauma of a life-threatening catastrophe or the emotional trauma of two conflicting feelings linked together in the same event—love and pain, love and violence, love and rage. One incident of physical or sexual violation constitutes abuse; emotional abuse is characterized by a consistent and repeated pattern of humiliation, sarcasm, ridicule, rejection, or threats. It is often impossible to neatly categorize the kind of abuse suffered because physical, emotional, and sexual abuse are often overlapping. Any kind of childhood abuse violates the child's quest for safety, which is second only to food and shelter in Maslow's hierarchy of needs (Maslow, 1970). The core of a child's world—the home—is not safe when the very people put on this earth to protect the child at the worst abuse and at the least fail to defend him or her. Childhood abuse damages and alters a child's perception of self, others, and the world. Those damaged and altered perceptions affect each subsequent developmental task.

THE DYNAMICS OF TRAUMA

A traumatic event initiates a two-part process. First, shock mitigates the immediacy of the catastrophe to allow survival. Then, the built-in drive to heal takes over, as the victim begins processing the trauma, telling the story, and spilling the feelings over and over again, until the shock lessens in intensity and the trauma is woven into the fabric of life. As the sometimes intrusive media reveals on an almost daily basis, processing happens spontaneously after the danger has passed. However, when processing is blocked by family denial, intimidation, secrecy, and shame, then the trauma becomes frozen in the shock stage—not finished, not diminished, not integrated. It may loom large in the conscious landscape, or it may be remembered only vaguely, but it continues to dominate the behavior, feelings, and thinking of its victim. It influences relationships, choices, and beliefs.

STAGE II RECOVERY

By the time the adult survivor reaches therapy, the tentacles of trauma extend deep into life patterns and self-image. Telling the story is no longer enough to resolve the trauma. Crazy, dirty, damaged, doomed, different, and defective have become self-defining adjectives. Coping mechanisms needed only to survive trauma have been overpracticed and are now self-defeating. Ongoing developmental tasks have been compromised or missed completely. The distorted reality of the abuser has become truth about self and world for the survivor.

Treatment must go beyond recounting the story of helplessness and horror, replete with the adult overlays of self-judgment and self-blame. Stage II recovery requires the survivor to achieve closure from the perspectives of both child and adult to effect meaningful transformation in coping strategies, self-view, and worldview.

EIGHT STAGES OF HEALING

In the context of Stage II recovery, recounting becomes a midpoint in the healing process. Recounting is based on a paradigm shift in self-experience from weak to strong and from crazy to normal, and it is followed by concrete and incremental steps that resolve the frozen trauma and repair developmental damage to complete the mental, emotional, and spiritual growth interrupted by childhood abuse. Healing is a process that has a well-defined beginning, a clear direction, and a definite end.

Defining Assault

Healing begins with a one-word intervention. The abuse is redefined as assault. The legalistic language used to distance society from the brutality of attacks on children needs to be replaced with the word that speaks reality and truth—assault. The strength of the word assault triggers a sea change that cracks the wall of denial and minimizing and begins to free the survivor from guilt and blame. Thus begins the journey from being a victim to being a survivor who triumphs and thrives.

Challenging the Distorted Reality

Implicit in every memory of interrupted trauma is the abuser's interpretation of the abuse, which almost never includes any admission of adult responsibility. Because the victim could not process the trauma, there was no exoneration from blame, no chance to hold the abuser accountable, and no independent or rational challenge to the minimizing or the denial or the gratuitous justification for the abuse. Each distorted belief about the abuse, self, and the world, internalized and embedded in the frozen memory, needs to be identified, confronted, and dismantled. The web of rationalization and intellectualization that has excused abusers and collaborators begins to disintegrate.

Using the PTSD Diagnosis As a Therapeutic Intervention

At some secret level, most survivors of abuse consider themselves crazy, and many have been given psychiatric labels that reinforce that belief. They are convinced that they are somehow dirty, damaged, doomed, different, and defective. As human responses to trauma are more completely explored and understood, it is becoming clear that the therapeutic community, with the best of intentions, has been capable of pathologizing and retraumatizing survivors, with fragmented diagnoses which identify only one aspect of trauma response and fragmented treatments which address only superficial symptoms of trauma survival. It is a disservice to tell survivors that they are anything less than normal, given their histories. Post-traumatic stress disorder is the one diagnosis that says, in effect, "You are having a normal reaction; what happened to you was abnormal."

To leap from symptoms of trauma to content of trauma is both dangerous and irrational, yet it is something both client and therapist are sometimes tempted to do. The phenomenon of traumatic

memory repression and the ensuing swirl of controversy and advo-
cacy around false memory have fueled the confusion between event
and effect. The symptoms of PTSD suggest that something catastrophic happened. They do not precisely define what that catastrophe was. They certainly do not determine that it was sexual
abuse. Although it is wonderful that the wall of silence around child
sexual abuse has finally been shattered, the resulting media and
self-help preoccupation diminishes the very real agony of survivors
of physical violence and emotional assault.

There is no single trauma, and no single level of trauma, that has
to happen before PTSD symptoms can occur. Sometimes an event
that is traumatic to one person is not as devastating to another, given
differences in surrounding circumstances and support. A competent
therapist does not make the search for new memories the sole or
even primary goal of therapy. If new memories surface, they must
be evaluated from psychosocial, cognitive, perceptual, conceptual,
and social learning developmental perspectives by a therapist familiar
with Erikson (1963), Piaget (1952, 1954, 1967), Bandura (1977),
and their disciples. The therapist's job is to guide the client to use
existing memories to understand behavior patterns, within the context of PTSD, not to force the client to search out new memories to
explain or justify symptoms.

Historically, the PTSD diagnosis was formulated to describe adult
responses to trauma during war. The diagnostic criteria for PTSD in
DSM-IV do not fully allow for the range of symptoms exhibited by
survivors of hostage situations, which is a child's experience in an
abusive family. Nor do the diagnostic criteria fully reflect the range
of symptoms that stem from trauma which occurs during the critical
developmental stages of childhood (American Psychiatric Association, 1994). Nevertheless, until the PTSD diagnostic criteria are expanded to include additional symptoms, such as those proposed for
complex PTSD (Herman, 1992), the PTSD diagnosis and all it implies about normal responses to abnormal events remains the best
and most accurate intervention available.

The therapist's knowledge of the neurophysiology and psychology
of trauma needs to be more than superficial to adequately answer all
the survivor's questions and doubts and to meaningfully reframe the
survivor's interpretation of symptoms. The PTSD diagnosis itself

catalyzes the shift in self-experience from crazy to normal and augments the shift from bad and guilty to blameless.

Understanding the Brilliance of Childhood Defenses

Defenses formed in moments of childhood trauma are deeply and stubbornly rooted and resistant to change. They are connected to survival at a primal level. They have been overused to the point of excluding the acquisition of more productive and appropriate coping skills. The repetition of what have become self-defeating patterns contributes to the survivor's sense of being crazy, dirty, damaged, doomed, different, and defective. Survivors need to understand that their defenses are normal, not just because they are typical patterns shared with other survivors; they are normal in the light of what is known about human responses and behavior. They are brilliant because they represent creative and sophisticated uses of human coping mechanisms. Redefining so-called crazy coping skills as brilliant responses to the chaos and confusion of an abusive childhood changes self-definition from weak victim to strong survivor. This gives the client the final building block for the paradigm shift in self-concept that underpins healthy recounting.

Recounting

Not until a significant alteration in self-view has occurred is the survivor ready to tell the story of trauma. Forced or premature recounting has potential for reinforcing guilt and shame, as the survivor once again confesses misdeeds and character defects in a story contaminated with all the altered reality of the abuser and the dysfunctional family. Some survivors need to be actively discouraged from detailed recounting early in therapy to avoid further locking in the distorted version.

Recounting is neither the beginning nor the end of healing. It is simply part of the process. Healthy recounting encourages survivors to examine their histories to understand what they learned, not to blame. Recounting does not just answer the question "What happened?" It answers the more important questions "How did I get this way?" and "How do I need to change?" Only when the story can be told from a base of reality, with understanding, power, and control, can it become the foundation for transformative Stage II recovery.

Reparenting to Resolve Trauma

Years of denial and layers of minimizing and guilt and shame overlay every abusive episode. Often memories are interrupted abruptly by dissociation that preempts storage and retrieval. Memories are devoid of rescue or resolution. To return to the frozen memory means to return to that moment of never-ending terror and impending death. Because the memory is frozen, the abuse continues at some level of the psyche. Resolution fantasy creates an imaginary ending which allows that frozen part of self to grow up, through and past the moment of attack, and to complete the trauma, using the needs and feelings of the child and the strength and capabilities of the adult.

Just as emotional, physical, and sexual abuse are often overlapping, healing is also overlapping. Each traumatic incident does not need to be resolved individually. Rather, working through one abusive incident with resolution fantasy produces a cascade of healing that applies across the board so that lasting recovery from years of trauma can be accomplished rapidly.

Repairing Developmental Damage

Recounting increases understanding of the crucible in which defenses were formed. Resolution of the traumatic memories frees the survivor from the tyranny of defenses necessary for suppression and survival. The door is open for elimination and alteration of behaviors that are counterproductive to healthy adulthood. Even survivors who got help as children may need to integrate the meaning of the abuse into later developmental imperatives and adjust coping skills acquired after the abuse but still based on inadequate understanding of its effect.

Recovery does not require a total change in being. All the tools needed to heal are already present in the victim's feelings and the survivor's tenacity. Skill gaps can be identified and filled. Defenses relevant only to surviving abuse can be gently relinquished from a position of strength and gratitude. Already brilliant survival skills can be modified so they more aptly fit adult needs.

Grief is an integral part of all work with survivors, and it is dominant during this period of letting go. Recovery requires survivors to accept responsibility for the people they are and the people they choose to become. Having a horrible childhood is not an excuse for being miserable as an adult.

Integration and Transformation

The final stage of healing occurs as the survivor accommodates to history. Although individual memories of trauma can be unfrozen and completed, the abuse is a fact of existence that cannot be changed. Accepting responses that will be normal given that history, recognizing that the abuse is a part but not the whole of formative influences and experiences, and letting go of the survivor identity that has driven and propelled healing allow the client to move beyond surviving to thriving and to claim a sense of wholeness and well-being that is the hallmark of Stage II recovery.

THE SURVIVOR'S INTERNAL EXPERIENCE

Not only do many survivors of abuse secretly consider themselves crazy, they also suspect they may have multiple personalities. Although dissociative identity disorder can be the outcome of severe abuse, the degree of separation from self for most survivors is less than absolute. The fear of dissociative identity disorder reflects not only the survival defense of dissociation but also the continual fragmentation and encapsulation of experience and identity that is demanded by the abusive and dysfunctional family (Herman, 1992; Shengold, 1989). The survivor splits off events and feelings to the point of disconnection from a coherent sense of self.

That internal experience is reframed on the contextual canvas of trauma and dysfunction as a trio of defensive states. The internalized abuser and the cognitive distortion which excused the abuse is separate from the tough and hardened shell of self which endured the abuse, which in turn is separate from the vulnerable and hurting child who had to be hidden to protect the secret. The triadic interaction is a script for therapy rather than a stage of therapy. The three disparate segments are used as vehicles for healing, and a major thrust of therapy is integration of these hitherto alienated defensive personas.

DIAGNOSTIC ISSUES

In the absence of a comprehensive PTSD diagnosis, the therapist is often forced to diagnose multiple disorders on Axis I to qualify treatment. However, responsibility to the client's recovery mandates that those conditions be related to the history of trauma, even without the sanction of DSM-IV. Newer research indicates that trauma is not just an emotional event. At its core, trauma is a neurophysiological event (Everly, 1993; Kramer, 1993; Van der Kolk, 1985). Aftershocks of trauma linger in the nervous system long after the traumatic event has passed, leaving lasting physical and emotional footprints that affect form and functioning. In the absence of diagnostic cohesion afforded by the proposed complex PTSD diagnosis, the survivor still needs to understand that anxiety, depression, dissociation, somatic and somatoform complaints, and disturbed cognitive, perceptual, and coping patterns are the logical sequelae of trauma, particularly trauma that is repetitive and anticipatory.

Depressive Disorders

Although it is beyond the scope of this book to even scratch the surface of the plethora of research in the emerging area of psycho-traumatology (Everly and Lating, 1994; Post and Ballenger, 1984; Van der Kolk, 1985) and the intricate connections between stress and neurochemistry, one documented neurophysiological effect of stress is elevated levels of cortisol, one of the stress hormones released by the adrenal glands, and corresponding elevated levels of corticotrophin-releasing factor (CRF) in the brain. In a "kindling" model, the effects of repeated stress and trauma are neurophysiologically cumulative. The organism becomes sensitized to stress, lowering the threshold for reactivity and responding, with ever-higher levels of CRF and cortisol to create physiological vulnerability to later stress (Kramer, 1993; Post, 1985, 1992; Post, Rubinow, and Ballenger, 1986). Ultimately, the condition may become autonomous, producing physical changes in the functioning of the nervous system independent of stressors (Kramer, 1993).

Elevated cortisol levels are significantly correlated with depression in adults, and studies done with survivors of documented childhood trauma indicate a connection between disruption in the stress hormone system and depression. Alterations in the neurophysiological climate have a downstream effect on production and availability of serotonin and other neurotransmitters linked to depression. Diminished serotonin levels and depression go hand in hand (Kramer, 1993).

In simpler terms, the demands of repeated severe trauma on the nervous system seem to prematurely deplete the brain's neurochemical resources to ward off depression caused by ordinary life stressors, just as muscle fibers and bone density deteriorate with age until minor injuries cause major problems. The body becomes hypersensitive to stress at a biochemical level, leading to chronic or episodic depression.

Anxiety and Panic Disorders

A connection between depression and anxiety is also emerging, again related to the availability of serotonin and other neurotransmitters, which serve as cell-to-cell chemical messengers in the central nervous system. The presence of serotonin promotes a sense of well-being and security; its absence engenders unease (Kramer, 1993). The experience of anticipatory, repeated trauma requires some level of fight-or-flight reactivity at all times, shortening the distance to all-out defenses in the face of life-or-death threat. That state of arousal becomes biochemically habitual, creating a state of constant anxiety and sometimes panic. Anxiety and panic reflect the disorder of arousal that has been postulated as the context for PTSD (Everly, 1990).

The subset of anxiety that manifests as obsessive and compulsive patterns can also be traced deductively to biochemical aberrations in neurotransmitters (Kramer, 1993). Those patterns can equally be traced to the rigors of existence in an abusive family. If safety and survival hinged on pleasing parents who could never be pleased, on performing beyond developmental capacity to perform, on measuring up to whimsical or arbitrary and unattainable standards, then evermore-pressured efforts to achieve perfection would spill over into obsession and compulsion.

Treating depression or anxiety and panic with medication is sometimes suspect in the field of PTSD. Even clients express fear that medication will cut them off from the real feelings they need to heal. In fact, depression and anxiety themselves block feelings. Depression and anxiety exaggerate and polarize feelings or numb them completely. Tears of depression are not tears of grief. Tears of depression are static and lead to despair, not healing. The heart-pounding breathlessness of anxiety or panic is immobilizing and invokes primitive and avoidant defenses to keep it at bay. Fear that can be titrated is fear that can be experienced and validated and calmed. Trauma survival is zone one or ten—numb or red alert. Recovery happens in zones two through nine. Prudently and appropriately prescribed medication can help clients access that broader range of congruent feelings so that healing can progress.

Dissociative Disorders

If dissociation is a major defense of the child ensnared in abuse, then it follows that dissociative disorder is often the diagnosis for the adult. There are significant differences between Type I and Type II trauma, between single-blow and repeated, anticipatory trauma. The latter is the stuff of childhood abuse. Unlike single-blow trauma, which tends to produce etched-in memories and trauma-specific fears, Type II trauma is characterized by vague or absent memories and more generalized fears and anxiety (Terr, 1991). The anticipatory cues to repetitive trauma—the footsteps on the stairs, the sound of the belt being taken from the shelf, the blank stare, the raised voice—initiate the self-hypnosis that is the core of dissociation. Practiced enough, either to cope with active abuse or to block recall of abuse later, dissociation becomes habitual and begins to occur independent of the original triggers. Again, medication can sometimes be helpful to prevent the automatic retreat into dissociation that thwarts therapeutic engagement and progress.

Somatic and Somatoform Disorders

Although there is controversy about body memory, about the capacity of sinews and muscle fibers to retain memory of trauma, somatic and somatoform disorders can be explained more logically within the context of repetitive fight-or-flight mobilization. A body subjected to frequent surges of adrenaline, which rushes blood to large muscles and heart at the expense of nourishing the digestive system, a body which then cannot discharge that incipient energy because there is nowhere to run, nowhere to hide, and no way to fight back, is a body that may incur damage at the sites of those biological imbalances. Thus, survivors seem prone to digestive conditions, such as ulcers, irritable bowel syndrome, and colitis, muscular-skeletal problems, such as fibromyalgia and chronic tension and pain, and vascular disorders, such as migraine headaches. Once developed, these conditions must be treated medically, but they also need to be conceptualized under the broader umbrella of trauma aftermath. Certainly hypersensitivity to stimuli and arousal and a history of physical threat or harm create fertile ground for the development of a somatoform disorder (Herman, 1992). The therapist has a collaborative responsibility to ensure that an obscure or difficult-to-diagnose medical condition is not being overlooked before a psychosomatic diagnosis is made.

The Question of Borderline

The high correlation between clients who carry a diagnosis of borderline personality disorder and those who have a history of childhood abuse cannot be ignored (Herman, 1992; Herman, Perry, and Van der Kolk, 1989). The history feeds the diagnostic criteria. If the years when interdependence and intimacy skills were learned took place in the zones of 1 or 10, if the dichotomy of loving parent and abusive parent had to be juggled mentally, then a polarized approach to adult interpersonal relationships should not be surprising. If threats of abandonment or loss of love punctuated the years when abandonment or loss of love meant death, then frantic efforts to avoid abandonment in adulthood should not be surprising. If the years of identity formation demanded roles and expectations well beyond a child's capabilities or included vicious attacks on self-esteem and self-worth, then adult confusion about self-image should not be surprising. If abuse was the norm and the here and now required every ounce of energy in childhood, then impulsivity and self-defeating patterns in adulthood should not be surprising. If pain and annihilation were what the child deserved, then self-mutilation and suicidal scenarios in the adult should not be surprising. If childhood reality and emotional climate shifted abruptly and dramatically, then mood reactivity and instability in adulthood should not be surprising. If abuse and rejection filled the place where love should be in the child, then chronic emptiness in the adult should not be surprising. If explosive rage was modeled by others and anger was forbidden to the child, then inappropriate anger in the adult should not be surprising. And, if self-hypnosis and retreating into fantasy and forgetfulness were the child's defenses against the reality of life-threatening hostility, then suspicion of the world's motives and ongoing dissociation in the adult should not be surprising.

The problem with the borderline diagnosis, not unlike the problems with the neurotic and the hysteric labels that came before it, is that the borderline diagnosis ignores the historical origins of troublesome patterns and pathologizes rather than seeks to understand them. The borderline diagnosis, similar to its predecessors, has also become pejorative, which subtly changes how the therapist approaches the client. The contrast for the therapist between borderline personality and trauma survivor is the difference between unfixable versus fixable, incurable versus curable, hopeless versus hopeful. Treating a borderline personality who needs to be framed and contained within limits and boundaries by a detached, uninvolved therapist is diametrically opposed to treating a survivor who needs to be comforted and validated by a therapeutic ally. The process represents the difference between repetition of trauma and healing to the survivor.

The therapist communicates expectations to the client with both overt dialogue and covert theoretical constructs that influence engagement and interaction. Therapeutic outcome hinges on this conceptual, diagnostic fulcrum. Sometimes the best expectation for the borderline personality is stabilization and some decrease in intensity of symptoms. A realistic expectation for the trauma survivor is healing and wholeness. Given the diagnostic categories presently available, the Axis II diagnosis must often be made in adjunct with PTSD. It is the therapist's obligation to go beyond the confines of DSM to help clients understand and then alter the borderline behavior patterns that are the logical outcome of their developmental histories.

Change does not come easily for people who see themselves as weak and defective because change occurs more readily from a position of strength and competence. If weakness and defectiveness are reinforced diagnostically, survivors will cling tenaciously to old defenses. When treatment is symptomatic, minor alleviation in symptoms is a satisfactory outcome. When treatment is founded on the bedrock of trauma resolution, massive improvement in Axis II symptoms can occur.

Other Personality Disorders

The connection that can be made between borderline symptoms and repetitive childhood trauma can also be made for other Axis II personality disorders, given each client's individual history. The creativity and skill of the therapist in eliciting and interpreting history is the cornerstone on which the client's recovery is based. Again, it is the therapist's task to help the client understand and then alter the self-defeating patterns that are the legacy of pervading dysfunction and abuse. Those patterns were learned to survive trauma, and they can be unlearned once trauma survival is not life's first and only priority.

TECHNIQUES AND STRATEGIES

The multiple stages and levels of the therapeutic agenda call for a wide range of theories and techniques. The process itself is psychodynamic and insight oriented. Assessment benefits from a multimodal perspective. Cognitive restructuring and rational-emotive interventions are the logical choices for disputing the faulty belief system. Resolution fantasy has Gestalt elements. The plan for repairing developmental damage is founded in cognitive and behavioral and reality therapies. The script for therapy using the survivor's internal fragmentation draws from transactional analysis. The eclectic therapist who has familiarity and expertise with a variety of theoretical models and techniques will have a broader and more flexible range of therapeutic tactics.

However, traditional talk therapy, the hallmark of most professional training, can advance survivor recovery only so far. The distorted perception of reality and process that is the inevitable companion to abuse precludes the presumption of common ground, which underlies the talk therapy contract. Work with survivors requires the therapist to move beyond the confines of the comfortable and habitual to explore creative and novel approaches. At times, therapy is still more art than science.

The survivor's therapist must first be educator, then model. Until the cognitive distortion is challenged and altered, until the survivor has some sense of normal behavior and responses, true therapy cannot proceed.

Education

The first order of therapeutic business is establishing a mutual baseline for what is normal. Survivors have adapted to inconsistency and unpredictability; they have learned to accept the bizarre as normal. Redefining normal for survivors means confronting the faulty belief system and providing accurate information about healthy childhood development and reasonable childhood expectations. It means providing accurate information about how the world works in the absence of abuse. One survivor couldn't object to a co-worker yanking on her hair to get her attention until she learned that the hair pulling used to punish her in childhood was assaultive.

One educational intervention, one challenge to years of learning locked in place by abuse, will not even scratch the surface. It is not enough to label false and dismiss out of hand the distorted belief system survivors have lived with for so long. That simply will not be credible to them. Each reason and explanation needs to be listened to and seriously considered. Only then can the pieces of self-blame and the excuses be concretely and individually confronted. If a bad childhood or job stress or an unhappy marriage caused abuse, then everyone who had a bad childhood or job stress or an unhappy marriage would be an abuser. Education is a constant in almost every session with a survivor.

Modeling

Survivors don't trust words. Words have been instruments of abuse and trickery. Their stories are an endless procession of empty threats and broken promises, of feelings discounted and denied, of events repressed and concealed. To approach them with words alone is to lose them at the outset.

The therapist enters into alliance with the survivor and immediately becomes a model for a radically new way of dealing with history and experience. The therapist defines the confusion and anguish the survivor is expressing as normal reactions to abnormal events. The therapist models rational and nonjudgmental consideration of symptoms rather than guilty confession or betrayal. The therapist may be the first person to furnish a healthy response to the story of abuse, the first person the survivor has encountered who can say words such as abuse, incest, and alcoholism without hysteria or rage.

Emotional modeling is built on education about normal, healthy behavior and responses. If survivors lack any conception of normal behavior, they also have little idea of normal emotional reactions. The therapist can begin with some level of self-revelation: "If that happened to me, I would be angry."

Again, words are not enough. Modeling means tying words to body. A skilled therapist needs to be part actor. The theatrics don't detract from therapy; they enhance it. When it comes to feelings, survivors need to be shown, not told. Survivors have disconnected feeling words from what is happening inside their bodies. They have pretended that they couldn't feel for so long that they have, in fact, become numb and unfeeling. It's not enough to talk to them about their anger. The word anger may be meaningless. Anger must be made tangible and visible for them. It must be demonstrated with clenched jaw, raised voice, tightened muscles, and frowning face. The therapist figuratively says, "This is how I look and behave when I am feeling angry. This is how it is for healthy people to feel and act."

Modeling needs to be tempered so survivors are not frightened by the same out-of-control emotions that victimized them in the past. A well-placed "I feel outraged about what happened to you," with some degree of firmness attached, is more helpful than the fury that might feel more appropriate to the therapist, when reacting to the horror at hand.

Modeling allows survivors to contemplate at a distance the feelings they might be experiencing themselves under their pretense and constraint. Feelings must be rendered safe and acceptable before they can be owned or expressed.

Sculpturing and Psychodrama

Ultimately, survivor therapy needs to be active and experiential. The trauma was experienced viscerally and physically, and it cannot be unfrozen and resolved without a return to the physical and visceral.

Sculpturing and psychodrama are logical extensions of modeling. To sculpture is to paint a picture with bodies and objects. It makes feelings and dynamics long ignored and buried come alive. Sculpturing is dramatic, but it takes drama to penetrate the blunted, constricted affect and the closed, tangled communication style that survivors have had to adopt. Again, these are people who don't trust words. Telling them what has been happening to them will be met with ambivalence and confusion. Showing them circumvents the verbal barriers and catalyzes insight and understanding.

The empty chair is the core of sculpturing. It represents the secret of the abuse itself. It takes the place of abusers and nonprotective adults.

Sculpturing allows survivors to make connections between behavior and feelings. Survivors resist verbal explanations of the price paid for covering up the abuse and adjusting to the abuser's anger. But when they are asked to tiptoe around the empty chair for only a few moments, they can feel for themselves the muscle strain. They can readily perceive the source of their tension and exhaustion, and they can begin to experience at a physical level the toll denial has taken.

Sculpturing allows feelings to be experienced in their true intensity. Shame is obscured in words. Crouched beside the empty chair, the survivor understands dramatically the aching denigration of shame.

Sculpturing flows naturally into psychodrama. Anger verbalized is anger discounted and minimized. But when the survivor, curled up beside the empty chair in a posture of helplessness and hopelessness, moves to stand up against the imaginary or role-played abuser, shaking a fist and declaring the truth about the abuse, anger is witnessed and validated. Powerlessness becomes power in a physical sense.

Sculpturing and psychodrama allow the survivor to recognize and vent feelings at a concrete level, permitting feelings of rage and shame to be redirected away from self and back to the abuse and the abuser, where they belong. Sculpturing and psychodrama move emotion from the realm of the conceptual and theoretical to the realm of the personal and possible. Survivors establish coherent and congruent ties between what they have been doing and what they have been feeling, and they carve for themselves a model for change.

"Conditional Tense" Therapy

Traditional talking, feeling therapy is at best ineffective and at worst counterproductive, when a client is barricaded behind the walls of *don't talk, don't feel,* and *don't trust.* The nature of the therapeutic contract flies in the face of the rules that dominated childhood. The therapist says or implies, "Come talk to me about your feelings and trust me." The very words are red flags. When survivors are asked to come into counseling to talk about their feelings and to trust, they are being asked to betray everything they have learned, everything they believe to be true, everything they have operated on for years. They are being asked to dissolve the glue that has held them and their families together, and that they cannot and will not do. Their resistance is not obstinacy. Those rules represent survival.

Rather than confront the rules head on, which leads only to frustration and despair, the therapist must devise ways to allow survivors to break the rules, without attacking the rules directly. Survivors need to be given permission to talk and feel and trust within the confines of their guarded communication system. The therapist needs to learn to think and talk in the conditional tense.

This simply means learning not to ask direct questions. Early interactions with the survivor are best framed conditionally. Questions such as "What happened?" or "How did you feel?" will invariably be met with bland defensiveness. "Nothing" and "Fine" are typical responses. This is not evasion; it is reality as survivors see and feel it, according to their rules. They aren't allowed to talk and they aren't allowed to feel. They know if they do, the whole fragile fabric of their existence will be rent asunder.

On the other hand, questions such as "If you could guess what happened next, what would that be?" allow them to share the secrets, without breaking the *don't talk* rule. The same holds true for feelings. "If you had to guess what you felt inside when that happened, what could that be?" lets them touch their own emotions, without breaking the *don't feel* rule.

Survivors don't have to trust to begin to process what has been happening and how they have been feeling. They are only being asked to speculate on what *might* have been happening or how they *might* have been feeling. Words and phrases such as "if you knew" and "if you had to guess" and "might" and "could" and "would" need to become integral and automatic parts of the therapist's vocabulary. They may be subtle and simple, but they are quick and effective wedges into the rigid shell the abuse has constructed around the survivor. They save time and energy and pain, and they pave the road toward recovery in ways that months of conventional probing and processing cannot accomplish. And by not demanding that survivors break the *don't talk, don't feel* rules before they are ready to do so, the therapist is established as a person who might be able to be trusted.

Humor

For the survivor, life is deadly serious. The ability to experience or express happy feelings has been buried, along with the pain and the hurt, and the reaction to humor is typically deadpan. Although some things that have happened and some aspects of family dynamics may indeed be funny, to laugh about these things is to insult. The survivor in early recovery feels belittled and threatened.

Yet every therapist knows that in laughter lie the seeds of wellness. Healthy laughter is retrospective. It derives from relief that this never has to happen again. Survivors' ability to laugh with and at themselves is a measure of progress and can play a pivotal role in recovery.

Humor simply needs to be dealt with like everything else in therapy: it needs to be defined. It is often enough to warn, "Now I'm going to tell you something that may make you laugh," or to ask, "Can I tease you for a moment?"

Once again, survivors need permission to feel and respond. The therapist must be sensitive to who survivors are and where they come from to use therapeutic tools effectively.

Avoiding Retraumatization

Survivors were forced as children to endure things they shouldn't have had to endure, to do things they shouldn't have had to do, to say things they shouldn't have had to say, and to believe things they shouldn't have had to believe. Although survivors need direction and encouragement in healing, pressure to meet some arbitrary timetable or imposed goal has potential for replaying the abuse. The abusive family redefined reality with their own "spin," and the childhood price for disagreement or dissent was death. Forcing premature renunciation of defenses is a threat akin to abuse. Forcing a survivor to recount the story of abuse, without the foundation of understanding symptoms as normal and coping skills as brilliant, revives the original trauma. Pushing a survivor to hurry through any stage of healing simply drives the survivor away. The therapist becomes the abuser, demanding unacceptable and unrecognizable beliefs and behaviors as the price for approval. Often the most helpful intervention is, "Take all the time you need." Healing from childhood abuse is usually not the stuff of brief therapy.

In direct opposition stands the managed care insurance company, with limited sessions and "crisis stabilization" criteria. Crisis stabilization is the abusive family's modus operandi, and "no longer suicidal" does not equal recovery for the survivor. The therapist needs to be a creative, informed, and reasoned advocate for the client, educating and modeling to the insurance review panel, as well as to the client, a realistic view of treatment and healing.

BOUNDARIES

If thoughts, feelings, and a person's very existence are invaded repeatedly and violently during the years when autonomy, integrity, independence, and identity are forming, the lines between self and others become an ever-changing kaleidoscope tied only to the moment, untethered to a stable sense of self or personal territory. If attachment is constantly threatened during the years when trust and security are developing, the search for safety and reassurance becomes a paramount drive. Boundaries are primitive—rigid or ambiguous or melded—often with volatile and mercurial fluctuations that seem unanchored to the immediate situation.

Engagement

The shifts from fixed to diffuse to enmeshed boundary styles make the engagement stage of therapy with the survivor like a high-wire act without a net for the therapist. Engagement is a period of continual testing. Life experience has taught the survivor that no one really means what he or she says and that no one can really be trusted. This is not a client who will respond with equanimity to changed appointment times or locales. This is a client to whom a promise made must be a promise kept. Both the client's and the therapist's interests are best served by consistency.

Hypervigilance to the moods and behaviors of others learned in childhood makes the survivor an astute observer. The survivor can read the therapist like a book. The survivor knows what the therapist is thinking and feeling, even before the therapist does. The survivor knows when the therapist doesn't know. That some of these judgments are based on distorted expectations and beliefs doesn't make them any less potentially damaging to the therapeutic relationship. The survivor's hypersensitivity can turn a casual comment into a crisis of trust. It is critical for the therapist to be congruent and to continually check out interpretations on both sides. Honesty is more important than perfection.

Therapists are human; therapists make mistakes. A major goal of therapy with survivors is to move them away from a black-and-white view of the world to a more realistic acceptance of the grays of human interaction. The most effective therapist is comfortable being only human. The therapist models acceptance of mistakes, apology, and accountability. "I made a mistake," or "I'm sorry— that may not have been a helpful thing for me to say," or "I will never deliberately hurt you, but I may say or do something that will hurt you accidentally" are powerful interventions. The human, not the expert, forges the therapeutic alliance.

Survivors come to therapy torn between a desire to heal and an intense loyalty to the abusive family. They come with a facade of adult insight and judgment, but the distorted reality and the dysfunctional rules from childhood dominate logic and cognition. It is important to form the therapeutic partnership exactly on the ground where the survivor stands. The therapist must enter the world of denial, delusion, and diversion that the survivor inhabits, while maintaining a firm footing in objectivity and rationality. The therapist needs to meet the survivor on the survivor's own terms and then lead the survivor out of his or her distorted world into reality. Therapist as aloof expert repeats the dynamics of abuse. Therapist as engaged partner facilitates healing.

Compliance and Resistance

If survival depended on placating and going along by denying feelings, thoughts, and needs, then agreement and cooperation in therapy may represent not progress but a retreat into trauma defenses. The first questioning of a statement or strategy is a moment to be celebrated.

Conversely, if survival depended on anger, defiance, and being tough, on giving no quarter and showing no emotion, then premature pressure to talk about and share feelings will mobilize hostility. Survival mandated *not* talking, feeling, or trusting. To label such defenses as pathology or resistance hinders engagement in the therapeutic partnership.

Survivors are strong and courageous. Their strength and courage can scarcely be imagined, much less imitated, by people from more ordinary backgrounds. These are people who have weathered crisis after crisis and who have felt pain and hurt beyond belief, yet they have managed to look and act "okay" for many years. These are people who have functioned amid severe dysfunction. These are people who have responded normally to abnormality and who have adapted to the unadaptable.

The words sick and well might best be eliminated from the therapist's vocabulary. Phrases such as "less useful" and "more useful," "less helpful" and "more helpful" are more accurate and more productive descriptions. These phrases acknowledge the defenses as contributors to survival, while presenting the continuum of gradual restructuring that healing will bring.

Transference and Countertransference

Obviously, the field of survivor therapy is rife for transference. The survivor's life experience establishes the therapist as a potential abuser from the outset. People who were supposed to help hurt instead. People who said they cared did not. People who said they would be there were not. People who were supposed to protect failed to stop the abuse. People who said they would listen ignored or criticized. Love and trust were dangerous. No one really cared. No one really listened. No one could really be trusted. Expectations that the therapist will turn and become an abuser can remain subtle undercurrents in therapy for months or years (Herman, 1992).

The survivor may escalate and flaunt self-abusive, self-defeating behavior in an unconscious effort to elicit disgust and disapproval from the therapist and to reap the punishment and abandonment that were the corollaries to victimization (Miller, 1994). Such a repetition compulsion connected to the cycle of abuse can mightily test the therapeutic bond.

On the other hand, when the natural order of childhood development is interrupted, when what is supposed to come from outside, mostly from parents, never materializes to be internalized, then it continues to be sought from without. The pressure on the therapist for love and approval that was denied in childhood can be immense (Herman, 1992). Desire to engage with the client needs to be tempered by clear and constant distinction between adult caring and unmet childhood needs. The therapist's healthy and necessary compassion opens a window of vulnerability that requires internal monitoring as well as articulation of boundaries to the client.

Repairing developmental damage is a requisite of Stage II healing. The trap for the therapist lies in being drawn into providing the parenting, instead of remaining the model for healthy parenting that the client uses to initiate parenting of self. Providing education about normal childhood development, modeling feelings and facilitating grief—"You deserved love and safety when you were little, and you have a right to be sad and angry now that you didn't get what you needed"—is very different from feeling and grieving for that wounded child.

Couples counseling augments the boundary issues. Trying to expand the therapeutic contract to include another person after survivor therapy has begun, trying to shift the therapeutic focus from the survivor to that space between survivor and partner, is fraught with potential difficulties. Although providing education to partners about PTSD and the recovery process is helpful and appropriate, a referral to another professional for couples work maintains clarity in the therapeutic alliance with the survivor.

The window of vulnerability is expanded or contracted by the therapist's own history and mastery of that history. The therapist who is a survivor risks confusion between client and personal material. However, that same therapist has the depth and breadth of survival skills and ego strength that come from both abuse and healing. The therapist with a more benign history may be open to charges of lack of empathy. However, that same therapist does not have to distract energy to separate personal history and issues from the client's.

Healthy therapists know their own issues and are sure they are not working at the same place on the same issue as their clients. Healthy therapists guide clients to live life as a continual process of growth and change, paralleling that guidance with their own positive life journeys of ever-increasing self-awareness and self-evolution.

Vicarious Traumatization

It is impossible for a therapist to be an empty slate in therapy. The therapist cannot remain devoid of feelings or detached from the process. The totally dispassionate therapist replicates the disinterest of the abuser, unfeeling and uncaring in the face of outpouring pain and sorrow. It is unimaginable not to be moved or affected by listening to any survivor's story. Strong feelings are the natural outcome of the investment in caring.

The therapist must have clearly delineated boundaries, both internal and external, and must differentiate between personal feelings and client feelings, both to self and to client. "I'm *sad* that happened to you," instead of "I'm *sorry* that happened to you," expresses the therapist's reactions, without implying the abuse is in any way the therapist's responsibility.

Caregivers can fall heir to the phenomenon of secondary PTSD or vicarious traumatization (Harrison and Kellogg, 1992; Herman, 1992, McCann and Pearlman, 1990). If PTSD symptoms are normal responses to immersion in trauma, then they are similarly normal responses for those immersed in hearing the stories of trauma. Therapists can be caught off guard by intrusive mental images and dreams. They can find themselves becoming emotionally numb, mentally overloaded, or defensive and avoidant. There is probably no way for a human therapist to avoid moments of vicarious traumatization; it seems part of the process by default. Even the therapist who keeps personal feelings absolutely separated from client feelings still has to deal with some intense personal feelings, still has to deal with bearing witness to trauma again and again and again.

Care for the Caregiver

Healthy therapists are willing to do exactly what they ask their clients to do—challenge any distortions in beliefs that are contributing to overinvolvement or overresponsibility and then process the trauma. (A therapist friend and I call each other periodically to remind ourselves, "It is probably not necessary for us to save the entire world this Wednesday.") Journaling, drawing, exercise, hobbies, distractions, and a healthy support system are just as important for the therapist as for the client. Having someone who understands and who can help in a meaningful and constructive way, processing reactions without violating client confidentiality—a therapist, a colleague, a support group, a clergyperson—is incredibly helpful. Therapists need to put themselves on their own caseloads through the day, scheduling times to pay attention to self, not others. The therapist who nurtures others all day needs to self-nurture at night. (If you do this work all day long, and if this is the only book you're reading this week, put it down, go to the library or the video store, and get something fun to alternate!)

THE THERAPIST'S ROLE

Of all the people who sit in the chair opposite a therapist, the concept of therapy as partnership is most important and most precious to the survivor of childhood abuse. Any hint of hierarchy echoes the original abuse. The choice to share recovery with a therapist does not alter the survivor's role as choreographer of healing.

Survivors hand the therapist all their power at the beginning of therapy. The therapist must hold that power gently and carefully, ever mindful of whose power it really is, and give it back, piece by piece, as the survivor is ready to reclaim it. The survivor regains power that was lost in childhood by taking control of pace and process. The choice to move ahead flows from growing trust in the therapeutic partnership; it is not imposed from above by the therapist's power. Clients have a right to expect guidance and suggestions and direction and encouragement, but they have a right to question "shoulds" or "musts."

There is no generic formula for healing because there is no generic survivor. Some survivors find themselves stuck unless they confront the abusers. Others are able to heal using journaling and role-play and psychodrama exclusively. A therapist who insists on confrontation may be requiring what is not necessary. For some survivors, forgiveness becomes a possibility during the final steps of the healing journey. Others find they cannot forgive what was done to that traumatized child and must commend forgiveness to a higher power. A therapist who pushes for forgiveness may be asking for something that cannot or should not be done. And no matter what, a therapist who hints or believes that in any way or under any circumstances abuse can ever be a child's fault is not a therapist who will be helpful to survivors.

THE TRAUMA THERAPIST

To be a therapist working with trauma survivors is both an awesome responsibility and a wonderful privilege. At a workshop several years ago, I was asked to condense survivor therapy into one sentence. I found myself saying and knowing to the depth of my being, "I help people give themselves permission to exist."

I compare my role as therapist to a long-distance runner's coach. The race is not run by the observer. I cannot do the work. The race is run, and won, by the survivor. I stand on the sidelines, point out the markers and mileposts, and cheer when the course seems productive. Sometimes I urge my clients on with gentle nudges. Sometimes my clients are running pell-mell downhill, and I slow them down and encourage them to pay attention to all the scenery along the way.

A favorite passage of mine in a book of meditations for therapists reads, "As a counselor, I don't direct the trip and plan the destination; I'm only privileged to participate as a lantern carrier. And I may be asked to exit the path at any point along the route" (Parkside, 1989, March 17).

I have found my clients know so much better than I their own individual paths to healing. It is my goal to help them free themselves to follow those paths and to help them see and celebrate their progress. It is my purpose to bear witness to both their pain and their healing.

I am sometimes outraged at the hurt inflicted on innocent children by the people who claim to care about them. I am saddened about the tears of a lifetime beginning to be shed at age thirty or forty or fifty, but I know those tears release the soul to mend. Some days I am tired and distracted by concerns of my own. Some days I learn more from my clients than I teach, and some days it is the reverse.

But I never fail to be energized by the power of healing that lies before me. And I never cease to admire those who strive to heal.

Chapter 2

Defining Assault

The first step in the healing process for survivors is acknowledging that they were abused as children. However, all the details about how they were hurt won't really help unless the abuse is first defined for what it was. Society and the helping professions talk about "exploitation of trust," about "unequal balance of power," about "inappropriate boundaries." This language dilutes and minimizes reality. For too long, crimes of power and control perpetrated by adults against children have been disguised under a protective umbrella. Words and phrases such as sexual imposition, molestation, and fondling and excessive discipline and maltreatment somehow soften the violence and brutality of these betrayals and contribute to the stigma of blame and shame that attaches to victims.

When something bad happens between an adult and a child, it is always the adult's responsibility. Molestation and rape are not about sex: they are about someone getting control by hurting someone else too tiny to resist. Beating and torture are not about discipline: they are about someone feeling powerful by attacking someone else smaller and less powerful. Sarcasm and ridicule are not about constructive criticism: they are about someone building up low self-esteem and inadequacy by ripping apart someone else's self-worth and accomplishments. The abuse must be labeled for what it truly was—*assault*.

There are many weapons of assault—guns and knives and sexual organs, sticks and belts and hands, mouths and faces and voices. Kicking, punching, slapping, or beatings with wooden spoons or yardsticks are assaultive. Spankings that leave marks are assaultive. Being made to stand on one leg for hours or kneel on a grate is assaultive. In some circumstances, even silence is assaultive. Words, looks, and gestures can be just as damaging as guns, knives, and baseball bats. In fact, they are perhaps the most vicious weapons of assault because they leave no visible wounds. Instead they tear the heart and leave it to bleed.

There is a fine line between verbal or physical attack and sexual assault. Pants-down spankings or repeated, unnecessary enemas are degrading. Lack of privacy and intrusion and name-calling and teasing all have undertones of sexual intimidation. Tickling until tears come is physically threatening. The abuser becomes tormentor to the child hostage.

If survivors discover that they were emotionally abused with words, silence, looks, or gestures, if survivors realize that they were physically abused with vindictive discipline, if survivors recognize that they were sexually abused with embarrassing punishments or sly touching or enemas, they may not want to believe these events were assault. They may find themselves wishing they had been abused "normally," that is, raped or beaten. That is natural. However, it is what the child experienced, not the technicalities of what happened, that defines assault.

It is important to include incest, molestation, and fondling under the definition of assault. Those three words, in particular, have a soft and gentle sound that suggests complicity, if not consent. It is too easy to move from incest or molestation or fondling to the idea that a child is "having sex with" an adult. There is no such thing as a child having sex with a parent or a trusted adult. A child is coerced and violated by a coercive and violating adult. Even the word victimized implies cooperation by the victim. Nothing a child does deserves physical, sexual, or emotional assault. Survivors were not in the wrong place at the wrong time; they were not doing the wrong thing or wearing the wrong thing or saying the wrong thing. *The only thing they did wrong was they were too little.* Assault denotes a victim and an aggressor—period.

Survivors need to think about their reactions if they had been assaulted with a knife. Would it for one moment be their fault? Would they need to feel guilty or ashamed? Would they be forbidden to feel angry and afraid? Would that kind of assault say anything about *their* behavior or *their* character? Newscasters don't talk about people being "molested" by guns or "disciplined" with knives. When someone has been stabbed by a blade or pierced by a bullet, words such as wounded, attacked, and assaulted are used. When a child's very soul is the target, how much more accurately these words apply.

The word assault helps to challenge the idea that the survivor somehow deserved or consented to the abuse. Even if it felt good, even if the survivor cooperated, no child consents to abuse. To consent, to say "yes," a child has to be free to say "no." There is no possibility for meaningful consent when the attacker is twice as big as the victim. There is no possibility for meaningful consent between an adult intent on hurting and a child who does not want to be hurt. The law does not allow children to make decisions about sharing their money; minors can't sign contracts or buy lottery tickets or dial 900 phone numbers. Certainly children are not able to make decisions about sharing their bodies. Even if children are bad or act up or talk back, they do not deserve battering or humiliation. Our society does not allow "cruel and unusual punishment" in the legal system. Nor is there justification for verbal or physical violence in the home.

The strength of the word assault also helps the survivor to separate from the abuser. Phrases such as "my abuser" or "my perpetrator" suggest a possessive link between the victim and the aggressor that makes healing more difficult. The victim does not need to feel any connection with the actions of the abuser because the victim did nothing to deserve the abuse. Survivors need to be encouraged to use only "the" in front of words such as perpetrator, assaulter, abuser, aggressor, or offender, when they are talking about the times they were being hurt. In fact, even the phrase "my abuse" implies a sense of ownership. "The abuse" is a more accurate and more realistic description.

When the word assault is first used to define what happened, the survivor may feel shock, followed by relief and understanding, as the pain, disgust, craziness, sadness, and self-loathing finally begin to make sense. Survivors need to say the words aloud: "I was assaulted. . . ." They need to say them again and again until they begin to believe them. When they do, they are moving toward healing. They are not only putting an accurate label on what happened; they are also validating the enormous reality of what happened—assault. With that reality comes the realization that it was never their fault.

In the early stages of healing, clients are more successful with assignments that maintain some distance from the immediacy of their own histories. To that end, journaling and artwork need to be more allegorical than literal in the beginning.

Client exercise: Draw a picture or write a fable or poem showing why the abuse was not your fault.

The journey from victim to survivor, from wounded to whole, begins with this simple but enormous step. Embarking on the journey is risky and frightening, and the path itself will be painful and rocky as well as rewarding. The journey's end, however, holds promise of freedom and fulfillment.

The past, ignored and buried, can be a sinister puppet master, subtly controlling every thought, feeling, and movement. Exposed to the light of day and freed from distortion and denial, the past holds the explanation for present behavior and beliefs and the key to changing patterns that have become destructive. The abuse will shift from being the essence of who the client is as a person to being simply something that happened. The abuse will cease to be the whole of the client's identity as a victim. It will become instead a part of the client's history as a survivor.

Clients have inside them all the tools they need to heal. They have the victim's feelings and the survivor's strength. With the redefinition of what happened as assault and the realization that they were not to blame, healing begins.

Jenny summarized this awakening in verse:

I Never Asked for It

I get so angry and confused;
It's been so long, and I still feel used;
I've been so hurt, and so abused;
But I never asked for it!

I let them tear me up inside;
I let them take away my pride;
I felt as if my soul had died;
But I never asked for it!

My parents thought that I was bad;
They couldn't see that I was sad;
They had to work for what I had;
But I never asked for it!

They let me do the things I did;
They let me hide the things I hid;
They didn't see me as a kid;
But I never asked for it!

I lived the way I felt I should;
I did the things I knew I could;
And nothing happened that was good;
But I never asked for it!

Love is something to achieve;
Faith is someone to believe;
Pain is the fiber of the webs I weave;
But I never asked for it!

- *Intervention:* Redefining abuse as assault.
- *Rationale:* Confront minimizing and denial. Reduce emotional connection between perpetrator and victim.
- *Result:* Decreased minimizing and denial; diminished self-blame and guilt.

Chapter 3

Challenging the Distorted Reality

I feel very sad and depressed. Blackness is all around me. I could sleep forever. I feel empty. There is a giant hole inside me—a silent scream. I feel helpless. No one can help me. Why bother even trying anymore because it won't get me any-where—just helpless and hopeless. I know I will never change. I'll always be crazy.

I feel like I'm teetering along the rim of the whirling black hole and the crazy feelings are all around me. I have to get out and get away before it gets me. I'm scared of being crazy.

I keep thinking I'm going to wake up soon and this night-mare will be over and everything will be okay—that I'll be somewhere safe. But there is no safe place. It's like being in a play and walking around the stage watching the sets change but not knowing where you're supposed to be or where you belong. Then you finally realize that you're on the wrong stage and this was just a sick joke someone played on you. And the sickest part of it is that you don't know what stage you're supposed to be on or where it's at. So you walk around the stages aimlessly—never sure where you're going. You just know you don't fit in. Instead of adding beauty to the play, you destroy every scene you walk through and every life you touch.

Jessica

What is normal for survivors of childhood abuse? Virtually ev-erything. It is normal for survivors to have every moment of every episode of abuse engraved in memory. It is normal for survivors to remember clearly only a few incidents, even when there is evidence that abuse was a constant in childhood. It is normal for survivors to remember only hazy details about the abuse itself. It is normal for survivors to feel like a puzzle with some of the pieces missing. It is normal for survivors to feel crazy, to feel doomed, to feel flawed and defective and damaged and dirty, to feel different, to feel split, to feel sinful, to feel bad, to feel depressed and suicidal. It is normal for survivors to feel uncertain about physical image, emotional responses, values and goals, or sexual identity. None of these feelings are deserved, yet they all make real sense, considering how they came to be. They are part of the survival kit every victim shoulders at the moment of assault.

Being abused as a child induces feelings of craziness. In an instant, the world turns upside down. The adults who are supposed to protect instead betray, and no one or nothing can ever be trusted completely again.

THE ROLE OF FAMILY DYSFUNCTION

It is not the violation itself that causes the deepest damage; it is the lack of protection, the secrecy, the inability to surface and get help that devastates. Children who are abused but can tell, children who can go to someone for comfort and support, children who are then protected and freed from blame *completely* will still experience nightmares, flashbacks, and fear. They will still feel crazy, flawed, doomed, dirty, and different. Those are normal human reactions to traumatic events. But over time, these children will be able to discharge the emotions and resolve the trauma. When an umbrella of family dysfunction overlays the trauma and forbids telling, feeling, or trusting, the trauma is frozen and *encapsulated*—locked away in a little mental box in a far corner of the mind. It can't be talked about. It can't be dealt with and resolved. Secrecy leads to shame. The attacker's guilt becomes the victim's shame, creating a legacy of self-condemnation and isolation.

Children in healthy families can become prey for abusers. Awful things happen in the world, and no family can guarantee a child absolute safety. But when a child in a dysfunctional family is the casualty, the dysfunction itself excuses the abuser and contributes to the child's conviction that it is self, not the world, that is crazy. If there is abuse and no one takes or assigns responsibility, the child has no choice but to blame self.

THE PRICE OF ALTERED REALITY

It is normal for survivors to come out of their dysfunctional families convinced that they are crazy. It is not the survivor who is crazy; it is the family circumstances that are disturbed. When abuse is happening in a dysfunctional family system, it becomes necessary to alter reality frequently and repeatedly. If children are being abused and there is no one safe to tell, how can those children go to school and function with the level of fear and pain and anger that must be present? The solution is both predictable and brilliant. Children have to convince themselves that what they saw, heard, and experienced wasn't that bad. If the family's minimizing meant that abuse was normal and acceptable, then anyone who thought it wasn't was crazy. Survivors who can describe every agonizing detail of the abuse will nonetheless report it with all the emotional intensity of a trip to the local hardware store: "It happened; it's in the past; it didn't affect me." Survivors may even have had to convince themselves that what they saw, heard, and experienced wasn't real. If the family's denial meant that abuse didn't happen at all, then anyone who thought it did was crazy. Some survivors have trouble recalling childhood events, not only painful moments, but also times that must have been happy and positive.

Sometimes minimizing and denial make later identification as a survivor of abuse difficult, if not impossible. If clients were targeted with a systematic pattern of verbal humiliation or teasing or criticism that shredded identity and crushed dignity, then they were assaulted. If clients were subjected to physical punishment or attack that put health or safety at risk, then they were assaulted. If clients were consistently touched or treated in ways that denied their right to be separate people, then they were assaulted. If clients were repeatedly ignored and isolated with the silent treatment, then they were assaulted. If clients were reminded regularly that they were the cause of all their parents' unhappiness, or if they were told again and again that they should never have been born, then they were assaulted. If clients were exposed to sexual talk or pornography, or if they became the emotional partner or sexual confidant of a parent, then they were assaulted. Even if they were not the direct target of violence or manipulation, they were still assaulted because they never knew when the violence or the manipulation was going to turn on them.

The word parent stands for any person in a position of power, trust, and access. Parents are the most powerful people in a child's life. A child naturally trusts parents. A child can't really get away from parents. To a child, anyone who is bigger because of size or authority is seen as an adult, and all adults are seen as equal to parents at some level. That includes grandparents, aunts and uncles, older siblings and cousins, neighbors, teachers, baby-sitters, coaches, youth group leaders, ministers, rabbis, priests, and any other people that fit the definition. The things that happened, if done by adults to other adults, would be defined as libel or slander or assault, battery, or rape. The perpetrators would be judged criminals. If no one was even acknowledging what was going on, it is no wonder survivors had to convince themselves that none of this was serious or even real. It is no wonder they had to convince themselves that they were crazy.

DYSFUNCTION REDEFINES REALITY

If children who are being abused don't learn very quickly to alter reality, then the family does it for them. Dysfunctional families constantly distort reality with denial, minimizing, blaming, and rationalizing. The very problems that underlie the family dysfunction are redefined. Catchwords and labels hide the truth. When people are drunk, they are "tired." Mental instability is explained as "over-sensitivity." Phrases such as "healthy appetite" and "picky eater" disguise full-blown eating disorders. Battering hides behind a "quick temper."

Triangled, indirect, and incomplete communication also complicates and obscures reality. People talk around other people. They send messages to one family member through another family member, often a child: "Tell your father I'm mad at him." Rarely does a message reach its destination intact, and often the messenger is blamed for the message. People read minds and react to imagined responses. Even if someone wants to talk about reality, the tangle of family communication prevents that from happening.

DYSFUNCTION REDEFINES ABUSE

Abuse is redefined to deny normal feelings and responses. Tickling that brings tears is redefined as "teasing." How can the victim be hurt or upset? Verbal abuse—ridicule, name-calling, humiliation, and intimidation—is redefined as "constructive criticism": "I'm saying this to help you." How can the victim feel threatened? Physical abuse and emotional abandonment are redefined as "discipline": "This hurts me more than it hurts you," or "I'm doing this for your own good." How can the victim be angry? Sexual abuse is redefined as "duty" or "love" or "education" or "bothering" or "messing with." How can the victim's skin crawl about something that is an obligation or a benefit or only a minor annoyance? Often the child is blamed for the abuse: "I wouldn't have to do this if you weren't so bad." When the child, not the abuser, is labeled the offender, the wrongness of abuse is covered up. The abuser feels no guilt; the child feels it all.

DYSFUNCTION REDEFINES FEELINGS

Feelings are also redefined to make them unacceptable. Sadness and tears are dismissed as "unnecessary": "I'll give you something to cry about." Anger is "bad" and "sinful": "Nice children don't get angry." Fear is "stupid" and "weak": "Don't be a sissy." Folklore and religion reinforce the rules against feelings: "Big boys don't cry"; "Little ladies don't raise their voices"; "Children are to be seen and not heard"; "Honor thy father and thy mother." Feelings themselves, even good feelings, wind up forbidden. Children who are excited and happy are accused of being "too dramatic" or "overreacting."

Sometimes certain feelings are assigned to certain family members. An alcoholic may be the only one allowed to express anger. The spouse may be permitted only sadness or self-pity. One child may be accepted only when appearing helpless, while another may be encouraged to feel superior. Sometimes one family member becomes the feeling bearer for the entire family, while everyone else remains depressed and numb.

The roles that have long been recognized in dysfunctional families reinforce confusion and denial concerning feelings. The Hero looks responsible but feels inadequate. The Scapegoat looks rebellious but feels rejected. The Lost Child looks independent but feels lonely. The Mascot looks silly but feels crazy (Wegscheider, 1981).

ROLE REVERSAL

When parents are inadequate as a result of their own history or sickness, when parenting is uneven or nonexistent because of family dysfunction, all children become *parentified* to some extent. They have to parent their own parents through drunken stupors, emotional outbursts, or suicidal depressions. Often they also have to parent younger siblings. If nothing else, children have to fill the gaps and parent themselves when appropriate parenting is missing. If children were responsible for parents or siblings or self at age three or five or ten, then they were also automatically responsible for anything bad that was happening.

Dysfunctional families reinforce delusions that further trap the parentified child. Well into adulthood, Liz firmly believed she consented to her father's advances because the sexual abuse didn't begin until she was in her teens. Until she began therapy, she couldn't identify his lifelong severe depression and his constant threats of suicide if she objected to any of his demands as emotional blackmail. Andrea believed her family's warnings about her father's heart condition and could not object to the abuse for fear of upsetting him. Many years later, she discovered the dreaded heart condition was a fantasy her family concocted to control her behavior and keep her in line. Even after she learned the truth, her childhood fear of killing him periodically returned to block her own recovery.

ABUSE PLUS DYSFUNCTION
EQUALS DESTRUCTION

To survive, children have to buy into the family's denial, minimizing, blaming, and rationalizing. They have to believe the backward definitions of "constructive criticism" and "teasing" and "discipline" and "duty" and "love." They have to learn not to feel. That's why survivors believe the abuse wasn't that bad. That's why they think it didn't affect them. That's why they doubt their own memories and wonder if they're not just exaggerating or imagining. The problem for most survivors is not that they don't know what happened; it's that they don't know what it means. That's why the first step in healing is defining the abuse as assault; that word allows clients to consider the feelings they had to suppress in order to survive, the feelings they have both a right and a need to feel to recover.

The very fact of abuse devastates any child. But abuse combined with family dysfunction—the altered reality, minimizing, denial, blaming, rationalizing, and redefinition of feelings and behavior—keeps the abuse secret and completes the destruction of the child victim. The home becomes a house of mirrors. The child seeks truth but is met with only shadows and reflections, deformed and distorted in the family looking glass. Reality is an illusion based on the shifting quicksand of dysfunction. The child becomes the offender in a crazy dance of survival, and that child carries into adulthood a legacy of shame and depression that can interfere with functioning, wreak havoc on self-esteem, and threaten life itself.

Until some basis for reality testing is established between client and therapist, until there are some shared assumptions about how the world really works and what the "teasing" and the "constructive criticism" and the "discipline" and the "duty" and the "love" really were, therapy will remain mired in that same quicksand of dysfunction. Investigating and challenging the distorted cognitive system of the survivor can be a daunting and repetitive task, but if it is glossed over, false beliefs and faulty perceptions may sabotage later process work.

Children who are assaulted and met with denial decide they are crazy. Children who are assaulted and not protected decide they are not worth protecting. Children who are assaulted and not defended decide they are not worth defending. Children who are ridiculed and humiliated decide they have no value. Children who are ignored and isolated with silence decide they are invisible.

Client exercise: Keep a log of your discoveries about the ways your family altered reality, and write your own redefinitions to more accurately describe what happened.

Catherine described in verse the bewildering insanity of an abusive childhood:

Inside Out

Came out backwards, in the front;
Didn't know that I was sure;
Thought that I was filthy, clean,
Tainted, and yet pure.

They all seemed so familiarly strange,
Too many and yet one.
Some were happy through their frowns,
Acting excited, very glum.

They thought me frozen, couldn't thaw out;
Little did they know,
That all the while they'd quietly shout,
In safety, my terror would grow.

My body feels torn and yet as one,
For it makes a bit of sense,
When down was up and shame was life,
What was the difference?

Be loyal to the faultless;
Trust in all the lies.
Do not speak—not one word,
Only 'til you die.

Well, death it was, while living still;
They buried me that day,
That awful day that I was born,
And wanted just to play.

I trusted all the anger;
I yearned to make it right.
I'll change enough for all of them,
If only for one night.

Do you see my disillusion?
Can you tell I'm struggling still?
If I am right and they were wrong,
I learned to live in Hell.

- *Intervention:* Challenging the distorted reality.
- *Rationale:* Identify and alter delusional thoughts and perceptions.
- *Result:* Decreased rationalization and intellectualization.

Chapter 4

Using the PTSD Diagnosis
as a Therapeutic Intervention

There were times Mom seemed interested in me, but I never knew how long it was going to last. Usually I couldn't even finish telling her something before she wanted me to be quiet or she just tuned out. I could stop mid-sentence and she wouldn't even notice. I never knew when it was okay to show her I loved her and when I would be yelled at. Sometimes I never knew if I would be wanted there or not. I just really felt like I was walking through a minefield and there were explosions all around me. At any moment I knew if I made a wrong move I'd set off explosions, too.

Jessica

The unpredictability and irrationality of childhood abuse, coupled with denial, is a fertile breeding ground for post-traumatic stress disorder. Just as soldiers coming out of the jungles of Vietnam found the experience didn't simply go away so, too, do survivors of childhood abuse carry psychic scars that return to haunt their lives, limit their options, and control their feelings and behavior.

POST-TRAUMATIC STRESS DISORDER

Post-traumatic stress disorder is predicated on exposure to trauma. Unlike most other disorders, the DSM-IV diagnostic criteria for PTSD cannot be satisfied solely by expression of symptoms; there must also be evidence of a causal event: "The person experienced, witnessed, or was confronted with an event or events that involved

45

actual or threatened death or serious injury, or a threat to the physical integrity of self or others, and the person's response involved intense fear, helplessness, or horror (American Psychiatric Association, 1994). DSM-III-R suggested PTSD might be conceptualized as a *normal* response to an *abnormal* situation: "The person has experienced an event that is outside the range of usual human experience and that would be markedly distressing to almost anyone" (American Psychiatric Association, 1987). The things that happened were beyond the realm of normal human expectation. It was the world, not the victim, that was crazy. Physical and emotional survival were threatened. Victims responded with predictable and normal defenses, and the symptoms they may be experiencing now are also predictable and normal.

The symptoms of PTSD in DSM-IV include the following:

- Exposure to trauma
- Recurrent and intrusive distressing recollections of the trauma; recurrent distressing dreams of the trauma; acting or feeling as if the traumatic event were recurring; intense psychological distress at exposure to cues that symbolize or resemble an aspect of the trauma; physiological reactivity on exposure to reminders of the trauma
- Efforts to avoid thoughts, feelings or conversations associated with the trauma; efforts to avoid activities, places, or people reminiscent of the trauma; inability to recall an important aspect of the trauma; diminished interest in life activities; feelings of detachment or estrangement from others; restricted range of affect; limited expectations about the future
- Sleep difficulties; irritability or outbursts of anger; difficulty concentrating; hypervigilance; exaggerated startle response (American Psychiatric Association, 1994)

There is now significant professional support for expanding the description of PTSD to take into account the effects of prolonged trauma in hostagelike or totalitarian situations. Some of these are now listed as "Associated Features and Disorders" in the DSM-IV diagnostic narrative (American Psychiatric Association, 1994). However, Judith Herman has proposed a new diagnostic category, complex post-traumatic stress disorder, that would recognize alterations in the areas of affect regulation, consciousness, self-perception, perception of the perpetrator, relations with others, and systems of meaning. Symptoms of Complex PTSD would include persistent dysphoria; hopelessness and despair; shame, guilt, and self-blame; sense of stigma or defilement; persistent distrust; transient dissociation, depersonalization, or derealization; suicidal thoughts; self-injury; idealization of the perpetrator; acceptance of the belief system and rationalizations of the perpetrator; helplessness; failures of self-protection; repeated search for a rescuer; isolation and withdrawal (Herman, 1992).

Within the context of the current DSM-IV diagnostic criteria, when PTSD occurs in an adult because of childhood trauma, the words "with delayed onset" are added to the diagnosis. Something wedges into the frozen, encapsulated trauma, and suddenly it seems as if the trauma happened yesterday. The survivor is flooded with all the feelings and reactions that should have been experienced long ago.

An adult survivor's responses echo the reactions of a combat veteran. The adult survivor of abuse lived childhood in a war zone, a war zone eerily similar to Vietnam. In that war, friend and foe looked the same, and there were no clear battle lines. The abused child could not predict when someone who should be a protector would suddenly change into an assaulter, and there was no fallback zone if the whole child's universe, the home, was unsafe.

Of the four factors that constitute PTSD—exposure to trauma, flashback phenomena, psychological numbing and reduced involvement with the external environment, and hyperarousal (Everly, 1989) —survivors seem to have the greatest difficulty understanding the last two. Most survivors can readily grasp the connection between past trauma and flashbacks, if only because of publicity about the plight of Vietnam veterans. The constriction of thoughts, feelings, memory, expectations, and connectedness and the augmentation in physiologic reactivity need to be more deeply explored and explained in the early stages of therapy.

PHYSICAL RESPONSES TO TRAUMA

Understandably and predictably, abused children react in ways that can be traced back to prehistoric times, when humans still lived in caves. Society is highly advanced, but the human body has not yet escaped its primitive heritage. When a bear suddenly appeared in the mouth of the cave, the early human had to have instant survival skills. The options were limited. The cave dweller needed strength to throw a spear at the bear or run out the back door of the cave—the old fight-or-flight reaction. A discharge of adrenaline, below the level of consciousness, readied the cave dweller to face the threat by altering body biochemistry. To fight or run, the body needs strength in the large muscles of the legs and arms and increased heart rate and blood pressure to rush blood to those sites. If life itself hangs in the balance, it's not critical that the body digest its last meal so blood flow to the digestive tract is shut down, causing the familiar knot of fear in the stomach. The body begins to produce its own painkillers—endorphins—so that injury will not interfere with escape. Finally, since physical defense is reflexive, the body goes on automatic pilot, funneling information through the spinal cord and bypassing the higher parts of the brain. There is no need to understand Shakespeare or quantum physics when life itself is on the line. Blood supply to the cerebral cortex decreases, impairing abstract thinking ability in moments of stress and threat.

This monumental shift in body biochemistry catalyzed by adrenaline is associated with two emotions—anger and fear. Even though humans no longer live in caves, they cannot prevent the rush of adrenaline in the face of rage or terror.

Similar to soldiers caught up in guerrilla fighting, survivors of childhood abuse never knew when or where the next land mine would explode. They never knew when or where the next verbal bullet would strike. From the moment of the first assault, they needed to maintain some level of arousal. They became accustomed to living with a certain degree of tension, trying to ensure it never happened again or, at the very least, ready to protect themselves or withdraw. They became skilled at preparing to dodge or deflect attacks, whichever seemed to work better in their particular family battlefield.

Even if actual assault happened only once or just a few times, the potential was forevermore there. If children are attacked and not comforted or rescued, they decide the attack was deserved, and they get ready to deal with the next one.

EMOTIONAL RESPONSES TO TRAUMA

The emotional reaction to threat is also predictable and understandable in terms of survival. Even though adrenaline is triggered by fear and anger, to maintain those intense emotions in the face of danger would quickly become life-threatening. When an animal is terrified, it bolts or freezes. Soldiers on a jungle path would be easy targets if they fled or froze in fear. They would be easy targets if they gave in to blind rage and thrashed through the underbrush hunting wildly for the enemy. That same destruction and death would have been the fate of victims of abuse if they had tried to run away when the aggressor was attacking. That same destruction and death would have been their fate if they had become angry and fought back at the aggressor. Fight or flight would have made things worse, maybe so much worse that their lives or someone else's life would have been at risk.

Adrenaline's job is to mobilize survival. To that end, it numbs and disconnects feelings to create the slow-motion sense of distance and detachment—having time stand still—that survivors of any trauma describe. It's only after the fact that the emotional reaction sets in. People have near misses on the expressway and drive home calmly, only to start shaking uncontrollably the minute the car is in the garage. People help others through an accident with paramedic-like precision, only to fall apart after the real emergency technicians take over. People stand by a friend during a loss like the rock of Gibraltar, delaying their own grief until the crisis has passed.

CHRONIC SHOCK

It is important to understand that physical mobilization and emotional disconnection can't be prevented in the face of trauma. Physical mobilization and emotional disconnection are *normal* trauma responses for human beings. It is impossible not to surge with energy physically, while freezing and going numb emotionally, if life and safety are threatened. The combination throws the body into a temporary state of shock, allowing people to function in the midst of trauma.

However, there are two parts to every traumatic event. The first part is what can be identified immediately—something catastrophic happens. The second part is the reaction, or *debriefing*—the shaking, the falling apart, the grief. Survivors of trauma need to talk, to tell their stories, to feel their feelings. They need to be listened to, believed, and comforted. People who have lived through catastrophe instinctively seek out ways to debrief. Victims of the Oklahoma City bombing debriefed with newscasters, bystanders, police and rescue workers, medical personnel, and families and friends because the explosion was over and the horror was acknowledged. Debriefing happens naturally after the trauma has ended, *unless something blocks that built-in healing process.*

What if there is never time for the aftermath of trauma, the physical and emotional debriefing after the near miss or the accident or the funeral? What if there is never time to react or decompress? What if the attack or threat of attack is ever-present, as in the jungles of Vietnam or in a violent and abusive family? What if denial keeps everyone from admitting that something awful happened? Then the trauma becomes frozen. The muscles never really have a chance to relax. They remain coiled and contracted, ready to respond. The feelings never get felt. They are stuffed and numbed until there are no feelings left at all. Numbing is not selective. If the scary, angry feelings must be smothered in order to survive, the joyful, happy feelings are smothered too. All feelings get suppressed, leaving only anxiety and depression in their wake. The muscle tension and the numbed feelings combine to create a condition of chronic shock that fills and limits the life of the adult survivor.

I've got to run and run and never stop and never look back. But I can't run because I don't know where to run to. There is no place for me to go. There is no safe place. I can't even hide inside of me, because I'm not safe—I'm what I have to get away from. Right now I don't think I have the energy to run—I just want to die—to just not be or exist. I want to go to sleep and never wake up. I'm so tired of trying. I'm just tired of being here. I'm tired of trying to understand things. I'm tired of trying to convince myself that I'm worth something when I know I'm not. I'm tired of being told to play the game when the game keeps changing and I don't know the rules. I just know that I'm the one who'll get it. I don't care. All I know is that I'm losing the grip on the edge of the whirling pit and I'm going to fall in and never come out. I'll just fall and fall forever.

Jessica

LEGACIES OF ASSAULT
AND POST-TRAUMATIC STRESS DISORDER

I'm really confused. It doesn't seem real anymore. Nothing's real. I keep waiting to wake up. I keep waiting and waiting, and I'm so scared that I'll never wake up. I feel like I've been waiting forever. I've just been doing nothing. I feel so numb. Nothing matters. Life doesn't matter. I don't matter. I don't know what's real. I'm not even sure I'm real or I exist. What difference does it make anyway? Who cares if I exist or not? I want to disappear and be invisible.

Jessica

The remnants of childhood abuse, the symptoms of post-traumatic stress disorder, are woven into every action of the adult survivor and into the texture of life itself. The chronic low-grade depression that results from suppressing feelings casts a dark cloud over existence. The same nerve endings that had to be numbed to fear and rage are the very ones that might feel happiness and excitement. Joy becomes a foreign territory, an emotion other people experience but out of reach for the survivor, who often can only be there and observe at moments of achievement or celebration. Survivors may imitate others and pretend feelings that seem appropriate, but the emotions are not real and underneath the gray-black pit of depression waits to reclaim them.

The only way survivors may still be connected to childhood terror is in nightmares and panic attacks and free-floating anxiety. The only way they may still be connected to childhood rage is in waking flashbacks and outbursts of anger that seem to come from nowhere and are just as quickly stifled.

PHYSICAL HYPERVIGILANCE

Survivors lived childhood under siege. They needed to be on guard all the time, always prepared to ward off attack or defend against violation. This need created a state of constant physical hypervigilance. They needed to know where other people's bodies were and what other people were doing at any given moment. They are still probably extremely alert to movement around them. They may startle easily and overreact to changes in their physical environment. This heightened perception makes them detailed recorders of their surroundings. It is not unusual for clients to notice minor changes in office arrangement, even down to the location of objects on the therapist's desk.

Although such overreaction seems a control issue, the adult survivor who insists on sitting in the same chair and resists changes in routine or environment may only be compensating for keenly developed senses, trying to keep from being overloaded with stimuli that are below the threshold of consciousness for those who never had to learn skills to cope with trauma.

EMOTIONAL HYPERVIGILANCE

Hypersensitivity to physical surroundings is only the tip of the hypervigilance iceberg. Because they were the targets of abuse, survivors not only developed constant awareness of bodies and objects, they also had to become emotionally tuned in to their surroundings. They had to train themselves to be alert to every variation in the unstable atmosphere around them. It was critical to instantly and accurately interpret the look in Father's eye, the tone of Mother's voice, the hints in gesture and body language that would predict emerging events. Their safety and their very survival hung in the balance. Was it safe to share a report card, or had Dad had too much to drink and did it need to be hidden for another night? Could they stay with the family, or did they need to escape to another room? Would Mother be all right tonight, or would she need to be defended from Dad's violence and comforted in the aftermath? What could be done to reduce the growing tension? Survivors needed to read minds, anticipate needs, and guess reactions. Survivors needed to think other people's thoughts and feel their feelings, even before they did.

In childhood, survivors became hostages to their families, lacking freedom to think or feel or even exist without the family's permission. As with other hostages, they became so loyal to their captors that they began to identify completely with them, their feelings, and their beliefs. Much the same thing happened to concentration camp victims who began to cooperate with their jailers in order to survive. History is full of accounts of victims of airline hijackings and kidnappings who come out of the experience expressing praise and sympathy for the villains (Ochberg and Soskis, 1982). Patty Hearst in the uniform of the Symbionese Liberation Army stands as this country's most vivid example (Herman, 1992).

Carried into adulthood, the focus on others at expense of self is labeled codependency. However, for the adult survivor of abuse, it represents a life-or-death skill not easily dismissed. If the survivor became a parentified child whose job it was to meet an adult's needs at the expense of self, it makes no sense to let others do for themselves what the survivor can do for them. When the concept of "tough love" or the advice of Alanon to "let go and accept the things you cannot change" comes up against the survivor's certainty that ignoring, accepting, or letting go puts life in peril, emotional and physical hypervigilance will always win. Again, this represents reality and sanity, not resistance, for the survivor.

BLURRED BOUNDARIES AND GLOBAL GUILT

I felt so guilty all day, and I'm not sure why. I guess I feel responsible for Mom's being sick. I told her—I told her over and over to go to the doctor but she didn't listen to me. I'm worried about her. I don't know what I'd do if something happened to her. I can't believe I'm crying about it. Nothing's happened to her, and she'll be okay. I keep hearing her say that I'll feel guilty when she's gone. I already feel guilty, and she's still here. Why do I do this?

Jessica

Hypervigilance is also reflected in boundary confusion. If, to cope with abuse, survivors had to know where everyone was and what they were doing at any given moment, it became difficult to separate themselves from others, to know where their own skin ends and others' skin begins. Survivors may still be terrified of real or imagined abandonment. They may fear they will cease to exist if they are left alone. They may be torn between wanting to be with someone all the time and feeling terrified of the intimacy that represents abuse to them. If survivors were physically hurt as children, their bodies' boundaries were violated violently. Closeness evokes panic, and yet closeness is necessary for caretaking and for permission to exist. Indistinct boundaries sometimes alternate with rigid boundaries—enmeshed one minute and isolated behind walls the next.

Not only physical boundaries are blurred; emotional separation between self and others is also clouded. The need to read minds and interpret and fix everyone else's feelings creates an emotional chameleon. Survivors can likely walk into a room and immediately sense the feeling tone. They may take on other people's feelings and feel them as their own. If someone is angry, survivors may automatically assume they have done something wrong. If guilt is constant companion to the child, chronic apologies are second nature to the adult. The confused lines between world and self lead to apologies with a twist of the bizarre. Sheila apologized if it was raining. Claire took the blame for letting her husband hit her.

Absence of boundaries around self, combined with the need to anticipate events and feelings, also gives birth to the "shoulds." Survivors may judge themselves harshly for failing to foretell the future. Betty was convinced she was dumb because she did not predict her husband's alcoholism, even though he was a teetotaler when they met and married.

For the survivor, the underlying themes of life are depression and guilt—depression as the result of emotional numbing and guilt as the result of not measuring up, not being perfect, not saving the family. In its most twisted form, guilt becomes survivor guilt. Clients may feel guilty for escaping and going on with their lives. They may subconsciously believe they really do not deserve to live and that someday they will have to pay the price for this survival sham.

VULNERABILITY TO REPEATED VIOLATION

My mother hit me all the time. I would go to school black and blue and look at other kids to see if they were black and blue, too. She would go crazy on me and completely lose it. She kept hitting and hitting like a wild woman. I still jump if someone moves quickly. She would hit me with whatever she had. I remember just shrinking and going numb. After a while it didn't even physically hurt anymore. Like all my nerve endings were dead and I didn't feel pain anymore. I know that even now it takes a lot to physically hurt me. Sometimes I don't even know if I've cut myself and am bleeding. She also let Daddy hit her and throw glasses and bottles. I thought that was normal. That's probably part of the reason I let my boyfriends beat me silly. I'm angry that she never taught me what a healthy relationship is.

Jessica

As if chronic depression and global guilt are not enough, the legacy of childhood abuse can also pollute ongoing personal history and events. The child whose physical and emotional boundaries were violated, the child who was not protected from abuse, grows into an adult vulnerable to further attack. Adulthood is sometimes filled with physically and verbally abusive relationships, date rape, exploitation, and stranger violence, which are then used to condemn self further. These are not reflections of inadequacy or sickness. These are the natural consequences of being assaulted and not defended as a child.

Shelley made a drawing of her three-year-old self during her first conscious memory of being beaten by her mother, while her father watched but did nothing (see Figure 4.1).

Swallowed up by her mother, with her father further obscuring and condoning the violence, Shelley used the only defense that would work at age three: *freeze—go numb—forget*. She had to freeze physically, go numb emotionally, and forget how awful it really was. She had no other choices. Her attackers were bigger and more powerful than she was, and she was totally helpless against them.

FIGURE 4.1. Shelley's Representation of Abuse

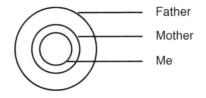

Father

Mother

Me

Shelley's picture shows how impossible it was for her to get away or to defend herself. There was literally no room for her to move. She had to deny her natural instinct to resist or run. Any struggle would have been squashed by her parents. Any attempt to break out and escape would have exploded their circles and destroyed them, and that Shelley could not do. She could never even grow and learn ways to protect herself. Her parents' rigid control saw to that. If she had fought back, she might have been hit harder and longer. She might have been badly hurt or killed. Even at age three, she sensed that danger and did what she could to prevent it. She absorbed the message in the drawing and stopped existing as a separate person.

Shelley's picture also clearly demonstrates why she could not tell anyone of the abuse or even allow herself to remember it in any of its real intensity. Although she didn't forget what happened, she had to forget her own terror and rage. Her abusers were, in fact, the people she had to depend on for survival, and their cooperation hid the violence from view and made it seem as if it never happened at all.

From that moment on, Shelley was locked into the primitive defense of her three-year-old self. She faced her mother's ongoing attacks with the same *freeze—go numb—forget* sequence she discovered at age three, and she approached her adult assaulters with exactly that same defense.

TWO PERSONALITIES IN ONE BODY

When I think of it, it's like Mom was possessed or something. Like there was this madwoman who was crazed and running around our house. She was like two different people, and she flipped like a light switch. It scared me because I didn't (and still don't) know how to control that switch.

Jessica

Even if the child was not literally frozen in the moment of abuse, like Shelley, there is still a subtle vulnerability to future attack planted deep within an assaulted child's being. Over the years of dysfunction and abuse, survivors build an incredible tolerance to inappropriate and inconsistent behavior. Recovery moves forward when they begin to uncover the schizophrenic reality that is at the core of every abused child's experience.

Children raised in physically or verbally violent homes, children not protected from attack, have not two parents but four. Children raised in abusive homes deal with two physical parents but at least four distinct personalities. Many survivors describe the abuser as "Dr. Jekyll and Mr. Hyde."

It is important for survivors to understand the specifics of the divided personalities with which they learned to cope. The dichotomy is easiest to identify in the actual abuser.

Client exercise: What words would you use to describe the abuser on a rampage, when there was yelling, screaming, hitting, or violating? Loud, vicious, and mean, or silent and threatening? Choose your own words.

What words would you use to describe the abuser after things settled down, when the abuse was in remission, so to speak? Quiet, distant, and forbidding, or apologetic and loving? Write your own words.

Hopefully, clients can identify that they have just described two separate personalities that inhabited only one body.

The four personalities in two bodies come from changes in the nonabusive parent. Even a parent who does not actively participate in abuse cannot help but respond with some shift in behavior or emotion when it occurs.

Client exercise: What was the nonabusive parent like when things blew up? Passive, withdrawn, and depressed, or angry and silently agreeing? Choose your own words.

What was the nonabusive parent like when things stabilized even momentarily? Happier and more energetic or tense and walking on eggshells? Write your own words.

Again, clients have just described two personalities dwelling in only one body. Focusing on counting physical bodies blocked recognition of this emotional multiplication. Even if both parents actively or passively abused, they each had their own unique styles. They each had their own set of dual personalities.

Add alcohol or drug abuse, mental illness, or an eating disorder to the equation, and the fragmentation increases exponentially. Rhonda recalled that her father's alcoholism caused as much disruption as the abuse: "When Dad was drinking he was funny and talkative, but when he was sober he was stern and cold. And when Dad was okay Mom was upbeat and involved in my activities, but when he was drinking she'd cry and lock herself in the bedroom."

It didn't matter if Rhonda's drunk parent was better or worse than Rhonda's sober parent. Her confusion grew out of the abrupt changes she witnessed and the conflicting personalities she was forced to try to fuse in her mind.

No one would pretend that healthy parents don't change. Of course they do. But, most of the time, healthy parents change in response to events around them. For example, if a glass of milk spills, even the healthiest and most nurturing of parents is likely to be irritated. Abusive parents, alcoholic parents, eating-disordered parents, or mentally disturbed parents change in response to their own internal emotional states. They can totally ignore the spilled milk one day and explode in rage the next. The child, when attacked, looks around for a reason to explain the unpredictability, inconsistency, and volatility. Finding none, the child can blame only self.

ORIGINS OF ADULT CHILD ISSUES

If the classic issues most survivors struggle with originate any-where, they are born right here in the schizophrenic turbulence of the abusive family. Problems with control, responsibility and per-fectionism, guilt, all-or-nothing thinking, trust, crisis addiction, tol-erance for unpredictability, and guessing at normal are the natural outgrowths of the need to make sense of the senseless (Woititz, 1990).

If the entire world was out of control, survivors tried to grab control wherever they could. The inexhaustible effort to make things right and finally measure up led to superachieving and per-fectionism or to just hopelessly giving up and blaming themselves. If the people in childhood were shifting 180 degrees, survivors began to see reality as black or white; there were no gray areas. Their ability to trust the stability of people and circumstances was damaged. If their families were constantly caught up in real or potential chaos, survivors became good at handling crises. If they had to adapt continually to the unexpected, they learned to accept the bizarre as normal and gained little understanding of cause and effect in relationships or events.

LEARNING TO IGNORE EXTERNAL REALITY

To cope with the multiple identities and the treachery of abuse and dysfunction, survivors had to learn to deny at least half of their own outside reality to avoid being overwhelmed by confusion. They had to ignore at least half of what they were seeing and hearing at any given moment.

That skill, learned of necessity in childhood, makes survivors vulnerable to abuse in the present. They may unwittingly put them-selves in harm's way, walking into dangerous situations unaware of risk, only to be blindsided by a sudden attack from a person they thought they could trust. They may ignore signals of potential vio-lence. They may not understand that the first time a friend introduced them to someone else the words held the threat of betrayal. If they are presented as "my man" or "my babe," there is a suggestion of ownership and disrespect. "My man" or "my babe" is an object without a name. "Lynne, my girlfriend," values individuality over the relationship.

CONTRADICTORY EXPECTATIONS

Their inconsistency came in many different ways—from what were acceptable grades to punishments to what were acceptable hairstyles and clothing.

What I had to do to be noticed by my mom was to do something wrong, be bad. She acknowledged me by yelling, hitting, or giving me the silent treatment.

To be accepted by my mom I had to stay away from my dad, have a boyfriend, and be doing what she wanted me to do. I had to be just like my sister, but if I was too much like my sister, then I was in trouble for trying to be like my sister. I also had to be popular and tell her everything she wanted to know, which was all about what my friends were doing, and if I didn't, then she would get mad.

To be noticed by my dad I had to be sick. If I was sick, then he was all over me, and I didn't like that—I would feel very uncomfortable. Also, if I was telling him what a wonderful father he was or if I needed help. If I was okay, then he ignored me.

I don't know what I had to do to be accepted by my dad. I think he just basically tolerated me—never accepting me because he doesn't really like me.

If I did what I needed to have my mom accept me, then he didn't want me around. I couldn't have both.

Jessica

When parents are caught in a web of violence, little agreement on family values or norms is likely. What one parent sees as acceptable or pleasing may be the exact opposite of the other parent's expectations. To be noticed by one parent may call for behavior that antagonizes the other parent. Sometimes the behavior that is noticed is very different from the behavior that wins approval from that same parent. The only way Jessica could get attention from her mother was by being punished for acting up and being bad, so her negative behavior got noticed. But obviously, misbehaving was not acceptable to her mother.

It is important for survivors to identify the specifics of that contradiction from their own experience.

Client exercise: What did you have to do to get your father to notice you? What did you have to do to get your father to approve of you? What did you have to do to get your mother to notice you? What did you have to do to get your mother to approve of you?

LEARNING TO IGNORE INTERNAL REALITY

To please one parent or the other, survivors had to deny at least half of their inside reality. To avoid being overwhelmed by confusion, they had to ignore what they wanted to do and who they really were at any given moment.

Survivors learned to discount their own discomfort, their inner warning signals of potential violence. The need to numb out painful feelings required them to deny natural fear. They had to extinguish instinctive fear reflexes to live in their families and to protect their families from outside discovery. Even today they may be envied for being fearless. In fact, they may be unable to recognize their bodies' cues to danger. That skill, learned out of necessity in childhood, also makes them vulnerable to attack as adults.

BLAMING SELF

The only way a child who is abused can cope is to blame self and justify the attack as deserved. The alternative is too frightening. Parents and caregivers are a child's link to survival in a hostile world. To judge them inadequate would be to lose them. And a child left alone, abandoned, or neglected, ultimately dies. Faced with that prospect, the child wisely takes the blame for the abuse.

Learning to ignore huge chunks of external and internal reality, coupled with automatic self-blame, leads to denial and minimizing and guilt for subsequent abuse in adulthood. Physical or verbal or emotional attacks happen repeatedly because they cannot even be defined as assault, and any suspicion that they might be violation is quickly replaced by "I asked for it," or "I deserve nothing better," or "It doesn't matter."

Survivors of childhood abuse who are later hurt as adults often blame themselves for letting it happen again and for not fighting back. They never realize that because they were assaulted and not rescued as children the only thing they have at their command to confront the next attacker is the same limited *freeze—go numb— forget* defense of the child locked in the moment of the first abuse. It is not about failing to fight back, it is about being absolutely unable to do so. And if they don't have a right to exist in the first place, nothing that happens to them counts anyway.

DETACHMENT

I don't know what's real and what isn't. It's so confusing.

Jessica

Finally, the *go numb—forget* portion of the child's survival system spills into the rest of life, creating a sense of unreality and detachment from ongoing events. Depression muffles feelings too painful to acknowledge. If survivors can't feel, they can't really connect in any meaningful way with what is going on around them. The struggle to not feel takes energy. Energy directed away from the present leads to preoccupation and difficulty concentrating. Emotional numbing blankets the survivor's ability to engage in life and relate to others. This increases guilt and depression and weaves the final threads into the cloak of feeling crazy that survivors wear as they walk through the world.

Client exercise: List your own symptoms of PTSD and connect those symptoms to events you remember from your childhood and to the family dysfunction you can identify.

REFRAMING PATHOLOGY

When the PTSD diagnosis is explained in the context of childhood abuse as trauma, when the dynamics of delayed debriefing are understood, and when the symptoms of PTSD, including the symptoms of complex PTSD, are framed as normal human responses to abnormal events, survivors can begin to shed the conviction that they are crazy. The realization that behaviors and symptoms have their origins in trauma, not pathology, frees survivors to form a more realistic and more positive self-concept on which to base recovery and relieves them from self-condemnation and self-doubt.

Maria had spent years in therapy with various diagnoses and felt she was severely disturbed and hopeless. Her history of abuse in childhood had been noted but never meaningfully addressed. Her reaction to this intervention was typical:

> Today I saw hope, that there was indeed a light within my reach. I want to jump up and down, cry, laugh, scream out to all the world—I AM NORMAL. I want to say it in a sing-song voice. I want to say it in my articulate, deliberate woman voice. I want to stop everyone along the way and whisper in the gentle voice of a three-year-old—I'm normal. I know where the tears that fill up inside me are from. I know what the fear is that puts a knot in my stomach. I am normal because I get scared when people get close to me, because I want to have sex when I feel lonely, because I want to give superficial messages that my life is together and that I've worked through so many issues. When in reality, these responses are normal for a child who needs to be protected as she continues to lie terrified and traumatized on the kitchen floor.

- *Intervention:* Using the PTSD diagnosis therapeutically.
- *Rationale:* Frame symptoms as evidence of frozen, encapsulated trauma, not pathology.
- *Result:* Shift in self-experience from crazy victim to normal survivor.

Chapter 5

The Survivor's Internal Experience

I'm in that pit and there's no notches in the wall so I can't get out. Then all of a sudden I'm out and I'm laughing and then it starts all over again, and it happens so much I'm confused. I was just this robot who didn't have the capacity to feel. I hate being numb. I hate feeling, too, so why bother? There's never any peace, never any rest. Always going, always going, no matter how slow it seems.

I feel like something is missing and I'm looking for it, but I don't know what it is or where to find it. I feel like I'm falling apart inside, and I can't move fast enough to pick up all the pieces. I get hold of one and three more fall. I try to get one of those, and then the one I just got plus three more fall. I feel like I'm fighting a losing battle.

Jessica

Learning to ignore huge chunks of reality and to suppress both awareness and emotion gives rise to a feeling of distance from life and a loss of wholeness and identity. It is also the taproot of a more significant separation from self. Sometimes it is a feeling that something is missing. Sometimes it is a clearer sense that there are several different pieces of self. Mary's poetry hinted at this division long before she identified herself as a survivor of abuse:

Three of me stare out at one of me staring in.
Which of the four is real, if any, I cannot tell . . .

SPLITTING THE SELF

For most survivors, splitting the self has nothing to do with split personality, or dissociative identity disorder. Splitting the self comes out of the struggle to survive ongoing deprivation or attack. To cope with the fragmentation all around them, survivors had to fragment themselves, too. They had to censor and compartmentalize their behavior, feelings, perceptions, and beliefs (Herman, 1992; Shengold, 1989). The shards of self that resulted are reflections of the events that formed them. They are normal and understandable defensive states, or *personas*, that can be shrugged on and off to suit the circumstances.

PIECES OF THE PUZZLE

If the client had to be a parent to parents or to siblings in childhood, there might be an efficient, controlling persona who can take charge and run the world or an undependable, indecisive persona who runs from responsibility. If the client was sexualized as a child, there might be a seductive persona who attracts and discards lovers like a candle lures moths to its lethal flame or an isolated, lonely persona terrified of intimacy. If the client had to disappear as a child, there might be a timid, apologetic persona who withdraws, turtlelike, at the slightest sign of conflict or danger or an exuberant, impatient, immature persona who emerges, ever so briefly, to dance in the sunlight. All of these are understandable responses to what was demanded in childhood.

THREE CORE PERSONAS

Underneath the masks shown to the outside world lies a trio of personas that more truly mirrors the disconnection from self dictated by trauma. Three broad themes run consistently through survivors' descriptions of themselves—part empty and mechanical, part impulsive and even fun loving, part dark and menacing shadow that overhangs life and threatens existence. Conceptualizing and naming the triumvirate of defensive states makes them less threatening and creates a commonality with other survivors. The first is the Adult; the second is the Child; the third represents the hurtful legacy of family dysfunction and abuse, the Destroyer.

When a child is being abused and no one is taking responsibility or protecting that child, the entire abusive drama is absorbed by the child. The child takes inside the triangle of players—the victim, the abuser, and the nonprotective bystander. The victim becomes the persona of the Child, the abuser and the abuser's distorted reality becomes the Destroyer, and the bystander who should have protected but didn't becomes part of the Adult.

Margret described these personas in herself as "the teacher's pet"—the perfect Adult, "the hippie"—the sensitive Child, and "the siren"—the self-destructive remnants of assault and abandonment, the Destroyer. No matter what characteristics each part takes on, childhood abuse cracks the self into three large splinters, each of which can shatter further as the abuse continues or intensifies.

Splitting the self was necessary for survival in the crucible of abuse. The survivor managed to mold three levels of self, three distinct and coherent internal pieces, to deal with the chaos outside.

The first part, the Adult, grew from the limited part of self that the survivor was allowed to expose. It reflects the false front the family showed to the world and the family's inability to value or protect their child. The second part, the Child, the vulnerable, real self, was forced into hiding by the third part, the Destroyer. The Destroyer is the sum total of family dysfunction—the disapproval, condemnation, altered reality, rejection and violence, which were internalized as rules for the game of life. The survivor intuitively and sensibly presented to the world only what the family decided was acceptable—the Adult. The survivor intuitively and cleverly hid a part of self—the Child—to keep feelings, creativity, and spontaneity intact. The survivor intuitively and wisely played by the family rules and believed the distortion and denial—the Destroyer.

Clients need to understand that the three-part defense—Adult, Child, and Destroyer—is not sickness or craziness. Rather, it bears testimony to the strength and brilliance of the children they were. It explains their ongoing ability to hold opposing beliefs and engage in incongruent behaviors. It is the triumph of their will to survive.

As clients grow more comfortable with the existence and origins of these defensive personas, they gain workable tools for healing. Clients have been waging unsuccessful internal battles for years. As long as the patterns based in abuse and altered reality are addressed as intrinsic evidence of a self that is bad and flawed, those battles remain ineffective and inconclusive. When the distorted behaviors and beliefs are separated from self and identified as learned, when they are framed as part of the externally acquired Destroyer persona, they can be successfully confronted and changed.

Integrating these three parts—nurturing and increasing the power of the Adult to protect and value the Child and using that alliance to challenge and discard the damaging and self-defeating pieces of the Destroyer—is a pivotal task in healing. The progressive dialogue among the three personas becomes the script for every ensuing stage of therapy.

- *Intervention:* Defining the survivor's inner experience of fragmentation as defensive states—the Adult, the Child, and the Destroyer—formed to survive abuse.
- *Rationale:* Establish a conceptual framework for integrative aspects of the healing process.
- *Result:* Increased understanding of contradictions and confusion in identity, behavior, and beliefs.

Chapter 6

The Adult

I feel like I'm sitting in this water bubble and I'm nothing. Everything goes on around me, but I can't join in because of the bubble. Everything's blurred because of the bubble.

It's like I'm a computerized robot, and I go through life doing what was programmed with no energy or emotion. The problem is that the robot's circuits have been overloaded—too much too quick—and now it's self-destructing. It's either going to explode out in millions of pieces and someone can get hurt, or it will burn inside and fizzle away until it no longer is here. It doesn't want anyone else hurt so it fizzles and burns inside, slowly self-destructing. There are times when it takes all of the little energy left to keep from exploding. The crazy part is it doesn't feel any of this because it's just a preprogrammed robot whose circuits are overloaded. It's not alive. It never really was. The programmers took its life away, and even if they wanted to give it back, it would be too late. It's already programmed to self-destruct. I've always known that the center of me was self-destructing. Even when I laugh and smile, I feel the fizzling and burning inside. When I say things are going good and I sound like things are going good, I know I'm really dying inside. I've always known I would never make it—I would never be normal or okay because you can't bring the dead back to life. I've always known I was different. I wasn't like the other kids in school. I know now it's because I died a long time ago. When you're dead inside you're not like other people. You laugh when you're supposed to and smile when you're supposed to, and on rare days you even cry when you're supposed to. But you're never really there. There's no energy inside—no life energy.

Jessica

69

The Adult is the surface or false, inauthentic self (Whitfield, 1987; Bradshaw, 1988). The Adult is the wearer of masks, the chameleon who takes on and rejects the surrounding emotional climate like a snake grows and discards skins. The Adult is the great imitator, the part that guesses at normal and makes self up from bits and pieces of the lives swirling around the survivor. Television, books, other people's personalities and behavior—all provide raw material for creation of this make-believe self.

THE ORIGINS OF THE ADULT

The description of chronic shock in Chapter 4 paints a clear picture of the empty shell Adult who has left Child and childhood behind. That Adult, devoid of many feelings, deprived of many responses, and drained of energy and life force, moves through the world like a robot, just an observer. The Adult is blocked from participating fully in events or connecting deeply with emotions. The Adult is often surrounded by a shadow of vague dread and doom. There is a fear that even this partial existence will be snatched away.

There is a quality of the wary watcher in the Adult—the one who looks okay, sees everything, feels nothing, expects little, and gets less. The Adult, never quite satisfied with self, is the part that struggles with all the issues attributed to adult children and adult survivors—control, responsibility and perfectionism, guilt, all-or-nothing thinking, trust, crisis addiction, tolerance for unpredictability, and guessing at normal.

These issues represent futile attempts to fix the unsatisfactory and incomplete Adult persona, which is the unhealed survivor's only available window to the world. Healing launched from the viewpoint of the empty Adult, which is only a portion of the total being, will also be incomplete and doomed to failure. Healing modes that fail to include the hidden Child or take into account the unstated family manual for living that is the Destroyer will produce piecemeal recovery at best.

THE ADULT AS PARENT

However, the Adult is not a void. The Adult is window to the Child and the self-destructive family mythology. More important, the Adult is the bearer of the parenting skills that will be used to reconnect with the Child and protect the Child from the threats and rules the family used to smother that Child. Although the Adult internalized the family's failure to protect and value the Child from the nonprotective bystander in the abusive drama, in reality, survivors were forced to parent themselves and others long before they were ready to do so. Although they learned to believe they didn't deserve to be protected and valued and they couldn't acknowledge their own parenting skills, they do have them.

In fact, they have been their own parents in many ways during these years. Recovery is not about learning all new self-parenting skills; it is about beginning to use deliberately the incredible skills already in place.

Survivors who are asked to sketch a picture of family dynamics rarely produce a healthy parental model. In healthy families, parents are placed somewhere above children most of the time, in a position that allows protection and safe control (see Figure 6.1).

Instead, dysfunctional and abusive families appear similar to Shelley's engulfed drawing in Chapter 4, or they demonstrate a parentified child (see Figure 6.2), or they show distance between people (see Figure 6.3).

In the latter two illustrations, there is no one in place to consistently or effectively parent "me." In all of them, the only one even close to the healthy parent position of protection and safe control is "me." Even in Shelley's picture, although parents are at least close, they cannot protect her or keep her safe because they are abusing. Abuse and protection cannot coexist.

FIGURE 6.1. Healthy Parenting

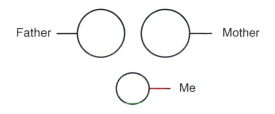

FIGURE 6.2. Parentified Child

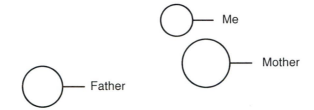

FIGURE 6.3. Interpersonal Distance

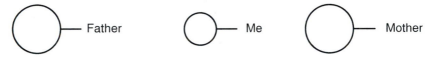

If no one was there, someone still parented the survivor. That someone *was* the survivor.

Before clients dismiss that possibility, they need to look at the evidence. They're here, aren't they? Someone kept them safe and alive during all those vulnerable years. Someone allowed them to get to this point. And if their parents weren't in the picture, so to speak, who else did it but them? By default, they became their own parents. They may have found other adults or older siblings to be surrogate parents, but *they* did that finding. And if they still want to discount their skills by insisting "Look at me! If I parented myself, I didn't do it very well," they need to go back to the evidence again. They're here, aren't they? Children who aren't appropriately protected or parented die. The tragedies of abuse and the accidents of neglect fill the papers and newscasts. Those fatal results didn't happen for them, so they must have done an adequate job.

OWNING SELF-PARENTING SKILLS

Survivors need to take credit for the positive self-parenting they have already accomplished and for the healthy self-parenting skills they already have in place.

Client exercise: Write a letter of congratulations to yourself, listing all the incidents that prove you have protected yourself and kept yourself safe, even through the times when you had no idea that was what you were doing.

Identification of self-parenting efforts and skills increases self-esteem and begins to build a sense of competence for the self-parenting tasks that lie ahead on the road to recovery. Acknowledging self-parenting skills is important because clients will use these skills to discover, nurture, protect, and celebrate that wonderful and delightful part of them that is the Child.

Chapter 7

The Child

Dear Little Girl,

I know you don't know who I am, but my name is Jessica. I see you a lot of times. You're always in or near the big black pit. I see you sitting in the bottom of it, sometimes curled up by the wall. You look so scared and tired. What are you thinking? What keeps you down there? What keeps you from pulling the notches out of the wall so you can climb out? Why is being in that pit so much safer than being out of it?

I was watching you from my special room. You were crying and you looked so scared, almost horrified and terrified. I hurt so much inside watching you. I felt the blackness of the pit. I called to you, but you couldn't hear me. I pounded on the window, but you didn't see me. I wanted so much to hold you and tell you that everything was going to be okay. I wanted to bring you into my special room, because it's safe there. But I couldn't, and I felt so helpless. I couldn't because you don't know I exist. You can't see me or hear me or touch me. You've blocked me out of your world.

The window I was watching you from kept getting smaller. It was being replaced with bricks. You were putting the bricks there. I want to help you, but I don't know how. I can't get to you because of the bricks. I don't think I'm strong enough to be able to go down into the black pit and bring us both back out. You can't come to me because you don't know I exist. You must feel so alone and so lost.

You can live past the fear. You won't disappear. I know that fear, and I know the fear of the pit. It's scary there and it's dark, but no one can hurt you. No one can touch you or reach you there, and that's part of what keeps you there.

*You can come out the top and see yourself. You'll know you're
there, and I'll know you're there. You won't be invisible anymore.
Maybe then we can both feel real. I can't do this alone. I need
your help. I hope you can feel how much I love you and care
about you. You're not alone anymore, and neither am I.*

*Love,
Jessica*

The journey inward to discover and reconnect with the true, authen-
tic self, the Child, is a path to the center of healing (Whitfield, 1987;
Bradshaw, 1988). The Child is the source of real identity and real
emotions, some painful, some frightening, some rageful. But under the
pain, fear, and anger, there is the innocence and playfulness and joy
that got buried, too. That joy alone is worth the journey.

THE ORIGINS OF THE CHILD

That the Child has been lost is confirmation of the reality of childhood abuse and validation of survival skills. Faced with assault and
family denial, a child has to deny the full reality of the abuse to stay
dependent on the family, which is, after all, a child's only hope for
survival in a threatening world. Given the choice between abuse or
abandonment, between discarding self or discarding family, a child
wisely offers self as a sacrifice on the altar of family continuity. The
only way to do this is to detach, if not from the actual memory of the
abuse, at least from the terror, anger, and helplessness accompanying
it. A child does this by dissociating, by disconnecting from senses
and feelings. This brilliant defense allows a child not to feel physical
or emotional pain at the time of abuse and not to remember that pain
in the future. The Child is left behind, frozen in time, and the Adult
moves on, empty and numb. The pain remains locked on nerve
endings as part of the buried persona of the Child (Grove, 1988).
The Child has to be buried for several reasons. The Child's developmental drive is a catalyst for growth and change, and growth and
change are not allowed in a dysfunctional family. The Child's curi-
osity is the source of questioning and thinking and challenging, and

independent thought threatens the uneasy balance of dysfunction. The Child's sensitivity is the origin of feelings that cannot be tolerated in the midst of abuse. Most of all, the Child is the storehouse of truth that would topple the rigid family hierarchy.

There may be several different pieces of the inner Child that dwell in this segment of self. The Child may have had to freeze and fragment repeatedly. If trauma occurred over and over again, feelings had to be repeatedly cut off from ongoing reality. If there was no chance for debriefing or resolution, emotions had to be continually shut down and encapsulated. There may be a series of wounded Children, each holding feelings for separate episodes of trauma. For example, the client may need to work with an angry seven-year-old who was physically assaulted and a frightened nine-year-old who was emotionally abandoned. Again, clients need to be reminded that this fragmentation is not craziness; it represents a brilliant application of the sensory and emotional disconnection that lays the foundation for post-traumatic stress disorder.

RECONNECTING WITH THE CHILD

For clients to become reacquainted with the Child requires some effort and imagination. Beginning to consider the Child as separate from self eases reconnection. Initially distancing from the Child is a technique that ultimately speeds healing. The Child has been lost for so long inside that unless the Child is held at arm's length and looked at in the light, it will be too easy for the Child to remain just a figment of the imagination.

Client exercise: Write a letter to the Child you were at any age that seems comfortable to you. Introduce the Adult you know to the Child you don't yet know. Tell the Child what you think must have been happening and what you guess the Child might have been feeling. Present the Child with your newly discovered self-parenting skills, and ask the Child to join you on the road to healing.

As clients consider the possibility of rejoining with the Child part of themselves, they may find childlike images or even voices nipping around the edges of their thoughts or dreams. These images and voices can be welcomed: they are the beginning of reconnection.

On the other hand, clients may find that even thinking about the discarded Child is frightening. The Child was frozen and laid to rest a long time ago and doesn't want to be resurrected. When Troy first tried to find the Child, he could only visualize a tiny being flattened under a sheet of ice, cold and lifeless. Missy's Child was stiff and resistant and didn't want to be held or hugged.

But the Child was buried to keep the whole alive. It was not a deliberate choice, nor was it a rejection of self. It was survival.

Clients may also have a sense that the Child is unlovable. They were taught to hate and reject themselves as children. If the eyes in which they saw themselves mirrored only distortion, then their self-view became distorted, too. If the people around them treated them in ways that suggested disgust and loathing, then they learned self-disgust and self-loathing, too.

The most important word in that last sentence is *learned*. Clients need to understand that what they learned is not who they really are. Just because they experienced hate does not make them hateable. Just because they were rejected does not make them rejectable. That was learned, and it can be unlearned.

Art can facilitate reconnection with the Child. For adults, drawing tends to evoke spontaneous and uncensored expression of feelings beyond the constraints of words and meanings.

Client exercise: Draw a picture of yourself when you were little, with the feelings you think you could have been feeling then. Try to draw it as you think you might have done at that age.

Some survivors use white crayons to outline themselves, making themselves invisible on the page. Jessica's empty picture showed only the anger and sadness and fear she felt as she struggled to not exist at all (see Figure 7.1).

Diane's smiling facade, while holding schoolbooks labeled "sad" and "lonely," illustrated her childhood Hero role that held the seeds of her perfect Adult persona (see Figure 7.2).

FIGURE 7.1. Jessica's Invisible Child

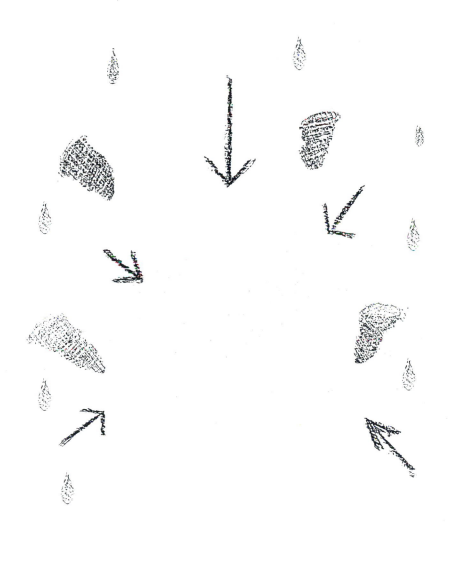

FIGURE 7.2. Diane's Hero Child

Lana's lonely cage showed how trapped she felt when she was little. It demonstrated the separation from true self which she was taught and which she mastered (see Figure 7.3).

Sadie's tearful picture also revealed the caged, walled-off world of the Child and the feelings that swirled around and had to be shut out (see Figure 7.4).

Client exercise: Now, close your eyes and try to visualize yourself when you were very young. If you have to use a photograph or the picture you just drew, do so. That might help you realize how truly cut off from this piece of self you have been. Imagine reaching down to give the Child a hug. If you can't do that, then imagine just touching hands with the Child. Let yourself feel, just for a moment, the possibility of oneness with your little self.

Catherine first approached the Child through her poetry:

To Little Catherine

I need you as much as ever,
I need you to see the light.
I need you to know the answers,
In the middle of the night.

I need you to do the seeing,
To hear and feel and love.
I need you to help discover,
A Higher Power above.

I need you to face discomfort,
When we go to school.
I need you to teach me how,
To disobey a rule.

The rules we always thought,
Were engraved in stone,
The ones that said to be afraid,
When we were alone.

You are the one I'll always need,
The one to teach me life.
For you're the one who knew just how,
To exist among the strife.

Now use your courage to grow beyond,
The pain and discontent.
Use your energy to live this life,
For it was heaven sent.

Don't be afraid we'll lose each other;
We were not attached through fear.
We lived their lie long enough,
And I love you, dear.

I care about just what you want,
Even though I cannot give,
Immediately you treasures,
I'll be here while you live.

I'll never leave you—no, not me;
I'll be right here for you.
And if you're napping, when you wake,
I'll be here—yes, it's true.

I love you every time you say,
I just can't make it one more day.
I love you even though you doubt,
And wonder what this life's about.

I love you when mistakes are made;
I'll always make time for you.
And I knew you could do anything,
When you learned to tie your shoe.

And when we die, nobody knows,
Where we will really be . . .
Though wherever we may travel,
It will still be YOU and ME.

Survivors need to connect the Adult and the Child and establish them as allies because, together, these two will fight and conquer the Destroyer.

FIGURE 7.3. Lana's Caged and Lonely Child

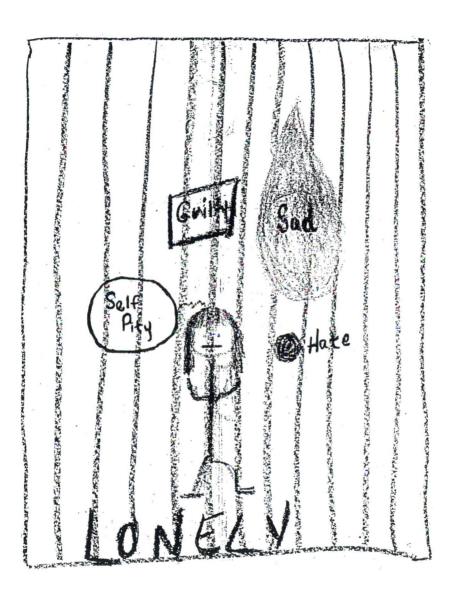

FIGURE 7.4. Sadie's Walled-Off and Tearful Child

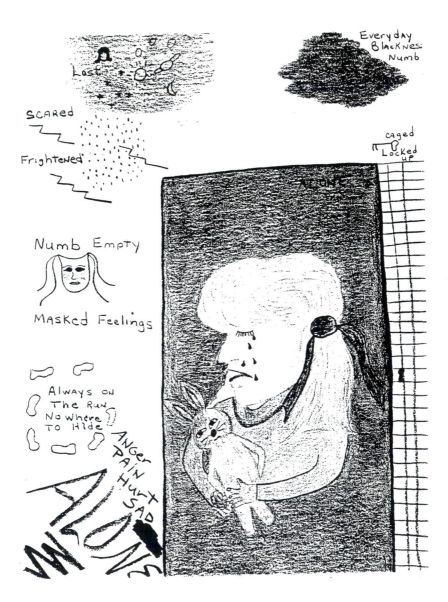

Chapter 8

The Destroyer

Even if I do get better, what difference would it make? No one at home is ever going to believe it. Everything will always be my fault. I should just accept it and shut up. What do I know anyway? What if they're right and everything is my fault?

This letter is to the thing that is keeping me stuck, the thing that keeps me silent and pulls me back. When I picture it, I see the Night Monster, and that doesn't make sense, because I thought the Night Monster was my dad. It also doesn't make sense that I'm afraid to draw it because I see it in my head, unless it's because putting it on paper makes it real, and I'm afraid of it becoming real. But then, to me, it is already real. So I want this thing, this Night Monster, to go away—to just disappear because I'm real tired and I want to be all alone. I don't want a Night Monster in my life.

Jessica

Survivors have their own unique names for this part of self—the Tape Monster, the Phantom Tapes, the Nothing, the Pit, the Black Hole, the Persecutor, the Bully, and the Power. The Destroyer is simply one particular survivor's label, but the idea of the Destroyer embodies so well both the threatening and the damaging aspects of this split piece of self.

No matter what it is called, the Destroyer is the locus of survivors' self-defeat and self-hatred. The Destroyer is the voice in the head, the conviction in the heart, and the tiredness in the muscles telling survivors that life is not worth anything and they are not worth anything, that they deserve to suffer and they deserve to die. The Destroyer is the sickening sensation in the pit of the stomach that makes them want to disappear. The Destroyer is the tingling in the neck and shoulders that tells them someone or something is watching and disapproving.

Although the Destroyer is as much a part of the survivor as the Child, there is one important difference: the Child is the core of self, while the Destroyer came from outside. When survivors are asked to think about the things the Destroyer says, they can often immediately identify faces and voices from the past as the source of negative messages.

The Destroyer can be traced to the adults from childhood, to the atmosphere the survivor grew up in, and to the institutions and perhaps the church that shaped those early years. It is made up of the things Father said, the look in Mother's eye, Grandmother's disapproval, the family's unspoken rules, society's customs, and religion's dogma.

THE ORIGINS OF THE DESTROYER

The Destroyer originates in a normal and natural stage of early childhood development that all children share. During children's very early years they are controlled from outside, by adults who are there all the time. Infants can't be left alone because they might roll off the bed or choke on a toy. Toddlers can't be left alone because they might touch a hot stove, run into the street, or hit a playmate. Adults need to be there to say "yes" or "no," to monitor behavior and control children's interactions with the world. During this period, children quite naturally experience themselves as the center of the universe.

But as children grow, they can be left alone more and more, and at some point, they must venture away from parents to school and to play. So children must find a way to carry their parents' rules with them, even when the parents aren't there to look to for help and advice. Children internalize their parents, literally take their parents inside them and furnish their interior landscapes with the parental road signs of life. They *introject* parental values and beliefs and rules (Miller, 1981). This is a survival tool for all children. It is critical that children remember to stay away from busy streets when Mommy is not there to hold a hand. It is important for children to know the stove can burn when Daddy is not there to snatch them away from danger.

FAMILY RULES

In healthy families, in which parenting is even and predictable, children internalize sensible and flexible rules that both keep them safe and allow them to grow. In healthy families, touch is safe, talking and sharing opinions are encouraged, and feelings are validated, not ridiculed or denied. In healthy families, there is predictability that allows trust to develop. The basic rules about touching, talking, feeling, and trusting are also adaptable, and children learn that their opinions, feelings, and decision-making skills influence the rules. For example, talking is allowed and encouraged, both within the family and with friends. However, children raised in healthy, functional families will have confidence in their own judgments. They will alter that rule depending upon circumstances. They will choose not to talk to a casual stranger about where family valuables are kept or when the home is empty.

In healthy, nurturing families, the rules are consistent and safe and growth oriented, and they are honored *most of the time*, for no family is perfect. Families operate on a continuum that ranges from dysfunctional to nurturing, and the family rules are reflected on that continuum (Black, 1981; Larsen, 1988).

Dysfunctional

- Don't talk
- Don't feel
- Don't think
- Don't have fun
- Don't trust
- Don't be selfish
- Don't be honest
- Don't be who you are
- Don't change or grow

Nurturing

- Problems accepted and resolved
- Feelings shared and affirmed
- Opinions valued
- Celebration honored
- Expectations met with positive predictability
- Boundaries consistent and respected
- Direct communication
- Unconditional love
- Risk and growth encouraged

Dysfunction is a natural response to unpredictability or inconsistency. All families, even the healthiest of families, can become dysfunctional in the face of unpredictability or inconsistency. A family will move toward dysfunction when one family member becomes inconsistent or unpredictable because of chemical dependency, mental illness, an eating disorder, or a serious illness. A family will move toward dysfunction if family circumstances become inconsistent or unpredictable because of death, divorce, chronic illness, or a threat to financial stability. Healthy families, faced with such situations, strive to return to their functional, nurturing base. Unhealthy families only tighten their grip on dysfunction.

In unhealthy families, rules about touching, talking, feeling, and trusting are dysfunctional most, if not all, of the time. Communication is incomplete and indirect. The rules are arbitrary because the family is closed and guarded concerning whatever secret is making the family dysfunctional. Secrets make families shame-based and unhealthy. Secrets, even secrets long forgotten, create a legacy of dysfunction that can be passed from generation to generation. In a dysfunctional, unhealthy family, the rules always favor secrecy, which guarantees they will be negative. The rules are fixed. They apply rigidly in any and all situations. They may provide safety, but they stifle growth and forbid change.

Children raised in dysfunctional, unhealthy families introject and internalize the negative rules and form their behavior codes and their value systems around isolation, perfectionism, and confusion (see Figure 8.1).

FIGURE 8.1. Functional and Dysfunctional Family Rules

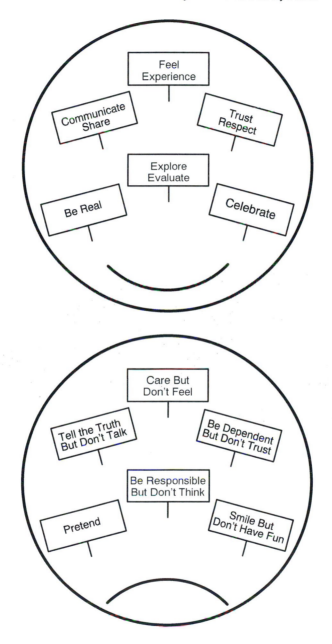

It is critical for clients to identify the specific rules they learned in their own families of origin. No two unhealthy or dysfunctional families are exactly alike. Not all unhealthy families live by all the dysfunctional rules. What was learned can be unlearned, but clients need to know exactly what rules they learned to challenge them. Generalizations and textbook examples will not serve.

Client exercise: List as accurately as you can the rules that governed your family.

FAMILY LABELS

Children introject not only rules but also what they learn about themselves during that center-of-the-universe period. They carry with them into the world core beliefs about themselves, based on the reflection they saw of themselves in their parents' looks and gestures and on who their families told them they were. If children are taught with words and actions that they are special, treasured, entitled to unconditional love and absolute protection from abuse, if parents convey a sense of celebration and confidence about their children's abilities and achievements, those children form a marvelous, affirming introject to carry through life: "You can make a mistake, try again"; "Who you are is just right"; "You are good, worthwhile, capable, caring—a success, a unique person, and a wonder."

However, in too many families, a child's introjected self-view is destructive and label-based: "You are a mistake"; "You will never be good enough"; "You are bad, lazy, stupid, selfish—a bum, a jerk, and a loser" (see Figure 8.2).

Dysfunctional families foster shame-based introjects. Because the family style is secretive and twisted, the introject becomes warped, forming the Destroyer. It is important for clients to identify exactly what they were taught to believe about themselves because they can unlearn only what they know they learned.

FIGURE 8.2. Functional and Dysfunctional Family Labels

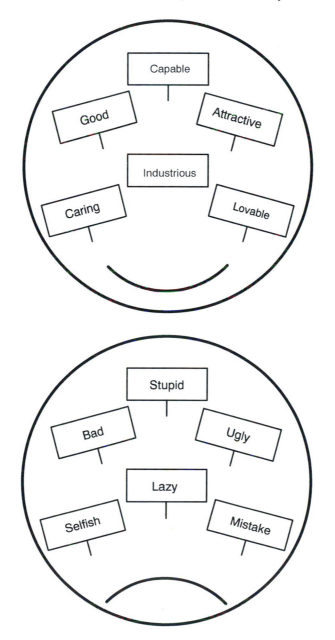

Client exercise: List the labels that were put on you and your behavior. Then think about how you learned about yourself in your family of origin. How did your parents praise you? How did you know when you had done something right? How did they criticize you? How did you know when you had done something wrong? What did they do and what did they say in each circumstance? Make separate lists for each parent.

It should come as no surprise that the praise list is often blank for children from dysfunctional, unhealthy families. If that list is almost blank for clients, then they had to guess what was good about them. If that list is almost blank, they likely decided that there was nothing really good about them. If praise was the absence of abuse, if they guessed they were being good because they weren't being hit or yelled at, they still lacked accurate messages about their own self-worth. Half of identity remained a mystery. And if information about one parent's feelings and opinions was always relayed through the other parent, the silent parent's list was really blank, too. All that information, or lack of it, has become part of the Destroyer.

THE DESTROYER'S SABOTAGE

Too many survivors of dysfunction and abuse work in the present, using twelve-step affirmations of themselves as adults, and then condemn themselves when attempts at recovery fail. They never realize that the Destroyer silences every affirmation. The Destroyer won't allow them to listen or believe because the inner Child still hears only the Destroyer. No matter how many times the Adult looks in the mirror and repeats, "I am good, capable, and worthwhile, and I love myself," the Destroyer *knows* differently. Its old message, whispered below the edge of consciousness to the Child, silently contradicts the affirmation: "You are *really* bad, stupid, inadequate and unlovable; don't even bother to pretend otherwise."

Obedience to family rules and acceptance of family labels meant survival in childhood. Talking or questioning meant tearing the family apart. It meant risking more severe abuse or even abandonment.

Carried into adulthood as the Destroyer, the restrictive family rules and the repulsive self-image lead to isolation and depression, guilt and shame. And carried to its logical conclusion, the ultimate meaning of the Destroyer's *don't talk* rule is suicide. Death guarantees the victim's mouth will be shut permanently, and the family secrets will be buried forever.

Even considering the possibility of the Destroyer is frightening. Its very existence says, "You have no right to challenge; you have no right to think or to exist." The Destroyer's messages are embedded in every thought, belief, and action. Worldview and sense of self have been molded by the Destroyer, which is entwined in self-worth and identity.

Yet the Destroyer does not come from self. It is a part of self only because it was learned. Unlike the Child, the Destroyer comes from outside, from the family's unhealthy myths and rules. Its message really is, "You have no right to challenge *me*; you have no right to think or exist *except on my terms.*" Knowing that gives clients power.

THE MANY DISGUISES OF THE DESTROYER

Understanding the origins of the Destroyer and its role as guard at the gates of self-concept allows clients to fight the Destroyer's attempts to undermine their efforts and their recovery. They may find the Destroyer hides itself in their thoughts and beliefs as images of inadequacy and catastrophe or as repetitive words and phrases: "Don't even try because you won't succeed anyway"; "Try but don't win"; "You deserve to fail." Survivors may also realize that the Destroyer operates wordlessly at a physical level, immobilizing their muscles and draining their energy in the face of challenge or change. Until clients identify the Destroyer, they are likely to have only intermittent success with present-tense strategies meant to bolster self-esteem and alter destructive behavior patterns.

CHALLENGING THE DESTROYER

To confront the Destroyer, clients need to make it separate from them. Once again, clients need to be reminded that this is not about being sick or crazy. Separation is simply a tool to give them control over the Destroyer.

The easiest way to separate the Destroyer from self is to draw. Trying to describe the Destroyer in words immediately invokes the *don't talk* rule. The inroads into the unconscious that the Destroyer has established are best attacked nonverbally.

Kevin pictured the Destroyer as a black, amoeba-like creature with claws and tentacles waiting to attack and devour him (see Figure 8.3).

Mary created a robed monklike figure to fit her image of the Destroyer. In her drawing, she discovered the power that her rigid religious upbringing added to the Destroyer (see Figure 8.4).

The Destroyer for Molly was a heavy and harsh crimson scribble. The color red symbolized the angry atmosphere of her family of origin (see Figure 8.5).

Patricia drew an ominous, disembodied head with a predatory, wolfish quality, which she immediately connected to the look on her mother's face during moments of taunting abuse (see Figure 8.6).

Client exercise: What do all those negative messages and labels and beliefs look and feel like in your imagination? Draw your own idea of the Destroyer.

Once clients have a picture of the Destroyer in their heads and on paper, they can use journaling to further separate themselves from the Destroyer.

Client exercise: Just as you introduced yourself to the Child, introduce yourself to the Destroyer. However, this introduction will be different. Tell it you know it exists, you know exactly where it comes from, and you know how it still operates in your life. Tell it you know it helped you in childhood by enforcing the family rules and keeping you from questioning the abuse aloud. You may even choose to thank it for keeping you safe when you were young. Then tell it you don't need it anymore. Even if you don't believe that yet, write the words anyway. You will come to believe as you move toward healing.

FIGURE 8.3. Kevin's Amoeba

FIGURE 8.4. Mary's Monk

FIGURE 8.5. Molly's Red Scribble

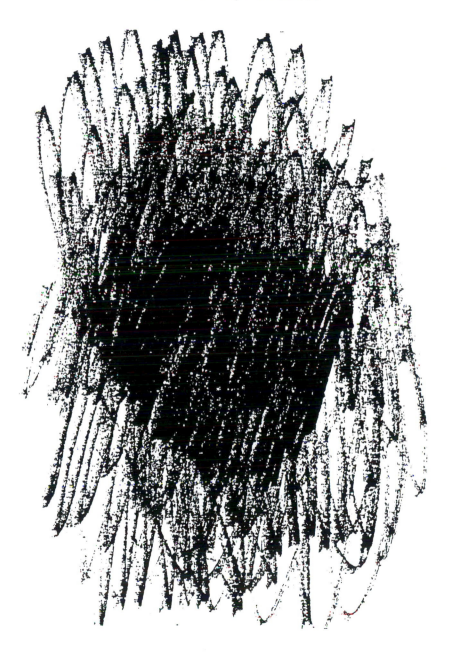

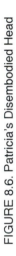

FIGURE 8.6. Patricia's Disembodied Head

98

The difficulty clients experience writing this first challenge to the Destroyer will let them know the power it has been holding over them and the life-and-death nature of the battle the Adult and the inner Child have begun to fight.

A poem was Mary's first suspicion of the Destroyer's existence:

Alien

Something
   is uncoiling
   inside of me,
Lazily stretching itself awake
   and
Sharpening its claws
   on my guts.
It will have teeth.
I can excise it
   in a few quick, agonizing strokes,
Or I can wait
   while it chews and claws its way out,
   one thin layer of me at a time,
   for a very long time.
Either way I am going to bleed to death.

Then Mary wrote her first challenge to the Destroyer's power:

I needed you when I was two and three, maybe even when I was five or ten. I do not need you now, telling me to shut up. Now I need to remember and feel and to talk about what I remember and feel. I don't need your voice in my ear and your hand down my throat, stuffing me full of food to keep me quiet. I am forty-eight years old. I am old enough to check out a situation and decide for myself what is safe and what is appropriate and what isn't. I am old enough to be responsible for the consequences if I make a mistake. I have learned how to make amends when I'm wrong. Now I'M TELLING YOU! Shut up! Get smaller! Go away! I don't need you anymore. I don't need any voice inside my head that isn't loving!

Externalizing the negative messages separates who the client is from what the client learned. It empowers clients to confront self-defeating behaviors and beliefs without the debilitating self-condemnation that has confounded previous efforts to change. Once they begin to uncover the Destroyer persona, it can never unexpectedly ambush them again. It may try to rear its ugly head and raise its ruthless voice as they climb toward recovery, but they can be on the lookout for its return, even as they add to their understanding of the ways it still affects their lives.

Chapter 9

Understanding the Brilliance
of Childhood Defenses

The thoughts and behaviors that make survivors feel crazy, inadequate, and different today reflect coping tactics they used in childhood. Rather than define themselves as sick, they need to recognize how clever they were as children. The word brilliant seems to most accurately describe their genius and their talents. As children, they developed incredible survival skills. They learned to function in ways that allowed both them and their families to move through life unnoticed and unjudged.

They found ways to deal with the confusion of two parents in one body. There was the successful, respectable parent for all the world to see and the monster parent who abused in secret. Denying, minimizing, freezing, going numb, taking the blame—they did whatever it took to make sense out of a nonsensical world. They did whatever it took to live. The alternative was to *really* go insane, to lose touch with all of reality. Rather than concentrate on what is wrong with them, survivors need to look at what is right with them.

Survivors learned what they learned because they had to. All human behavior makes sense, given the context in which it was learned. Survivors had to make many choices as children, choices that were not really choices at all. Forced to choose between destruction of family or destruction of self, they sacrificed themselves, paying the price for keeping the family together by losing pieces of themselves and their feelings. Cleverly, wisely, and brilliantly, with no training, no guidance, and no support, they repeatedly chose behavior that gave them a chance to make it though the minefield. And they did this all in the midst of denial. They perfected survival skills despite the altered reality that said the family was fine and they didn't need survival skills at all.

The coping mechanisms clients used in childhood were both awesome and understandable. Their defenses had a twofold purpose: they created an illusion of control and provided some sense of hope. The fact that clients may still be using many of those same defenses today says nothing about their mental stability. It simply says they haven't had the opportunity to learn other behaviors. Although clients may not identify with every defense that follows, they need to appreciate the strategies they did use. They need to recognize their strength as survivors because they will tap that strength to modify and add to their life skills as they move toward recovery. They need to acknowledge the ingenuity and creativity of the defenses they mastered because owning the brilliance of the Child is the final brick in the foundation for transformative Stage II recovery.

DISSOCIATION

I remember when I was little, I used to go outside in the backyard and lay on the hammock. I always felt like I was floating above myself and looking down on me. I used to wonder if other kids did that, too. I remember going to school and watching the other kids to see if they would float above themselves. I was sure that the teacher would yell at me if she saw me floating in class. I remember being relieved I never got caught. It bothers me that it still happens.

Jessica

From the natural physical and emotional responses to trauma discussed in Chapter 4 comes dissociation, a major defense of the child victim and the adult survivor. Dissociation grows out of the body's ability to shut down nervous system receptors to avoid physical pain and emotional overload. This survival mechanism is common in people operating under traumatic conditions. The accident victim who rescues another and doesn't recognize she is hurt until the paramedics start tending to her, the firefighter who runs from a burning building on an ankle that later proves to be broken, the cook who touches a hot stove and thrusts his finger into cold water before the burning begins—all share in dissociation to some degree. The adrenaline rush triggered by crisis allows the human body to temporarily freeze pain receptors in the sensory nervous system. This allows escape in life-threatening situations, when feeling pain would paralyze and prevent survival.

Children under physical attack are just as human as the adult accident victim. They shut down sensory awareness to mask the actual pain of hitting and battering and rape.

At a corresponding emotional level is shock—part of the first stage in the grief process. Someone who loses a loved one moves efficiently and calmly through the funeral, planning and organizing and comforting everyone else and bearing up wonderfully. That behavior is not based so much in bearing up as it is in denial. The death hasn't really happened yet at an emotional level. Emotional numbing allows feelings to be delayed and disconnected from the immediate loss.

Children under verbal attack are just as human as the adult mourner. They shut down emotional awareness to numb the pain of sarcasm, criticism, and humiliation.

Add to that emotional and sensory shutdown the two personalities in one body and the need to ignore huge chunks of external reality. Add to that emotional and sensory shutdown the conflicting standards for notice and approval and the need to ignore huge chunks of internal reality. The scene is now set for a child to cut off reality completely, to silence senses in order to survive.

Disconnection from physical and emotional awareness is the prologue to denial. If they didn't feel it or react to it, children could convince themselves it didn't happen.

Disconnection from emotional and physical awareness is the core of dissociation—the survivor's continuing ability to disengage from ongoing events, to put feelings on one side of the room and shell of self on the other, to leave true self behind and move out into the world to function but not feel, to endure but not enjoy, to perform but not perceive.

Survivors often describe *depersonalization*, the uncanny sensation of watching their bodies drift through life as they sit on the sidelines and watch. Sarah describes herself behind a camera filming her life. Jessica calls it "floating"; Ginny refers to it as "trancing out"; Jason talks about "checking out"; Mitzi's label is "splitting."

Dissociation sometimes feels like daydreaming. It can happen during conversations—clients may find themselves "coming to" with little or no recollection of content, although the reactions of others indicate that nothing unusual has occurred. It can happen under stress—clients may cut out emotionally and have difficulty reconnecting. It can happen during intimate moments—clients may find themselves detached, not fully present or participating. It happens frequently in therapy sessions when the abuse is being addressed. Reminders of trauma trigger that same self-hypnotic sequence mastered in childhood to escape the abuse. The therapist needs to remain alert to cues that dissociation is occurring and be prepared to anchor the client in the present, either verbally or with a tactile object the client associates only with safety and adulthood.

Some of the memories of abuse likely reflect the defense of dissociation. Mental images of assault may be distanced and devoid of feelings. The survivor is not included in the picture. Instead, the survivor seems to be viewing from afar things that are happening to another child, not self.

It is only a small step from numbing sensory nerve endings so there is no feeling to numbing motor nerve endings so there is no moving. Even animals held too tightly struggle to free themselves. What if a child is being physically or verbally held down by an attacker twice as big, an attacker who has absolute control over that child's life and safety? For some victims, such as Shelley in Chapter 4, the physical escape mobilized by adrenaline is not an option. Shelley could not resist. Resistance would have made things worse. Not only did she have to disconnect from her senses and emotions so she could not feel pain or rage or terror, she also had to disconnect from her muscles so she could not move. She had to extinguish her natural instinct to fight back.

When this learned motor nerve numbing is carried into adulthood, tremendous energy is used to stay continually frozen. This creates chronic fatigue in muscles, which then become drained and lifeless, like an exhausted runner at the end of a long-distance race. The resulting immobility leads to depression. Unable to function or carry out even basic life tasks, survivors sometimes consider suicide or death as the only solution possible or deserved.

Dissociation undoubtedly contributes to adult survivors' suspicions that they are crazy. After all, floating and trancing out and wanting to die are considered signs of mental instability. All these phenomena need to be reconsidered in the context in which they were learned. Dissociation allowed survivors to function and remain relatively intact in a world gone mad. It allowed them to control and minimize the impact of the assault, to filter the trauma through the unfocused lens of detachment. Dissociation allowed them to separate core self from the abuse. Dissociation protected true self from being harmed. It is incredibly comforting for survivors to realize that dissociation means *the spirit, the soul, was never touched by the abuse.* The alternative to dissociation—to experience the true level of physical and emotional pain—would have been devastating. Dissociation, similar to every other defense an abused child discovers, is nothing short of brilliant.

FORGETTING AND FANTASY

I keep forgetting things, at work and in school, and also just everyday things. It's really beginning to bother me. I get frustrated a lot when that happens. I wish I could stop forgetting.

Jessica

Incomplete recall for childhood events is further evidence of childhood brilliance. To hold on to the feelings and the details of the abuse from day to day and to know there was no one safe to tell or no one who could protect or rescue would have created such an emotional and mental overload that functioning at school or at play would have been impossible. How could clients have gone to school and performed at all, weighed down by a replay of the previous night's violence racing through their minds? That truly would have driven them crazy. Abuse blurred around the edges fades into oblivion.

More important, concentrating on every moment of abuse would have put up a barrier between them and their parents, the people they needed to survive. To stay in the family, to maintain some degree of hope, they had to diminish some of the horror and terror. Forgetting is not the same as repression. Forgetting is the deliberate effort to dull the intensity of the memories.

Interludes of peace encourage forgetting. Rarely is childhood all horrible. There are usually good times in between the bad. People have a natural tendency to minimize past pain and focus on present happiness, similar to the woman who puts aside the discomfort of childbirth for joy at the sight of her newborn infant.

Some children add fantasy to the forgetting sequence in their flight from reality. They create elaborate imaginary realms in which peace and predictability reign. Claude escaped to a gentle and nurturing family. Shasta's fantasy life still included rigid expectations and beatings, but punishments for breaking the rules were fair and even-handed. Ann Marie's letter to her childhood self praised the brilliance of her retreat into a world she fashioned in the crystal doorknobs and the ceilings of her foster home:

> Dear Little Girl,
>
> Looking through the glass doorknobs and pretending it was a place for you was a very smart move. No one had put a claim on the doorknobs. They were all yours and your foster mother did not mind. Later you discovered that no one cared about owning the ceilings. Then you claimed them and used to spend time with a mirror pretending you were walking on the ceilings. Such an escape! It was very smart of you to claim a territory. At least that way you found places that were yours and that no one else cared about, even though you knew you did not belong there.
>
> Ann Marie

Needing to master the arts of forgetting and fantasy in childhood paves the way for later difficulty concentrating and remembering. The adult survivor is criticized for being thoughtless, inconsiderate, and absentminded. This adds to the sense of inadequacy and craziness and ignores the life-saving origins of inattention.

Children caught up in violence, incapable of caring for themselves in a hostile world, must choose to believe in the illusion of family security rather than face the awful possibility that there is no safety. They must ignore evidence to the contrary to remain part of the family, for without the family, they know they cannot live. In the end, abused children forget because the pretense of caring and consistency is more reassuring and more survivable than the reality of assault.

CHOOSING ABUSE VERSUS ABANDONMENT

I remember that after a while I just kind of did whatever and said whatever, and if they happened to notice, then I got in a lot of trouble, and if they didn't notice, then I guess I just wasn't there. Sometimes I would do things just to see if they would notice. I started playing a game and it kept me entertained. It was something—in some strange way—that I had control of. I never knew how they were going to react, but I knew it was a game and somehow it made it seem like the joke was on them this time. They didn't know it and never will—but I knew it and they couldn't take it away from me.

Jessica

Survivors need to challenge any lingering belief that they deserved the abuse. Survivors who know they deliberately defied and disobeyed as children may insist, "I asked for it." Acting up, rebelling, talking back, and making trouble need to be reexamined, taking into account the dysfunctional system in which they were learned.

The exercise about parental praise and criticism in Chapter 8 helps clients recognize that praise was absent or at least inconsistent in childhood. If that was the case, they knew at a very early age that positive affirmation was unavailable or unpredictable.

All human beings need to be touched. Children are no different. In fact, children need more touch than adults do. Infants need to be touched physically. Babies in orphanages, whose needs for food and shelter are met, nonetheless die if they are not held and cuddled by their caregivers. As children grow, their need for touch can also be satisfied with words, or verbal *strokes*. But if clients already knew that positive physical and verbal touch was missing, if they already knew that beating and ridicule and scolding were the only ways to get noticed, then they were forced to choose between negative verbal and physical touch or no touch at all. If positive strokes from caregivers were not possible, then negative strokes were better than nothing. No interaction means a child does not exist.

In reality, clients were forced to choose between abuse and abandonment, which children experience as emotional death. Greta learned to laugh at her parents' threats to send her to an orphanage, laughter which enraged her parents. Greta opted for verbal blackmail and physical punishment rather than total silence. At least the sound of her parents' voices and the beatings, awful though they were, gave Greta hope and assured her that her parents were still there.

Ann Marie followed her foster mother around the house and was cursed for being a "shadow." Her poem described the hollow non-existence she fought desperately to avoid:

Shadow

> Shadow, shadow, on the wall,
> Can be big or really small.
> Shadow needs only a little light,
> To show up good during the night.
> Love and hugs a shadow does not need.
> That's why a shadow can't be me!

Continued into adulthood, the pattern of seeking attention from friends and lovers with repeated problems and crises often leads to the abandonment it is meant to prevent. The desolation that follows increases the survivor's sense of distance and difference and offers no explanation for the powerful pull of negativity learned in the emptiness of childhood.

A child who is abandoned dies. A child who is not touched dies. The need for touch is part of being human. Core survival instincts take over to seek some affirmation of existence, even if that affirmation is negative. If clients were getting attention, even if that attention was painful and damaging, they at least knew they were alive. Acting out, which looks crazy on the surface, makes sense when it is viewed at the deeper level of family dysfunction. It is, in fact, another proof of childhood brilliance. In the impoverished emotional climate of abuse, a child learns rebellion guarantees touch and life.

SELF-PUNISHMENT

I remember standing at the top of the stairs to the basement. I remember feeling like I was looking down on the steps from the ceiling, and then everything was black until I heard my mom screaming. I was lying at the bottom of the steps. I remember my mom telling my dad I passed out, but I knew I hadn't.

There was another time when I was four. My mom had the iron on in her room, and she walked away and told me not to go near it because it was hot and I could get hurt. I remember the same funny feeling and then everything was black. I remember my mom screaming and I didn't know why. When I looked, I was standing in her room, which I was afraid of, with my hand pressed against the iron. I don't remember it hurting.

Last night I cut myself with a razor blade. It hurts but in a weird way it feels good—like I know I'm here.

Jessica

Rather than acting out, some victims of childhood abuse choose "acting in." These children harm themselves rather than wreak destruction on their surroundings. Some survivors continue to deliberately hurt themselves as adults, cutting themselves, banging their heads against walls, burning themselves, bruising themselves, pinching themselves, pulling hair, and picking scabs.

Sometimes the ways survivors hurt themselves echo the abuse itself. Adults who were beaten with sticks or branches as children cut whiplike marks into their skin. Adults who were attacked with belts as children burn welts into their bodies. Adults who were battered or saw others beaten when they were little bruise themselves. They seem to be trying to tell the story of what happened to them with their bodies, when they can't tell it in words.

In a climate of preoccupation, in which clients were often shoved aside, their feelings were also ignored. They weren't listened to or comforted. Physical pain overrides emotional pain. Hurting themselves took away anxiety and fear and sadness, if only for a while. And if they learned to anticipate abuse, if they could feel the tension building toward an outburst, then they also learned that relief would follow pain. They learned that they could relax only after they were hurt. They may still want to hurt themselves before they can sleep. They may still want to hurt themselves when they get upset or scared. They may still believe that they deserve to be hurt. That was what they were taught, and that is what they learned.

These self-harmful gestures rarely reach suicidal proportions. They are driven by a desire to end loneliness, not to end life. If survivors are suicidal, the ideation is often more passive than active: "I would never do anything deliberate, but if something happened to me, it would be no big deal."

The self-punishing sequence can become a recapitulation of the abuse, with the survivor playing all three roles—the victim, the abuser, and the nonprotective parent. The survivor passively endures self-inflicted trauma, feels unable to interrupt the cycle, and often fiercely resists discovery or intervention. Trauma reenactment syndrome can be a sequelae of childhood abuse (Miller, 1994).

The repetition compulsion seems an attempt at trauma mastery, fueled by an unconscious fantasy that this time things will end differently, that this time there will be relief and resolution. The fantasy is doomed to failure by the power of the original abusive scenario that remains frozen and unresolved.

Despite highly publicized but irresponsibly quoted statistics that seem to predict adults abused as children will inevitably maltreat their own or other children, survivors much more frequently direct anger and abuse toward themselves in some variation of trauma reenactment syndrome. Correlations between childhood victimization and offender behavior in incarcerated felons—the population most available for study—have no bearing on the lives of functional survivors. In fact, the vast majority of survivors grow up to be fierce protectors of children, determined that no other child will ever be hurt as they were (Sanford, 1990).

Some professionals also lump alcohol and drug abuse and eating disorders under this broad category of adult self-abuse. However, there is too much evidence that substance addictions are separate diseases. Alcohol and drug dependencies and eating disorders need to be addressed as primary problems once they have taken hold in a life. Any recovery work from childhood abuse will be blocked if substance abuse continues unchecked.

The mood-altering qualities of substances cannot be underestimated. To dull the wrenching hurt of abuse, a child's drug of choice is likely to be anything that works, anything that takes away the pain. Even the adrenaline rush produced by risk-taking behavior, the clutch of fear about getting caught, allows the body to alter mood with a self-supplied biochemical shift. The anesthetic effects of alcohol and drugs are obvious. Food, too, can be mood altering. Sugar (candy, ice cream, chocolate, pop) provides a "high" comparable to cocaine or amphetamines. Flour (pasta, bread, cake, noodles) sedates and puts the body and brain "on the nod," similar to heroin or narcotics. Ann was no more than three when she first fled to hide under a bush outside the back door with a piece of bread for company and comfort.

Other forms of self-punishment and self-abuse are more subtle. Echoing the risk-taking behavior of a self-abusive child, adult survivors drive too fast, shop and spend compulsively, shoplift, gamble excessively, and have unexplained accidents. Living life on the edge, surrounded by self-created chaos, survivors seem to be repeating all that they struggled to escape. Yet it is not too puzzling, given the family left behind, that confusion and crisis continue to reign. If childhood was one disaster or potential disaster after another is it any wonder adulthood seems no different, either in quantity or quality? Until they learn other ways to do things, survivors are drawn as if by magnets to the familiar, even if the familiar is uncomfortable or downright destructive.

Beyond that, risk taking has ultimate logic in the illogical existence of an assaulted child. Such children are often described as accident prone. In reality, if a child's life and safety do not seem to be valued by those put on this earth to provide protection, then that child's life is not worth much. Risking physical or emotional harm comes naturally. The grown-up who emerges from that child, still believing self not worth protecting, will continue to risk, oblivious to any connection between present and past.

For survivors of sexual abuse, patterns of self-punishing sexual behavior emerge. Sexually abused children tend to grow into adults who are sexually avoidant or promiscuous or adults who are preoccu-pied with sexual self-satisfaction. All three add to self-condemnation. All three are attempts to reclaim power in the same arena in which it was taken away: "No one will ever touch me again," or "I'll attract you and then reject you," or "I'll control my own pleasure."

Hurting self became a powerful way to control an uncontrollable reality. The self-blame that resulted from self-punishment fanned the flames of the fantasy that clients held the answer to their fami-ly's problems and their own abuse. That gave them hope. If every-thing was all their fault, then surely they could fix things by being better, trying harder, going faster. When their efforts failed, they simply intensified their search for the magic solution.

If the self-destructive behavior left marks or scars, they were sure to be punished for that. They knew they would be humiliated or criticized or hit. If they hurt themselves, at least they could predict the reason for the abuse and make themselves believe they deserved it. Greta first began to consider this possibility in a letter to her little self about her childhood "sin" of eyebrow and eyelash pulling:

> Dear Little Greta,
>
> I'm writing to tell you that I know now that the eyebrow and eyelash pulling was not your fault. I know you always thought it was and you were bad. That's just not true. It was your only way of coping with your life at that time. It seemed like a crazy way of doing it, but it really wasn't. The alternatives were all worse. Pulling your eyebrows and eyelashes made the abuse more predictable. You would know what to expect. It really helped you with reducing the fear of the unknown. You know the fear of "what is going to happen to me next" has always been your biggest fear. This way you could predict a lot of the abuse. You didn't think about doing this because you were too young, but you did it as a kind of instinct, like the cat waiting for you at the alley when you came home from school.
>
> Love,
> Greta

Self-abuse was just another way of getting the attention and strokes that were needed to survive. If acting out was too dangerous, if someone else could have been hurt or if the price clients might have had to pay for open rebellion was life-threatening, then how clever to rebel inwardly. No one got hurt but them, and the payoff of being noticed outweighed the pain of hurting themselves. In fact, turning destruction inward on self is in some ways more sophisticated and more brilliant than turning destruction out onto the world. The results of outward aggression can't always be predicted, but the degree of self-harm is always controllable.

Of all the normal survivor characteristics, self-punishment probably feels the most crazy to clients. However, self-punishment, too, is brilliant. Even if hurting self as a bid for attention failed in childhood, it always met a core need. If they were hurting, if they were in pain, they at least knew they were alive. The power of this defense spills into an adulthood filled with doubts about their right to exist. Hurting self serves the same purpose for an alienated and isolated adult as it does for an alienated and isolated child. Hurting self says, "I am real." It is also an incredibly clever way to control a chaotic reality and a reenactment of the abuse that clients were taught was only their due.

RITUAL

I was a perfectionist by always needing to look perfect. This has changed, but in junior high and high school I was obsessed with my looks. I had to be skinny. I weighed 98 pounds in junior high and believed I was obese. In high school I weighed 120 pounds. My hair, clothes, and makeup had to be perfect. I also did and still do need to have everything in exactly the right place.

Jessica

An abused child's world is chaos. Children who are abused know they can't count on anyone or anything. They know reality is disorganized and uncontrollable.

Children share a normal human need to control or at least organize that chaos. That need to control and organize seems hard-wired into the human brain. If a series of pictures is flashed before their eyes, people remember the main objects at the expense of detail. People whose homes are devastated by a natural disaster focus on the hunt for one object, as a symbol of the total loss. People concentrate on the tree to minimize the confusion of the forest.

All children use ritual to some extent. "Don't step on a crack or you'll break your mother's back" gives a child a sense of control over a little person's fear of imagined loss and abandonment. A child raised in violence uses ritual to defend against real loss and abandonment.

For the survivor of abuse, the ritual often had a quality of perfectionism. There was a certain sequence in daily routine: "I always put my left sock on first," or "I always walked to school by the same route." There was a superstitious interpretation of daily events: "If my mother got up first, things were going to be okay," or "If my teacher smiled at me when I arrived at school, then I could relax." There was a rigid ordering of daily tasks: "I listed everything I did on my calendar," or "I'd clean my drawers from top to bottom, never the other way around." There was a careful arrangement of personal possessions: "Every stuffed animal had its own special place on my shelf," or "Every item in my school desk had to be lined up just so."

By clinging to ritual in a small corner of their lives, clients tried to convince themselves that control in the larger scheme of things could not be far behind. By rigidly structuring their own daily activities and space, they carved out tiny oases of safety in an otherwise unsafe world.

The boundaries that divide healthy organization from perfectionism, obsession, and compulsion are unclear. Some adult survivors are plagued with preoccupations or addictions concerning eating, sex, shopping, spending, speeding, housekeeping, working, or exercising. Food puts feelings to sleep. Adrenaline numbs feelings. Staying busy keeps feelings at bay. At the center of most compulsive sequences seems to be the psychic hole of emotional abandonment, which survivors vainly attempt to fill with food, sex, people, possessions, money, or frantic activity. Ritual, in the form of compulsive behavior, may still be a way for clients to dull feelings and regulate reality.

These compulsions probably have some of their roots in the fantasy power of childhood rituals.

Once again, an abused child, tiny and helpless, armed with nothing but imagination, finds in ritual a brilliant shield against the terror of a universe out of control. An abused child uses ritual to bring order out of chaos and to secure a wedge of sanity in the insanity of abuse.

PHOBIAS

> *It's thundering real loud now. I remember when we used to sit in the garage and watch the rain and listen to the thunder. It was nice because no one talked. I used to pretend the thunder was talking to me, but when it got loud it was like it was yelling at me. Then Mom would get mad and yell, and we would have to go inside. But she couldn't take away what the thunder said. She couldn't take away what was in my head. She tried. She always yelled because I was in another world. She never stopped to think why. The thunder told me there was someone out there, watching me and protecting me. But when it got loud I thought it was mad at me. I got real scared. I never understood why.*

Jessica

Many survivors recall terror as children, terror that played itself out as fear of specific events or objects—fear of animals, fear of storms, fear of the dark. These fears are often carried into adulthood as phobias that are so intense they block efforts to carry on ordinary life activities.

As children, clients had valid reasons and identifiable targets for fear. However, to direct fear where it really belonged was dangerous and forbidden. To acknowledge that they were terrified of a parent would have meant that there were no protectors and no safety. To admit fear of assault would have meant admitting that assault was happening. Family denial and the need to remain connected to their parents made it impossible for genuine or straight fear to surface.

Yet children sometimes are unable to suppress all fear. Its under-current laps at the edges of consciousness and cannot be totally erased.

If clients could not admit they were afraid of the adults around them, then how brilliant to invent objects and events to be phobic about. Fear of abusers got channeled to bears and monsters and thunder and night.

There is an underlying logic to an abused child's phobias. The phobic objects resemble the abuser in some ways, and there are common threads among many survivors' phobias. Most contain some element of irrationality and threat. Tornadoes, thunderstorms, beasts, or pitch dark—all of these represent the fury and menace of the abuser.

Fear directed to objects helped clients to deny the abuse and adapt to that schizophrenic reality. Jessica both loved and feared thunder, which represented her mother. Her other abuser, her father, filled her waking fantasies and her dreams with terror as the myste-rious Night Monster. Lorraine still feels frantic when the wind howls outside because it reminds her of her grandmother's rage.

Assigning the fear outside the family, placing it on something vaguely similar but in no way openly tied to the abuser, allows an abused child to discharge some terror, without further crumbling the already shaky foundation of the family. It lets that child release some feelings, without losing hope that the fragile bond with the family will remain intact.

FAMILY ROLES

My family really tries to pretend that they're my family, but they're not because I don't matter to them—only what I say matters—not me. It's like as long as I am their puppet on a string they'll let me be a part of this so-called family.

Jessica

Adapting to assigned roles was also a brilliant survival tactic. Role behaviors serve to lessen the stress of an altered and two-faced reality. They help to organize and control chaos. They contribute to family and personal survival.

The parentified Hero child, who protects, controls, performs, and achieves, is responsible for keeping the family intact. The Hero's triumphs in the outside world give the family proof that they are worthwhile and acceptable. The Hero's caretaking within the family provides stability and often prevents outright disaster. The Hero who functions as a negotiator between parents or between a parent and a sibling defuses potential violence. The Hero who becomes surrogate parent to siblings keeps childish immaturity and careless-ness from becoming tragedy. The Hero who becomes a rescuer or a shield for another victim saves injury and possibly lives. The Hero who becomes a surrogate spouse to a parent calms the turbulent family waters and quiets the backlash of abuse.

The victim of abuse is most often the Scapegoat, assigned by others or offering self as a human target. The family Scapegoat also becomes the blame bearer for the group: "We'd all be fine if it weren't for this child." Dumping all the blame on the Scapegoat allows other family members, particularly the abuser, to escape judgment. Greta recognized this: "I was just a pounding pillow for my parents' anxieties." Blaming the Scapegoat justifies the explo-sions and prevents exposure, and the family is convinced exposure of the abuse would be fatal. Even little children know that people who hurt others are taken away and punished. What would happen next in the child's mind? "If Daddy or Mommy went away the family would fall apart. I'd be left alone, and then I'd die." Having the Scapegoat handy keeps the family from ever having to face reality and its consequences.

The Lost Child, the one who escapes physically to another room or emotionally into imagination, lessens stress on everyone, includ-ing self. The Lost Child does little and demands less: "What a relief! That's one child we don't have to worry about." The Hero and the Scapegoat each pull some energy from the system; Lost Children fade into the woodwork and leave behind little trace of their presence.

The Mascot, whose job it is to relieve family tension whenever it begins to build, plays a critical role in keeping the family dysfunc-tion from going public. The Mascot transforms the electricity of conflict into the energy of entertainment. Mascots often become the bearers of family craziness. Like the court jesters in Shakespeare's plays, their wise observations about their surroundings can then be dismissed as the mutterings of fools (Wegscheider, 1981).

Clients need to recognize how the role they played helped keep the family together. They also need to understand how that role behavior helped them cope with the abuse and dysfunction.

> *Client exercise:* What was your role in your family? What behaviors did that role require from you? How did your role help your family keep the abuse a secret? How did playing your role help you to survive?

Every role in a abusive family is essential. It is as though family members struggle together to form one incomplete and inadequate identity. Each role contains some elements of a healthy personality, but merged together, the roles create only a shadow of the wholeness that no one person is allowed to achieve.

Playing the assigned role, changing or combining roles when that was called for, compromised clients' development and identity at the expense of family continuity and cohesion. If clients still find themselves slipping into one of those roles today, that does not make them emotional cripples. It simply means that they adapted brilliantly to the crippling reality in which they found themselves.

FAMILY RULES AND MYTHS

I keep being so confused. Like about my dad not having an aneurysm when I was always told he did. I guess any other child in this situation would feel angry. But I don't feel any anger—just sad. I don't know why they would tell me that if it wasn't true, and I don't understand why I can't get angry. Maybe because I shouldn't be angry. My dad didn't know that my mom was saying this. He looked real puzzled the day I asked him what kind of problem he had at the doctor's. He just said that there was nothing wrong with him and asked why I thought there was. I didn't tell him about Mom. That would have made him mad at Mom. I think of all the times Mom used that so I would be good. I can't believe I was stupid enough to buy into it.

Jessica

Obedience to the family rules was also a brilliant way to reduce stress, control chaos, and ensure survival. To talk, feel, trust, think, change, or grow in a system that could not tolerate talking, feeling, trusting, thinking, changing, or growing would have created unbearable conflict. Clients might have been abused more. They might have been banished altogether. Not fighting back created an illusion of consent that made the abuse seem less terrible. Not telling kept the family together. It was better to submit, unquestioning, to the family rules, better to surrender than to challenge the family fables, better to carve a niche in the world with only the tools and methods allowed by the family.

Beyond the general dysfunctional rules outlined here and in Chapter 8, each family creates some of its own myths. In healthy families, myths can add to the reputation of a colorful ancestor. Uncle Jeb, the circus clown, has new stories added to his legend at each family gathering. In unhealthy families, myths are used to browbeat people into secrecy and submission. "People in this family are strong and solve their own problems" keeps victims from seeking outside help. The fantasy that some adult in the family is in frail health guards against any challenge to family authority. "Men in this family can hold their liquor" enables alcoholism. The idea that women "fall into flesh" as they age excuses eating binges.

The most vicious myths are the ones that justify the abuse. Children need to be disciplined to ensure their safety and socialization. Discipline, however, is loving control in a child's best interests. "Spare the rod and spoil the child" condones brutality. The idea of the bad seed or the black sheep, the idea that a child is somehow evil and corrupt from conception, singles out the Scapegoat, targets that child for attack, and justifies the assault. And the myth of the seductive child is just that—a myth. Although children are undeniably sexual beings, an innocent child does not understand deliberate seduction. Children deserve to be able to trust the adults in their lives and to experiment with their growing sexuality comfortably and safely with those adults. Seduction is either learned because it is taught, or it is discovered by a child as a means to get negative attention rather than no attention at all. No child asks for or consents to sexual assault. Consent is not possible when the attacker is twice as big as the victim and holds all the power and authority. Claims that a child is "too pretty" or "so sexy" are used to brainwash both the victim and the family. But they are just excuses that make a child unfairly responsible for the actions of an irresponsible or criminal adult.

Often myths deny a child's right to exist. When a child is repeatedly told, "I'd be better off if you had never been born," or "You ruined my life," or "You were an accident," or "You should have been a boy," or "You should have been a girl," that child needs to apologize for being born. The child tries to be perfect but can never be good enough. In disgrace, the child sometimes retreats from the world's eyes, starving or bingeing or self-punishing in an attempt to change the unacceptable self.

Client exercise: What rules and myths did your family have? How did they affect you in childhood? How do any of those myths still influence your life today?

If clients failed to challenge the unhealthy rules and myths in their families, if they still find themselves going along with some of them today, that does not make them weak or out of touch with reality. It simply means they made a brilliant decision not to battle against overwhelming odds, odds that may still seem overwhelming.

CONSIDERING CHANGE

The patterns clients learned in childhood served them well then. But just because their present behaviors are normal for survivors and reflect brilliant childhood coping strategies, that does not mean they have to keep doing the same things. If those coping strategies are causing problems today, it is because they are relevant only to surviving abuse. They are no longer useful in the real world. Although they were helpful and even lifesaving in childhood, they are less helpful and may even be life-threatening now.

Clients will find it easier to let go of defenses that are no longer helpful if they first acknowledge how necessary they were in childhood. Simply recognizing that behavior patterns are no longer useful will not make them disappear. Clients have probably realized and tried that for years. Defenses rooted in survival cannot be shrugged off so easily. Fighting weakness is a negative approach that engenders resistance. Honoring behaviors as evidence of strength renders them more malleable.

> *Client exercise:* Write a letter to all the defenses you have identified, describing exactly how each one helped you to survive in childhood. Then write a letter to the Child, thanking the Child for discovering such brilliant coping skills.

Recovery boils down to a choice between staying stuck, to avoid rocking the family boat, or confronting and changing old beliefs and behaviors. Because clients have always had to choose their families first and put themselves last, recovery is a frightening prospect indeed. They do, however, have the right to decide. They have the right to get well for themselves.

Recovery involves a paradigm shift, a complete change in the angle of the window through which clients view the world. Up until now, their existence has taken second place to family secrecy and survival. Any thought or action that put their needs or feelings first had to be denied. Recovery is based on the value of self and on individual wholeness and fulfillment, and the false front of the abusive family will be threatened by that.

Clients will feel guilty as they begin to challenge the rules that have run their lives. Guilt comes when there is a conflict between belief system and behavior. The family's belief system would not allow challenge. It demanded silence and forbade independence and growth. Clients need to understand that it is the belief system they were taught, not them or their behavior, that is at fault. For too long, they have used guilt to condemn themselves and their own behavior. They can begin to use guilt as a signal that change is needed.

They can begin to break down the walls of the false belief system that has kept them prisoners, a belief system which is no longer necessary or productive in the adult world.

The belief system that supported survival does not yield readily to challenge or change. Clients may benefit from "acting as if" their beliefs are already different. They can ask themselves what they would be doing if they believed they were worthy of protection (not to blame for the abuse, smart, capable, competent) and then do those things. The actions will influence the beliefs.

The power and energy needed to initiate recovery lies in the clever and courageous Child. Recognizing and celebrating the brilliance of the Child shifts self-experience from weak to strong and completes the framework for the trauma resolution process work to follow.

- *Intervention:* Reframing survivor defenses as brilliant.
- *Rationale:* Decrease self-condemnation for adult behavior sourced in trauma survival; build positive base for altering self-defeating patterns.
- *Result:* Shift in self-experience from weak to strong.

PART II:
THE PROCESS OF HEALING

Chapter 10

Recounting

I guess I need to write about this because I can't stop think-ing about it. I saw Mary today and we talked about what happened with Dad. She called it incest. I don't like that word—it scares me. I remember waking up and Dad being in bed with me. I remember the way he looked at me differently and the way he touched me differently. It explains so much—why my mom says, "What's it like to be your father's wife?," why I hate sex and feel so guilty, why Mom is so resentful of my relationship with Dad, and why I was always so spacey in school. I'm so scared and so sad. How do I act toward my dad now? How do I act toward my mom? She probably knew it was happening. There's this very large part of me that keeps saying I'm crazy and none of this happened. I feel so terrible and awful. If I don't believe I will live through this now, how could I have lived through it then?

Jessica

Telling the story of trauma advances healing and moves recovery into a new dimension. However, not until self-experience has begun to shift from dirty, doomed, damaged, different, defective, and un-fixable to normal and brilliant can clients tell the truth about what really happened. That is not to suggest that up until now clients have not been telling the truth. They have been painfully honest, to the best of their abilities and awareness, but truth has been distorted by denial and minimizing and blaming and rationalizing, by emo-tional and sensory disconnection, and by all the clever defenses they used as children. Most of all, truth has been forbidden by the Destroyer.

Truth has been facts with no feelings. Truth has been panic and anxiety and depression unconnected to facts. Truth has been what the family said it was. Clients had to accept the family's twisted definitions of "constructive criticism" and "discipline" and "teasing" and "duty" and "love." Even if they can tolerate only brief flashes of memory, even if they can't imagine any feelings connected to the abuse, the steps they have already taken have started the healing process. They are now ready to tell the story from a different place, a place that recognizes the truth of assault and the brilliance of their survival skills. The story now includes both what happened and what it means. The story is no longer confession and revictimization; the story is now vindication and reclamation of power. Defining assault, challenging the cognitive distortion, understanding symptoms in the context of trauma, and celebrating the brilliance of childhood defenses are the foundation for recounting. Recounting both draws from and solidifies these preceding stages.

BLAMING IS NOT HEALING

Telling the truth is not about blaming. It is simply revealing what was learned about the world and what was learned about self. The decision to heal includes a deliberate decision not to blame. That does not preclude putting responsibility for assault squarely on the shoulders of the person who was responsible—the assaulter. It does mean that clients are no longer going to excuse their present self-destructive and self-defeating behaviors by blaming childhood. That was then; this is now. Blaming keeps survivors stuck in the past and robs them of their present and their future. What was done to them was done by others, and they developed strategies to cope with those events that were useful and helpful then. The task of changing patterns that are no longer useful or helpful is theirs, and only theirs, in the present. Life often requires people to take responsibility for fixing things that aren't their fault. The car has to be repaired whether it was purposely backed into a pole or it skidded accidentally on a patch of ice.

UNDERSTANDING IS NOT HEALING

It does not really matter why the abusers treated the victims as they did. If it seems important for clients to seek reasons, they should be encouraged to investigate the family history. But even if they figure out exactly what made the abusers so mean and vicious, that does not change the fact that *the abusers were mean and vicious to them.* Finding reasons and analyzing can divert survivors from the work at hand and put healing on hold.

It is possible that the abusers were doing the very best they could, given the tools with which they had to work. The client may know that the abusers themselves were victims of abuse. The fact that the abusers were the products of violence and neglect and dysfunction certainly affected them and narrowed their parenting and protecting abilities. Knowing the abusers were doing the best they could does not, however, change the fact that at times *their best was horrible for the client.* Survivors have a right to recover, even if the people who hurt them weren't intentionally trying to be cruel. The broken leg gets a cast no matter who or what caused the injury.

FORGIVENESS IS NOT NECESSARY

Entering the work of healing with the sole goal of forgiving abusers will block recovery. If clients are doing this work only to forgive, they are denying at the outset every feeling they have yet to feel.

Forgiveness is a choice to be made at the end of healing, when survivors truly know how the abuse affected them. They may find there is some damage that is unforgivable. What was done to them may be so awful that there is no possibility of human reconciliation. They can commend such deeds to divine judgment, if their belief system allows.

Survivors do not have to forgive to heal. All the work can be done in the absence of forgiveness. They can free themselves from the need for revenge and find release and peace, without granting pardon, if pardon is not due. Forgiveness naturally follows an apology. It is difficult, if not impossible, to forgive if denial and blame persist. If clients were told they caused the abuse, if they were accused of being bad or evil to justify assault, they may need to work at forgiving themselves for imaginary sins defined by the confusing family dynamics of dysfunction. The culmination of healing is forgiving and celebrating self, not forgiving and celebrating the abusers.

THE IMPORTANCE OF RECOUNTING

Telling the truth, recounting exactly what happened, both factually and emotionally, is not a pointless exercise to make survivors relive the pain and panic of childhood. Although it is tempting to skim over the details of the abuse, clients need to remember specifically and feel completely to break the bonds of denial and distortion. Recounting is important for three reasons.

Recounting Provides Meaning and Direction

First, it is impossible for survivors to heal unless they know exactly what has caused the need for healing. Unless they know what they are healing from, they cannot know how they need to heal. Superficial truth will produce only surface recovery. Core pain will fester and reemerge to limit life once again.

Recounting allows clients to identify areas of developmental loss. They need to understand the strategies they learned that were relevant only to surviving abuse because those now need to be unlearned. They need to know the skills they missed learning because those now need to be learned for the first time. During the recounting stage, clients need to be reminded that it is not betrayal to talk about how they learned to cope with the world.

In addition, recounting accurately and specifically makes the abuse real. Clients need to replace that vague sense of doom, that suspicion that they have no right to exist, that questioning of their own perceptions and reality with a solid conviction that it was their world, not them, that was crazy. The abuse is not some figment of their overactive imaginations; it is a real part of past history and present experience. When the facts of the abuse become real, the need and the right to heal become real also.

When clients finally tell the whole story, they will be able to challenge conclusively the distorted beliefs they were taught as part of the abuse. They will know with certainty that what happened wasn't "constructive criticism" or "discipline" or "teasing" or "duty" or "love." It was assault. They will then understand completely that it wasn't their fault. Clients didn't consent just because they didn't tell then. They didn't consent just because they didn't say "no." They were too little to say "no." They were too little to fight back. They were threatened or they just knew something terrible would happen if they told.

Because the prospect of telling is frightening, clients need to be assured that they will live through the process. They survived the actual abuse. They can survive telling about the abuse.

Recounting Allows Control

Second, the very act of recounting drives the healing process. Survivors can and need to control the pace of telling. They had no control at the time of assault: they must have absolute control over recovery. Recounting reverses the helplessness of the original assault. For the first time, the survivor is completely in charge of what is happening, when it is happening, and how it is happening.

Forced recounting repeats the trauma of abuse. Taken out of the survivor's hands, recounting can become emotional assault. For that reason, hypnosis seems inadvisable for most survivors of abuse. Despite the urgency to know and tell everything immediately that some survivors feel, it is better to let the details and feelings surface when they are ready. What clients can tell now is what they need to tell. If there is more that is important to tell, they will do that in their own time. As they rejoin and draw strength from the Child and as the Adult and the Child together take a stand against the Destroyer, clients are preparing a framework into which feelings and details can emerge gently and naturally. They are preparing a framework that will make healing manageable, not overwhelming.

Recounting Affirms Strength

Finally, exact and specific recounting is important to complete survivors' understanding of the present patterns that may still be perplexing and frustrating them. Even though Ann remembered escaping outside under the bushes with a piece of bread when she was three, she did not fully connect her eating binges to childhood abuse until she told the complete story of oral rape. She discovered that she was still filling her mouth to protect it from violation. Marsha continued to castigate herself for hitting and bruising and burning herself until she recognized that the abuse always stopped and the tension always lessened after she was hurt. She had learned before she could walk or talk that her own physical pain provided swift relief from anxiety and fear. Jeremy found that his puzzling habit of sleeping with his hands tucked securely underneath him made sense when he described the circumstances of his brother's nighttime attacks. Trina believed she was partly at fault because she didn't fight back against her uncle's touching. She realized her stiff and frozen body was the way she tried to resist.

Recounting lets clients truly believe in the brilliance of the Child. As clients recall exactly what was happening when their coping mechanisms were forming, their disgust for the defenses they have been condemning will change to awe and admiration. They will begin to truly see themselves as powerful survivors, not as powerless victims.

For survivors to believe they are sick and crazy is not only inaccurate, it makes healing an insurmountable task. It is almost impossible for people to make changes when they are feeling weak and defeated. Defeat saps strength and leaves them exhausted. Exhaustion keeps them plodding along in the same old rut, head down and eyes to the ground. They can't see another path even if they stumble over it.

Recounting is the catalyst for Stage II transformation. Understanding that they were and are brilliant survivors—that they did what they had to do in order to stay alive—provides clients with a solid launching point for healing. Recovery is not about suddenly becoming a strong person. Recovery is about using the strengths that already exist to shift perspective on self and the world.

Recounting holds the keys to those strengths. Recounting gives clients facts and feelings which will guide that change in perspective. Clients already have all the answers to healing inside them. Their own histories can bring meaning out of chaos. They can reclaim control over the abuse because the ability and the choice to tell that history is theirs and theirs alone. They have the energy and the brilliance of the Child who crafted their survival defenses; and they have the power of the Adult survivor.

ROADBLOCKS TO TELLING

I really thought I wanted out of this pit, but when Mary asked me how much did I want out, I thought I didn't really want out. I'm trying to think of all the reasons I don't want out:
I'm afraid of the memories.
I'm afraid of the anger I'll probably feel.
I'm afraid my dad won't love me anymore.
I'm afraid I won't love him anymore.
I'm afraid I'll fall back in the pit.

Dad,

All I want is a dad—a real dad—not the father you are. You terrorized my life for twenty years, and now I have to deal with what's left of it. If I ever felt what's in me, then I know my world would be wiped away. It would go away, and then I'd be even more alone than I am now.

Jessica

The old tapes from the Destroyer, the family rules and myths, the role clients played, as Hero who kept the family together or as Scapegoat who took the blame or as Lost Child who ignored or as Mascot who dismissed everything as a joke, the self-blame and guilt, and the underlying conviction that they or someone else will die if they tell—all these combine to forbid disclosure.

Telling feels like betrayal. If they tell, clients may fear that they will lose the family. They may be convinced that something terrible will happen. They may feel sure that some horrible fate will befall them or someone they love. They may fear that listening to the secret will destroy or doom the therapist.

If communication was indirect and incomplete in childhood, it is difficult to consider telling the truth completely and directly. Efforts to talk, feel, and trust are immediately subverted by the old rules against talking, feeling, and trusting that kept clients alive when they were small. This makes sense because the family's code of secrecy and silence was woven into the story of the abuse itself.

The defenses clients used to cope with trauma were also woven into the story of the abuse. When clients begin to think and talk about what happened, the memories and the defenses cascade from storage simultaneously. If they dissociated to survive, clients may find themselves spacing out more frequently after they have recounted some part of the abuse, even if they have recounted it only in a journal. Old phobias or rituals may reappear, or they may want to hurt themselves.

Sometimes the blocks are bizarre. Margot recognized talking about anything except current events or the weather was defined as "mudslinging" in her family. Of course she had trouble talking about her father's vicious beatings and her mother's failure to stop him.

Again, clients need to be reminded that it is not betrayal to reveal the facts about what happened to them when they were children. It is simply telling the truth after so many years of lies and deceit and distortion.

It is undeniably comforting to continue to believe that family and childhood were safe. But if clients were abused, all they're holding on to is an illusion. That fantasy about the past is contaminating both the present and the future.

This is a time for reinforcement, for journaling which insists to the Child that disloyalty does not mean death, for drawings which affirm the Adult's ability and desire to safeguard the Child. Slowly but surely, the alliance of Adult and Child will help clients get past their fear of telling. Slowly but surely, they will be able to tell what they need to tell to heal.

ROADBLOCKS TO BELIEVING

Nothing fits—nothing makes sense anymore. I think of my father and my mother and it's not them. They wouldn't do that. It's like it happened to some other child by some other people. Not me. Not my parents. I don't feel anything—just numb. I talk about it like it was nothing. That girl was probably scared, but I don't feel scared or terror or anything. I say it but I don't feel it. When I saw my parents on Sunday I felt nothing. When I looked at my dad there was nothing inside me. No hurt or pain or sadness or anger or happiness or anything—just nothing. No recognition that he's the one who abused that girl and no recognition that I am that girl—just nothing.

I think I'm trying to make a crisis out of all of this. It really is silly. I mean, come on. I'm not a victim of abuse. Sometimes I can be such an idiot. I can really see myself looking for a crisis. I wasn't depressed. I was just so tired from trying to climb that wall, and the wall just kept getting taller and taller. I think all I need is some sleep. And maybe a kick to make me see how silly I can be.

Jessica

Believing what they are saying is sometimes harder for survivors than the actual telling. Mental pictures of the abuse may be only vague outlines. They may seem more like dreams than reality. The observer quality of traumatic recall caused by dissociation makes the mental pictures seem like fantasies. It seems to clients as if those things happened to somebody else, not them. If the memories feel at all real, they will be tempted to insist they are overreacting or imagining.

The family's denial, minimizing, blaming, and rationalizing were embedded in the abuse. Every thought about what happened is tainted by the family's distortion of reality. Beyond that, no one wants to believe that the people who were supposed to love and protect were abusers. It is natural to doubt recollections of abuse. It is natural to question whether what happened was so horrible that it deserves to be called assault.

THE NATURE OF TRAUMATIC MEMORIES

Although this is clearly not a book about repressed factual memory—the healing process begins when clients redefine as assault the things they already know happened—it would be irresponsible to ignore the phenomenon of memory repression associated with trauma. Recent findings indicate that most people who were abused as children remember all or part of what happened to them, but it is also possible for memories of abuse that have been forgotten for a long time to be retrieved (Denton, 1994). "Inability to recall an important aspect of the trauma" is part of the post-traumatic stress disorder diagnostic criteria (American Psychiatric Association, 1994). That description of PTSD was based on symptoms displayed by Vietnam veterans, people who had experienced trauma in adulthood. If adults have gaps in memory for traumatic events, how much more so children, who often don't know what's happening or what it means, who have no mental framework to fit the experience, and who have to continue to depend on the abusers for life itself.

A common misconception about repressed memory concerning trauma is that it involves only facts. Memory has several parts, each or all subject to repression in catastrophic circumstances. The BASK model of dissociation (Braun, 1988) is a helpful explanation of the mechanics of memory repression. An event occurs at multiple levels of perception. BASK stands for behavior (B), or what happened, affect (A), or what emotions were attached, and sensory (S), or what sensations the body felt. The behavioral, affective, and sensory components of an experience comprise knowledge (K) of the event. Any one or a combination of the BAS elements can be disconnected or dissociated and then repressed around trauma, significantly altering a survivor's later understanding of the event. Memory includes any one or all of these elements—what happened, what emotions were present, what the body experienced.

Repressing feelings or sensations while retaining some factual details about what happened is particularly common in trauma, especially for trauma that happened when a child was older. Thus, the survivor who remembers the beatings is convinced that they didn't hurt or that there is no anger or fear attached. The younger the child, the more likely that larger chunks of the traumatic experience will be missing. Near total repression is also more common when the same kind of trauma happened again and again, and the need to dissociate could be anticipated. Dissociation cuts off perception, and what is not perceived is not remembered (Terr, 1988).

As the preface pointed out, all the strategies suggested in this book are self-controlled. None are directed solely to retrieving repressed factual (what happened) memory. However, when clients allow themselves to consider the reality of family and childhood, when they allow themselves to think about the things that happened and to connect with the feelings buried back then, when they allow themselves to tell the story of abuse, that process can trigger memories of other events that have lain dormant for years. Some of these memories may contain unexpected factual information. Others may release surprising emotions and sensations. When clients finally let themselves acknowledge that bad things happened when they were little, it is logical that things not safe to think about until now may come to light. They are looking through the family scrapbook with clear eyes and new glasses. Details they didn't notice before may now stand out in sharp relief, and new interpretations may emerge. Given cues, everyone can recall incidents not thought about in years. High school reunions are awash with memories, as friends last seen at graduation evoke reminders of long-ago events: "Do you remember when . . . ?" Memories long forgotten can be recalled by a picture of a circus, the smell of fresh-baked cookies, or a visit to a former school.

New episodes of trauma or a flood of distressing and emotionally charged flashbacks to events previously viewed without feelings can come spontaneously when there are prompts or reminders from the environment—the birth of a child, contact with someone from the past, a return to the places of childhood. Memories can start to flow with the elimination of substances that have been sedating or mood-altering—alcohol, drugs, excessive or restricted food. Memories can be triggered by either stress or safety—another trauma, such as a natural disaster or an assault or finally finding support with a caring and considerate partner. Currently, there is much debate about the accuracy of memories retrieved through hypnosis or memory-enhancing drugs. The contraindications for hypnosis logically extend to drugs. However, memories that occur naturally in response to environmental or situational triggers or memories that result from thoughtful and conscious reflection on the past are less questionable, and many survivors enter therapy only after such memories begin to surface.

Clients can distinguish between *recall* and *retrieval*, between memories they've always held on to at some level and memories with completely new content. When any aspect of a memory is retrieved, but particularly when factual (what happened) memory is part of what comes back, clients need to understand that is psychological reality. There is a difference between psychological reality and courtroom objective reality, between how the child experienced what happened and what factually happened. Evaluating any long-repressed factual memory that is retrieved is a task which requires discrimination. Realistically, forensic investigation—"what happened next?"—simply cannot produce anything like a videotape twenty or thirty years after the fact. At best, clients can get close to what happened. The fishnet of memory is constantly being tossed in the currents of new experiences and new information. The webbing allows some details to escape and traps others. Added layers of life and learning color and cloud what is already stored.

Moreover, the memory is influenced by the way it was interpreted as it happened. A child may lack conceptual references to understand what is going on. Just as the family's twisted reality changed the definition of events, attempts to fit abuse into the context of the known can result in distortion. Survivors of earthquakes demonstrate this confusion in their first reactions to the shock: "I thought it was a sonic boom," or "I thought it was an explosion." They try to explain the unexplainable to themselves in ideas they can comprehend, ideas that come from previous experiences and learning. An adult describing pressure and pain that felt like it was splitting the body apart to a very tiny child may not be describing what is legally defined as rape.

What clients are remembering is their own psychological reality, what they experienced in a child's mind. They have a right to heal from that psychological reality because that reality reflects what meaning the event had for them, even if it doesn't always meet the criteria for courtroom evidence.

The age at which the memory was stored also affects its content. For example, what is known about very young children's cognitive processes suggests that clients dealing with very early memories may never really know what happened first, second, and third, or how many times something happened because very young children can't sequence events, and they lack the ability to sort salient features or to form continuous memory. When children retell the plot of a movie, they skip from end to beginning to middle, interrupt the account with elaboration of unimportant details, and leave out critical scenes. This has nothing to do with repression. It has everything to do with normal human growth and development (Piaget, 1952, 1954, 1967).

Young children also don't have appropriate words to attach to what is happening. Children who remember "going bye-bye" with the family will define the trip as a "vacation," when that word is later added to their vocabularies. But when a memory has to be encapsulated and locked away, the story can't be reinterpreted as new information and concepts are added. Again, this has nothing to do with repression. It results from not being able to think about the memory or change it along with the maturing thought process. Survivors processing retrieved memory for the first time often struggle through single syllable descriptions of an event—"He gave me ice cream; I took the ice cream; I ate the ice cream"—only to discover that the adult word bribery and the adult concept manipulation apply. The words and concepts have been frozen along with the memory.

Clients need to assess the accuracy of their existing or new memories from these viewpoints. Do the words they use to describe what happened, when they first allow themselves to think about it again, reflect appropriate vocabulary for the age at which it happened? Are the parts of the memory organized in ways consistent with the mental abilities of a child that age?

If the work has added new details or fragments, clients also need to assess the accuracy of their discoveries by comparing new material to uncontested memories. Sometimes pieces they have always retained clearly mesh with freshly retrieved events. Sometimes new fragments fit obviously into known history. Clients can look for corroborating evidence in the things they are certain about. If their aloofness is part of family folklore, that may help them consider the possibility that they needed to hide from assault. Body reactions in adulthood, such as intense discomfort around an adult, can mask childhood fear of an abuser. Sometimes the factual memories they are questioning can be verified by other family members, teachers, friends, or Child Protective Services records.

Evaluation and validation of memories is often a difficult and ambivalent task for clients. It is also an opportunity to enrich and strengthen the therapeutic partnership. Clients must rely on the clinician's expertise and support to be able to make their own determination. Clients need gentle encouragement to believe their memories, tempered by a reasoned and informed assessment of the validity of those memories. The therapist's knowledge of the stages of childhood cognitive, conceptual, and perceptual development assumes equal precedence with clinical skills during this stage of therapy. The therapist must balance science and art, navigating the waters between intellectual objectivity and creative interpretation with wisdom and grace.

Recounting is a time for both honoring and evaluating memories and for exploring the feelings those memories contain. Recounting allows debriefing from trauma and begins the process of integrating the trauma into ongoing history.

- *Intervention:* Recounting the story of trauma.
- *Rationale:* Debrief from trauma and begin integrating trauma into ongoing history.
- *Result:* Decreased guilt and shame.

Chapter 11

Rediscovering the Child

Little Girl,

Hi. I decided I needed to talk to you. Maybe because I think you know some things I need to know. I think you've been separate from me for a long time, and I want to get to know you. You look real sad. What was happening to you? Why are you crying? I see you sitting outside my special room by the tree. I think you still have feelings you're not letting go of. I need you to share them.

Jessica,

Why are you writing now? You never cared about me before. You treat me bad. You don't like me. You say I'm gross and disgusting. Why should I tell you anything? You'll just hurt me like they do. You don't like me. You don't take care of me. I take care me (sic). I protect me. You don't—you never will.

Little Girl,

I need to ask you what you need to be safe. What can I do to help you feel safe?

Jessica,

I need Mommy and Daddy to stop. I don't like it—go away, go away. Not safe. Not safe. Please—no—go. Not safe. No— no—no—no—no.

Little Girl,

Mommy and Daddy did stop. They're not hurting you now. They'll never hurt you again. I'll never let them near you. I'll protect you from them.

Jessica,

No—not gone. They hurt—hurt. You can't protect me. They hurt you. Still hurt you. Never stop—never stop.

Little Girl,

They're not hurting me anymore, and they can't hurt you anymore. You're not bad. What they did is bad and wrong—not you. You are good.

Jessica,

No—no safe.

I'm very mad at that little girl. I wish she'd either come to me and be a part of me so I can feel and believe that what happened to her really happened to me, or I wish she'd just go away. I can't stand this in-between stuff. It should be one way or the other.

Jessica

Rediscovering the Child and rediscovering the feelings, the subject of the next chapter, are simultaneous and complementary processes that require therapeutic guidance during the transition between recounting and resolution. They are both accompaniment to recounting and preparation for resolution.

The Child is window to the past, strength for the present, and hope for the future. It is the Child who holds emotions and perceptions and sensations locked on the ends of nerves that were numbed and frozen during moments of repeated trauma. Pieces of the puzzle will begin to fall into place as clients make that Child feel safe enough to trust and venture forth.

Empty encouragement to trust will not work, nor will promises of safety that are only words. Connecting with the Child is a spiral of truth and belief that spreads upward and outward from the steps already taken toward recovery. As clients begin to believe the Child's feelings, the Child opens the floodgates to provide more. That, in turn, increases acceptance of the Child and the Child's truth.

Clients need to affirm that they are proving themselves to be dependable parents for the Child, with their willingness to listen to the feelings and to tell the full story of the abuse and with their willingness to define what was called "love" and "duty" and "discipline" and "constructive criticism" and "teasing" with the word that speaks the truth—assault. They are no longer participants in the mind-boggling game of altered reality and denial. They are establishing a circle of love and safety around the Child by celebrating the brilliance and wonder of that tiny victim.

Focusing on the Child enables clients to move from the position of caretaker for others to caregiver for self. They no longer have to blame themselves and deny their own existence to keep the family functioning. As they begin to sympathize with the hurting Child, they can put the responsibility for abuse where it really belongs and free the Child from guilt and shame.

The more clients validate the reality of what they lived through, and the more they affirm their own brilliance and innocence and goodness, the more they will find themselves worthy of self-love and self-care. The more the Child senses that self-love and self-care is proof of belief in the Child's existence and brilliance, the safer the Child will be to reveal evidence of that existence and that brilliance in the form of feelings and true connection with self. As self-acceptance grows, that hidden piece, the Child, will find freedom to come forth and claim a rightful place in the sun.

The journaling and drawing clients did in Chapter 7 set the stage for the Child to rejoin the present. However, one invitation after years of silence and avoidance will not be enough. Clients will need to continue writing and drawing to encourage the Child's awakening. They will need to be patient and persistent in their attempts to reconnect with the Child.

ALTERNATE HAND JOURNALING

A technique that can help with reconnection is alternate hand journaling (Kritsberg, 1985; Bradshaw, 1990). Jessica's example at the beginning of this chapter can serve as a guide. If clients are right-handed, they will write to the Child with the right hand, but they will let the Child respond with the left hand. They may produce awkward printing or an almost unreadable scrawl. Neatness is not the point of this exercise. It is a tool to connect with the Child. Since each side, or hemisphere, of the brain controls the opposite side of the body, using the left hand to write for the Child allows clients to access the right hemisphere of the brain, the side that is the seat of creativity and imagination, the natural dwelling place of the Child. If clients are left-handed, they will still benefit from trying this alternate hand method to journal with the Child. The switch to the nondominant hand focuses concentration on coordination rather than content and releases unexpected discoveries. If alternate hand journaling does not seem to work, clients can be encouraged to use different colored markers or pens for each persona.

Jessica's alternate hand dialogue introduces a little person who uses childlike language and incomplete sentences, in contrast to Jessica's articulate adult style. As Jessica's journaling also indicates, the first contact with the Child may not be the joyful reunion hoped for. The Child may be resistant, and clients may feel upset or discouraged by that. It is unrealistic to expect instant trust and affection from a part of self that has been ignored or hurt. Even if the worst the Adult provided for the Child was benign neglect, that Child was taught to disappear. The Child learned not to talk because no one was really safe or caring. Speaking up and believing someone will listen after so many years of silence may not come easily or quickly for the Child.

In time, alternate hand journaling will provide positive connection with the Child and direction for the recovery process. Greta's exchanges with the Child confirmed her suspicions that her mother's "discipline" was really assault, and the childishly scribbled replies contained a personal blueprint for reparenting around the aspects of self-care Greta was finding troublesome.

Dear Little Greta,

I need to hear from you. When you write please print. I would like to hear about your feelings and what you feel and need now and how I can help you feel safe.

Dear Greta,

You asked me to write you about my feelings. I will try my left hand. I was scared when Mom threatened to get a switch. She used to hit me with it. It was awful! I was so scared. If you want me to feel safe don't let them do that to me anymore! You can make them stop!

Dear Little Greta,

I love you. I will protect you. What do you need today? What can I do to make you feel safe? Please answer me in a letter and be sure to answer the two questions I asked and tell me anything else you need or want to. I will love you always no matter what.

Dear Greta,

I love you too! I need to stay with you and do whatever you do. Keep thinking about me. Don't forget me! Give me time to do things without having to hurry. Tell me you love me. Tell me I can take as long as I need to tell you things and to do things. Keep me warm. Let me take a nap when I'm tired. Let me go to bed early when I'm tired.

Some of the Child's feelings may be very painful, and survivors may not want to listen to that pain. However, to access the good feelings that Jessica found at the end of this chapter, they must be prepared to accept the hurtful ones, too. Being willing to tolerate only one aspect of the Child makes clients like the abusers who drove the Child underground in the first place. Uniting with the delightful, wonder Child is impossible if they are not open to embracing the wounded Child also.

The instrument of reconnection between the Adult and the Child is feelings. As clients prove themselves trusting and trustworthy listeners, they will find emotions and perceptions and sensations coming more clearly. Those emotions, perceptions, and sensations are sourced in the core self, the Child.

THE PROCESS OF REMEMBERING

Sometimes emotions or perceptions or sensations appear directly in alternate hand journaling. More often, they occur in a variety of other forms. Clients may be aware that the abuse has haunted their adult existence for years, disguised as flashbacks and dreams, panic attacks, phobias, and chronic pain. Even as they work to make sense of what they already know, they will likely find new fragments emerging or old memories becoming more defined and detailed.

Visual Flashbacks

One way survivors remain connected to the abuse is visual flashbacks, those still or motion pictures of specific incidents of trauma. Flashbacks have been an acknowledged part of the post-trauma response since the symptoms of post-traumatic stress disorder were identified. The classic example is the Vietnam veteran who hears a car backfire and is suddenly overtaken with images and reactions left behind on the Mekong delta.

Some visual flashbacks are so brief and vague they defy description. Like freeze-frame images, they flicker through the brain during waking moments and disappear almost before they can be recognized. Some are so relentless they take over thoughts so that there is no escape. For some survivors, the flashbacks are ruminating rather than intrusive. Memories of the abuse continually hover in the background of conscious thought, an ominous backdrop to life.

Neurolinguistic programming techniques can provide swift and simple relief. Clients can be coached to visualize putting the picture on a small screen in a movie theater and then imagine themselves backing slowly away until the image is so small that it is barely visible. They can change the picture from color to black and white and dim and blur the focus, or they can move to the projection booth and watch themselves back away from the screen so that the flashback itself appears only in peripheral vision. These distancing techniques can help survivors detach from the compelling power of the flashback (Bandler, 1985).

Most visual flashbacks are just that—mental pictures unattached to any emotion. Those are the memories that survivors recount flatly, like the plot of a boring book or the outline of a dull documentary. Whatever events took place happened to an unimportant character in the script. The survivor is involved only intellectually, not emotionally.

Auditory and Tactile Flashbacks

Some memories of abuse are not visual. Instead, they are sounds or sensations. Words or a voice or a sound may suddenly come into the survivor's consciousness out of nowhere. The survivor's skin may tingle, or the survivor may feel touched or hit when no one is near. Auditory and tactile flashbacks can be accompanied by a sense of violation. Such memories are just as real as visual flashbacks, even though there are no pictures. The abuse may have happened in the dark, or the victim's eyes may have been tightly closed. The words themselves may have been the weapon of assault. The sounds may have been part of the abuse.

Often the words and phrases now associated with the Destroyer take over their thinking during a flashback, and survivors feel powerless to shut those off. Warnings such as "You're crazy," or "You should be ashamed," or "You should die" repeat internally. Again, neurolinguistic programming interventions can be effective. Clients can be coached to change the pitch and the volume, to make the voice soft and mellow and loving. It is difficult to be frightened of threats made in warm and melodious tones. They can make the voice high and rapid, like a record being played at the wrong speed. It is difficult to take seriously threats from a character who sounds like Daffy Duck (Bandler, 1985).

Body Flashbacks

The panic and anxiety attacks, phobias, and chronic pain that free-float through survivors' lives are also flashbacks of sorts. Unattached to pictures of the abuse, panic and anxiety attacks, phobias, and chronic pain nonetheless hint at the feelings that were suppressed at the time of abuse. They contain the body reactions associated with the trauma, separated from visual or auditory or tactile recollections. Although such flashbacks are really the brain remembering what the body experienced, no survivor who has viscerally experienced those overwhelming reactions will be able to relate to any description other than body flashback.

Suffering from an anxiety or panic disorder is not proof of childhood abuse. However, if clients know they were abused, they can begin to understand their anxiety and panic symptoms in a new way. The heart-pounding, gulping, gasping sensations experienced in anxiety and panic episodes repeat the suffocating terror of a child under attack who dared not breathe for fear of further harm. They reflect the frenzy of a rejected child trying desperately to please. Panic and anxiety attacks echo the paralyzing feelings that were suppressed to sow the seeds of post-traumatic stress disorder.

Phobias about storms and monsters mirror the chaos of the abuse and the fury of the abuser. The intensity of the fear associated with the phobic object is a clue to the instinctive need to recoil and run that had to be denied in childhood.

Chronic pain speaks to the tension of childhood in the combat zone. It indicates muscles knotted into a flight-or-fight reaction. It points to nerve endings frozen by buried feelings.

Rather than judging themselves disturbed or crazy and fearing body flashbacks, clients can begin to use them as tools for healing. They offer a chance to complete the trauma interrupted in childhood. They are opportunities to accomplish the debriefing after danger that was never allowed. First, clients need to connect the feelings they are experiencing to some memory of abuse or abandonment, even if they can only guess at a specific incident that might apply. The cascade of healing described in Chapter 1 will take hold. What they needed then and did not get was someone to be there, listen, and believe. Clients must act on their commitment to become a healthy parent to the Child. They can tell the Child they know it was scary and that they are now here to be comforter and protector. Then they can ask themselves what they would do for a frightened child and do that for themselves—turn on a light, wrap themselves in a blanket, rock with a teddy bear. If they identify the *freeze—go numb—forget* sequence associated with abuse, it is all the more important to do something physical when such moments of terror occur because movement unblocks frozen nerve endings. Movement replaces messages of immobility with messages of power. Writing belief in the Child's feelings and their own efforts to comfort and protect the Child helps to validate and discharge the emotions, and the act of writing itself patterns energy onto nerves and muscles.

Dreams and Waking Nightmares

The nightmares are back. I dreamed that millions of people were being killed—just blown away. It was awful. I woke up so tense it hurt to move. I was terrified. Now I'm exhausted.

I feel like I'm on a supersonic train. I'm the only one on it and it's going really, really fast. I keep running from car to car and no one's there. It's deserted. I can see through the windows and everything is a blur. I catch glimpses of this little girl crying and hysterical. She looks so hurt. I keep trying to run to another car, but it's so hard. I feel like this train is going to keep on going forever.

Jessica

Some dreams replay actual incidents of abuse. Other dreams, particularly repetitive dreams, are allegories that can stand for the whole of childhood. Jessica's dream of millions of people being killed spoke to her own repeated emotional death as a child. Kira dreamed of driving down a street in a car with no driver and being shot at by hidden snipers, only to find the route to escape was to drive back down the same street with herself at the wheel. She interpreted the original trip as the terror of childhood in a rudderless family and the repeat journey as her need to mentally revisit the scene of trauma in order to recover.

Jessica's train fantasy was a waking nightmare, a variation on the theme of body flashback. Similar to dreams, panic attacks, and phobias, waking nightmares allow some feelings to surface and be discharged separate from the mental pictures of the actual abuse.

Abreaction

The most intense kind of flashback is abreaction. Survivors re-enter the traumatic space. They relive the experience physically, psychically, and emotionally. They can curl up in a ball, unable to talk, gasping for air or absorbing palpable blows. The therapist very literally bears witness to trauma during abreaction.

Although some clients have abreacted trauma spontaneously for years, the fear of getting caught in abreaction and not being able to come back seems very real to them. That fear creates resistance to approaching traumatic material. Both client and therapist benefit from preparation for the deep process work necessary to resolve trauma. The same anchoring techniques discovered to interrupt dissociation can be used to limit abreaction. Verbal or physical cues to the present and to adulthood can be planned and rehearsed. Used in session or independently, such cues become tools for clients to reclaim control and power.

Triggers for Flashbacks

It is important for clients to identify the triggers for the snatches of memory the Child is releasing, so they will no longer be blind-sided by pictures or by panic. When they observe what was happening around them before the flashback occurred, they may discover that a particular smell or sound or event touched off the flashback.

Roberta experienced a vivid flashback to sexual assault when she was touched in the dark. Jill's disturbing flashbacks were triggered by the sound of a door closing, a sound that was part of every episode of abuse.

The scent of an aftershave or perfume, the smell of a particular furniture polish, the time of day, the season of the year, the way the sunlight slants into a window, a tone of voice, a specific word or gesture, loud noises, a certain body posture, the texture of a fabric—almost anything can be a cue for a flashback. Identifying and understanding their own triggers gives clients some power over the flashbacks when they occur.

MOVING DEEPER

Sometimes no matter how lovingly clients treat the Child, no matter how faithfully they communicate in journaling, a real sense of connection to the Child remains just out of reach. They know there is something there, or they know there is more, but they can't quite get to it. As the drive to heal increases, such a plateau can be frustrating.

Enlarging upon techniques that have already proved helpful is an obvious option. However, the creative therapist can take this opportunity to push the therapeutic envelope beyond conventional strategies and guide the therapeutic partnership in new and dynamic directions.

Drawing

Just as pictures enabled the first approach to the Child, art can facilitate a deeper connection to the Child. Sometimes drawing a picture of a place or room associated with the Child is helpful. Sometimes drawing a picture of the feelings that might be holding the Child back opens the door. Sometimes drawing a picture of a memory will free the Child. Drawing with the nondominant hand often lets the Child break though.

Using the Conditional Tense

When the Child is stuck despite the client's best efforts, it may be because the Child is listening to the old rules. If that is the case, asking that part of self still locked in the prison of *don't talk, don't feel,* and *don't trust* to talk and feel and trust won't work. The Child still believes that what is being asked means disloyalty and death.

Instead of demanding that the Child talk and share feelings directly, clients can frame their journal questions to the Child in the conditional tense. Asking "What do you think *could* have been happening to you?" and "How do you guess you *might* have been feeling?" allows the Child to share the secrets without breaking the rules. Clients may even have to ask the Child and themselves how they think another child might have felt in their place. They are only asking the Child to let them know what *might* have been happening and what the feelings *could* have been. They are giving the Child a way to tell without telling, to talk without talking, to feel without feeling. That establishes them as people who can be trusted, people who will not force the Child to go against the rules that kept the Child alive and the family intact.

Assessing the Retrieval System

If conditional tense therapy does not produce results, it may be that the questions are not sensitive to the client's storage and retrieval mechanism. Human beings tend to store information in three basic sensory styles—visual, auditory, or visceral. Storage and retrieval styles can be quickly assessed. An open-ended question about benign material provides information for evaluation: "Tell me about your trip to the office today." Content will indicate primary storage and retrieval preference. Clients who describe traffic lights rather than sirens are likely more visual than auditory. Nonverbal clues are also revealing. If their eyes wander over the room as they try to remember, clients likely store information visually, as pictures. If they cock their heads as though to catch a distant voice, they likely store information auditorily, as sounds and words. And if they hunch over and figuratively go inside themselves, they likely store information as sensations on the ends of nerves (Bandler and Grinder, 1979).

Once the predominant storage modality has been determined, the therapist can use words to bypass the censors and uncover memory contained in the first two systems. "Can you lift the veil?" or "Can you see behind the curtain?" may induce visual memory. "Whose voice do you hear?" or "What words are being said?" may prompt auditory memory.

It is important for the therapist to be aware of personal storage preference because therapeutic metaphors and language will reflect that modality and may confuse a client with a different sensory orientation. Visual word pictures will be frustrating and ineffective with a predominantly auditory client.

Sometimes the rules are so highly evolved and so tightly drawn that the Child will resist even the most gentle permission to speak and share. Memories that are stored viscerally, as sensations in the body, are not easily accessed with words. If that is the case, clients can be coached to *listen to the body*, as they try to reconnect with the Child.

Listening to the Body

Because so many of the abused child's emotions and perceptions and sensations are bound on the ends of those chronically shocked nerves, the body holds answers to rediscovering the Child and the Child's feelings. Thinking and talking and journaling are sometimes not enough to unlock deeply buried pain, which remains out of reach of cognitive, verbal techniques. It becomes necessary to learn the language of the Child.

THE LANGUAGE OF THE CHILD

I just want to feel calm and not like a tornado whirling around.

Jessica

For a lifetime, clients may have dealt with chronic tension or pain they were told was psychosomatic. The physical symptoms can be signals from the particular nerve endings that are holding on to feelings. Headaches and stomach problems and difficulty swallowing and shortness of breath may be indications of nerves blocked by layers of emotion. The Child's experiences are not always stored as film clips or sound bites. They sometimes seem to be stored as sensations in the cells of the nervous system. Discovering the images or symbols associated with those sensations can reawaken those buried feelings. The symbols are the language of the Child who concealed the feelings there.

Uncovering the symbol that holds the Child is the key to core connection. This body technique is an adaptation of therapist David Grove's work with the wounded Child (Grove, 1988).

Symbol identification begins with listening to the body and becoming aware of the vast storehouse of information it contains. As clients begin to think about the lost childhood, the abuse, or some of the physical symptoms they experience, the therapist coaches them to locate exactly where in the body they feel tension or sensation or pain—exactly in the middle of the stomach, on the surface of the skin, in the back of the neck, just behind the forehead, deep in the chest?

Then the therapist asks, "When it's like that there, right there in the middle of stomach (surface of skin, back of neck, just behind forehead, deep in chest), what's that like?" The client is cued to imagine some *thing*, not person, to compare the feeling to. What kind of object could be causing that kind of tension or pressure or pain?

The therapist helps the client mentally nurture the outline of that object, allowing it to expand and resonate through the corridors of consciousness. Clients will find vivid images racing and exploding through their minds. They need time to capture all the richness of the symbol, to let it assume color, shape, size, texture, and temperature.

The therapist then moderates the investigation of the symbol's modalities, careful not to impose imagery from outside but only suggest qualities for consideration.

Is the symbol gray and colorless or brilliantly colored? Is it round or square or elongated or jagged or shapeless? Is it big or small? Short or tall? Is it soft or hard? Rough or smooth? Firm or squishy? Solid or transparent? Heavy or light? Is it hot or cold or lukewarm?

Clients may discover a red, hard knot in the throat, or a huge, gray boulder in the stomach, or a green puddle of slime in the abdomen, or a heavy, iron weight on the shoulders, or a cold, dense mist in the head, or a black, gaping hole in the chest, or brown, gritty dirt on the skin. They may identify several different symbols, each holding court in separate parts of the body.

If clients have trouble producing an object as symbol, the therapist can arbitrarily pick a quality for elaboration: "Hot like what?" or "Heavy like what?" To ensure a critical quality is not being ignored, an open-ended question needs to be included in the investigation: "What else about that boulder (puddle, weight, mist, hole, dirt)?" Sometimes asking what the object wants to say produces surprising results. Dick's symbol was a red, boiling mass of molten lava, but it wanted to say "Help!" Dick realized the anger that isolated him from the world disguised the helplessness he felt as a child when he was being beaten.

Then clients need to consider the meaning of their own symbols. What does each characteristic say to them? For example, do they associate the color red with anger? Do they connect dirt with shame? Do they associate cold with fear? Do they connect hot with rage?

If symbol work wedges into encapsulated trauma and provokes panic or abreaction, the symbol can be made to move. It is the client's own image, and the client can make it change. The therapist guides this process with questions: "What do you want the mud to do?" "How could that happen?" "Who or what could help?" The therapist can suggest imagery-based solutions: "Could the sun dry the mud and make it crumble?" The therapist need not be afraid of polluting the client's imagery at this point. Since the imagery is coming from the Child, suggestions that don't fit will be rejected, but they may inspire a solution that works to defuse the reaction. The need to override the panic or abreaction outweighs the need for purity.

It is critical for clients to pinpoint their own specific symbols. Their imagery decodes the secrets the Child has been keeping all these years. Once guided through symbol and imagery work, clients quickly appropriate it as their own and can begin to initiate it independently.

Client exercise: Draw your symbol as you imagined it, so it becomes even more real for you.

April sketched a tightly coiled spring around a volcano that covered her entire being, which she first related to the tension and anxiety that filled her childhood. Her drawing allowed her to recognize her family's invasion of her entire being, first with an eating disorder and later with other perfectionistic compulsions. Her family defined her reality, feelings, thoughts, and actions. Of course, connecting with the Child was difficult for her. She was allowed no mind or soul of her own (see Figure 11.1).

Mary identified the Child in the blood oozing out from under the riveted steel wall of silence and isolation that closed her throat and tightened her chest. The wall represented childhood abandonment and emotional denial. She described the footprints as evidence that the little girl had walked away, a challenge to the *don't talk* rule from childhood that was part of the Destroyer for her (see Figure 11.2).

Although each survivor has unique symbols, there are surprising similarities in survivors' images. Knots, fists, walls, rocks and boulders, tornadoes and volcanoes and whirlpools, fogs, and empty caverns are themes that run through imagery work with those who have been abused. There is often a slimy quality, such as mud or lava or ooze, in the symbols of sexual abuse survivors. When a

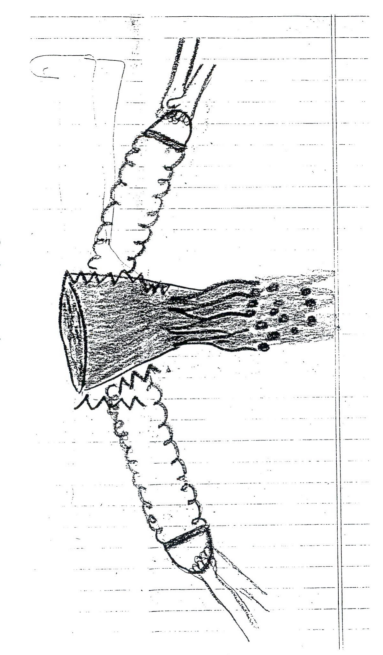

FIGURE 11.1. April's Coiled Spring

FIGURE 11.2. Mary's Steel Wall

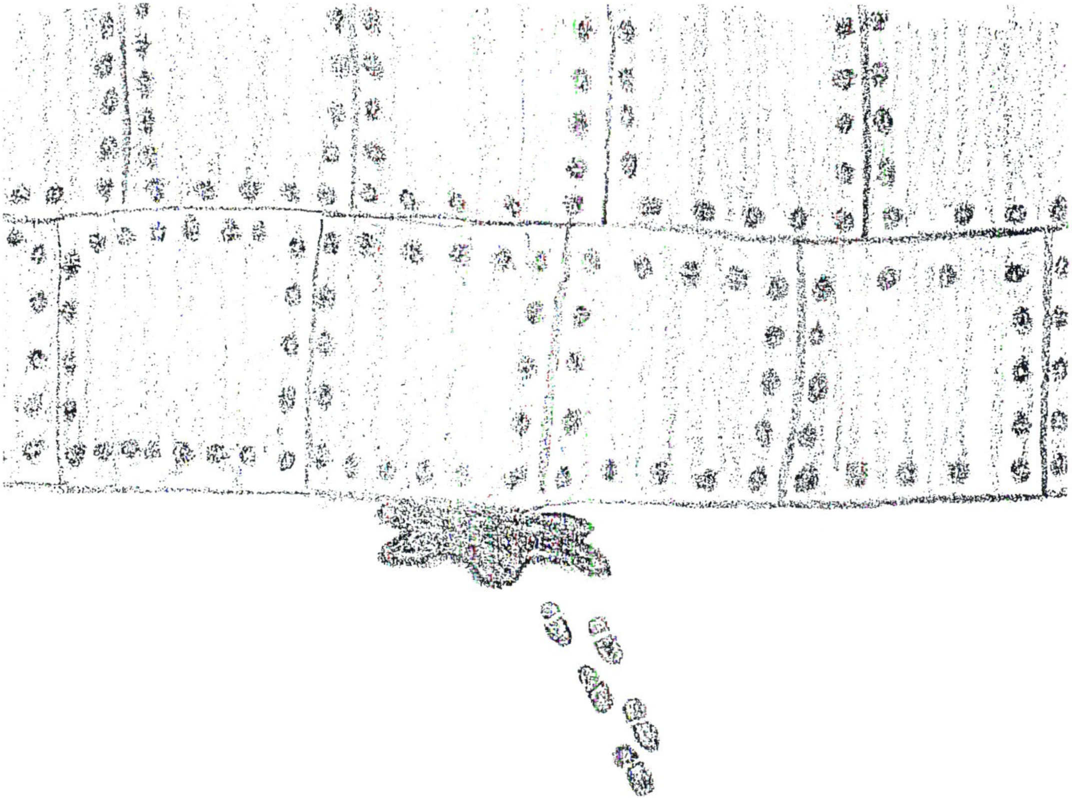

child is abused and then blamed for the abuse, the aggressor's guilt is internalized by the victim in these symbols of shame.

Patricia drew the tornado that appeared in Jessica's journal (see Figure 11.3).

This is not to suggest that such imagery is foreign to adults who have not survived abuse. Anyone asked to mentally investigate a body sensation might imagine it in quite similar ways. However, survivors of abuse are aware that the symbol is not transient. It is a constant and consuming part of their internal geography.

Just as with journaling, there is often a time lag between the first time the symbol is identified and the beginning of connection. Working with the Child's symbol, which is the Child's language, loosens the nerve endings associated with the Child, but it may take a while for the feelings to be freed. It may take some time for that hidden part of self to appear.

Connection may come with a quietly growing awareness or with a blinding flash. A sense of oneness with the Child held captive behind Mary's wall emerged in spontaneous poetry:

> This, then, is not an illusion:
> The red face,
> The grunting noises—
> Oh, my little self!

Clients can begin to pay attention to the reappearance of the physical cues they now associate with their symbols. The circumstances that surround their reappearance hold clues to the Child.

Many survivors recognize that their symbols are in some way connected to their concept of the Destroyer and the Destroyer's attempt to silence the Child. After all, the symbol marks the place in the body where the Child and the Child's feelings were suppressed. The Destroyer's role was to enforce the family's denial of truth and feelings that belong to the Child.

Ruby found the Child buried under a granite rock in her stomach. Leigh realized the Child lay almost suffocated under gray-brown mud in her chest. Bunny discovered the black, opaque fog in her head was depression that stripped her of energy and kept her away from the Child's feelings. Tom recognized the Child was trapped

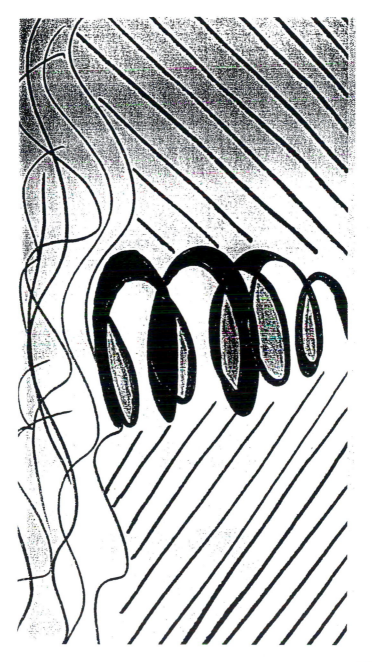

FIGURE 11.3. Patricia's Tornado

behind metal doors that clanged shut in his throat and made it difficult for him to speak or to breathe.

Survivors will find the symbols, and the feelings associated with them, recurring as they move through recovery. Their return should be celebrated, uncomfortable and painful as it may be, for it is a sign from the Child that the nerves are truly unlocking to free what has been imprisoned for so long.

Clients will be fatigued during this explosion of feeling. The work itself is emotionally exhausting. When muscles and nerves that have been tense and contracted, holding a lifetime of feelings, are suddenly relieved of their burden and able to relax, they become slack and drained for a period of time. Suppressing feelings is like holding a helium-filled beach ball under water. It has sapped energy. However, all the energy that has been directed backward into the past is now available in the present.

COMBINATION OF FACT AND FEELING MEMORY

The culmination of all this work comes when the feelings clients have reclaimed join with the facts they already know, and they begin to allow the abuse and the emotion so long severed to flow through them together. Combining facts and feelings finally gives meaning to the abuse. Combining facts and feelings allows them to fully understand why the abuse was assault, why is truly wasn't their fault, and how intensely it hurt and frightened them. This integration of fact and feeling will happen when they have created a safe harbor for the Child. Then the Child can risk telling and know that trust will not be betrayed and feelings will not be discounted.

Integrating feelings with facts can be frightening. Survivors may feel safer continuing to intellectualize and avoid the feelings. Survivors may feel safer staying in the observer role and pretending that the abuse happened to some other child. Survivors may even feel safer continuing to believe that they are disturbed or crazy.

If the reconciliation work has been done gently and consistently, combined fact and feeling memories will come when clients are ready, emerging gradually into the fertile field the Adult and Child have prepared. Combined fact and feeling memories are a validation of the client's strength and a testimony to the client's readiness.

Even if the connection feels at first like a sudden jolt, clients will quickly see that it is the result of the gradual progress they have made over a period of time.

That is not to say that joining facts and feelings is not painful. Again, clients lived through the abuse and not only felt but suppressed all feelings. They need to be reassured that they will live through the feelings now. The Adult and the Child have built a strong and secure place where the feelings can finally be discharged, and the emotional experience interrupted so long ago can finally be completed. The Child can now do what could not be done at the time of abuse—talk freely, feel completely, be believed, and find comfort and freedom from blame.

Greta's journal traced this journey:

> The memory came back! No! No! No! Shaking the head. Afraid to die! Afraid to make Mama die. Not to tell! The same memory as always, only this time I felt the fear! Big-time fear, crying, terror. I had to talk to someone. I called Mary B. She said to write it down, then be with people. Reassure Little Greta.

Dear Little Greta,

> It's okay. Nothing can hurt now. I won't let it. You're not going to die for telling. You didn't make your Mama die! You never told her! She didn't die until 30 years later! Even if you had told, it wouldn't have made anyone die! They just told you that so you wouldn't tell. They were the ones being bad, not you! You were good. You didn't do anything wrong! You were innocent! They are gone. They can't hurt you anymore, ever! It's just the emotion of fear connecting with the memory of fear. When I talked with Mary B. she told me that and I believe her. It makes sense. You're okay. I will keep you safe. I love you. I believe you. I will take care of you always.

> Love,
> Greta

Jessica's continued alternate hand journaling released not only painful feelings necessary for healing but also joyful feelings that would lead to wholeness:

Dear Jessica,

Hi. I'm the little girl you saw sitting by the tree. I want to share a good memory with you. It was summertime and you and Mom were sitting outside at the picnic table. It was sunny out, but the table was in the shade. Mom was wearing one of her sleeveless dresses. I think it was the green one with big flowers on it. She was sitting next to you and she was coloring a picture of Cinderella. She colored so nice. She would color softly in some places and darker in others. It looked so pretty. Cinderella's dress was magenta. I don't remember what you were wearing or what you were coloring, but I remember that you really wanted to be able to color like her. I remember you looking at your mother and thinking about the beautiful picture she made.

Love,
Little Girl

Jenny's poetry made her experiences and feelings real:

Why Did You Abuse Me?

Why did you take your love away,
   when I most needed you?
Why did you tell those lies to me,
   and tell me they were true?
Why did you let me hurt myself,
   and hold the pain inside?
Why did you raise your hand to me,
   when I broke down and cried?
Why did I have to hide from you,
   when I had made you mad?
Why did you smack me in the head,
   and tell me I was bad?
Why did you trust a little girl,
   with so much for her age?
Why did you hold your feelings in,
   and turn them into rage?

Why did you make me eat my food,
   and tell me I was fat?
Why did you say mean things to me,
   and look at me like that?
Why did you dress me like a boy,
   and laugh at all my fears?
Why did you show no sympathy,
   when I came home in tears?
Why did you mention sex to me,
   when I was only ten?
Why did you teach me how to please,
   and how to comfort men?
Why was it a secret,
   when a problem came about?
Why did you ignore me,
   'til I had to scream and shout?
Why did you let me date so young,
   the man you let me see?
Why did I have to lie to you,
   when he assaulted me?
Why did I have to be with him,
   to feel that I was free?
Why did I have to hurt myself,
   to make you look at me?
Why did I have to hide my pain,
   when I was raped and used?
Why did you do nothing,
   when you saw that I was bruised?
Why did you believe me,
   when the truth was in my eyes?
Why did you continue,
   to let me weave a web of lies?
Why did I have to write it down,
   to tell the truth to you?
Why did you not call me,
   when my letter begged you to?
Why do you ignore me,
   when I'm over at your house?

Why are you insistent,
　　that I find myself a spouse?
Why are you so busy,
　　when I call you on the phone?
Why do I still miss you,
　　when I'm out here on my own?
Why do I still think of you,
　　and ache to feel your touch?
Why did you abuse me,
　　when I needed you so much?

- *Intervention:* Using imagery to reclaim feeling memory.
- *Rationale:* Circumvent verbal blocks around feelings.
- *Result:* Access to broader range of congruent feelings.

Chapter 12

Rediscovering the Feelings

Dear Little Girl,

I'm supposed to write to you to let you know that it was okay to have mixed feelings about Mom and Dad. I have mixed feelings about them, too. They both did a lot of things to hurt you, but yet they acted like it was normal, and you had no right to be upset, and under no circumstances did you have a right to be angry at them—at least that's what they wanted you to believe. They told you that you should be grateful they let you be born and they didn't send you away. They didn't tell you they were the ones who should be sent away. They said you were so awful and disgusting that no one would ever like you, and you would always be alone, and that you had to be nice to them or they would go, too. Yet they weren't nice to you, and when you really needed them, they were gone. They yelled at you because you were withdrawn, yet they yelled at you if you made too much noise. They said they loved you, and then they hurt you and said it didn't happen. How could you know who to trust? I still don't. It was okay to hate them and love them, too.

Jessica

As the Child releases feeling memory, clients may find themselves overwhelmed by a jumble of emotions. The overriding feeling may be confusion, or they may think they feel nothing at all. Putting accurate labels on all those feelings seems an insurmountable task.

This confusion is understandable and predictable, given the training ground of dysfunction. One of the developmental steps most often missed in an unhealthy family is learning the language of feelings.

Children are born with the ability to register emotion. Even a tiny infant who is dropped a few feet and then caught will reflexively cry out in fear and alarm. But children are not born with words in their heads to match the sensations their bodies feel. Words for feelings are learned as part of language development. Clients learned words to describe objects because someone pointed to a ball and said "ball" or handed them a spoon and said "spoon." But it is unlikely that anyone pointed to the lump in the client's throat and the tears in the client's eyes and labeled that reaction "sad."

A healthy parent both mirrors and teaches emotion during a child's early years. When her son comes in from a backyard play session crying but obviously uninjured, a healthy mother's face crinkles in sympathy and she responds, "Oh, you're crying. You must be sad. Did someone hurt your feelings?" When his young daughter tries unsuccessfully to button a shirt and stomps her foot and yells, a healthy father reflects, "You sound angry. It feels frustrating to work so hard on that button and not have it do what you want. In a while you'll be able to button your blouse easily. It takes practice because it's a difficult job."

If clients grew up in families where sadness and tears were unnecessary, where anger was bad and sinful, where fear was stupid and weak, and where happiness was overdramatic and overreacting, then their feelings were killed before they could be born. If they were threatened with "I'll give you something to cry about," or if they were shamed with "Look in the mirror and see how ugly you are when you pout," then feelings were downright dangerous. Feelings were forbidden, and they were left with only confusion and emptiness.

What really happened is that clients were never given words to label the sensations their bodies felt. As emotions begin to surface in their full intensity, is it any wonder that the only names they can give them are "confused" and "numb"?

When Tim entered group he was convinced that he could not feel love. As group members hugged him, he described what was happening in his body: "My insides get tingly and the top of my head feels like it's coming off." As Tim described those physical changes, he realized he had always been able to love. He had just lacked the word to link sensation to feeling.

LEARNING TO FEEL

To heal, clients will have to teach themselves to feel again or teach themselves to feel for the first time. They are in a better position to do that as adults than they were as children. They now have knowledge of the world's feeling vocabulary, gathered from a lifetime of exposure to other people's emotions.

The Vocabulary of Feelings

There are many words and shadings in the human feeling vocabulary. All of the words used to describe feelings can be divided into four broad categories: *mad, sad, glad,* and *afraid.* Every word that defines a feeling, no matter how simple or complicated, fits under one of those headings. Words and phrases such as irritated, inconvenienced, displeased, upset, furious, enraged, seeing red, incensed, resentful, angry, ticked off, bitter, infuriated, offended, and rankled all express levels of *mad.* Words and phrases such as unhappy, sorry, distressed, wistful, serious, somber, desolate, grief-stricken, wretched, torn up, melancholy, inconsolable, depressed, broken-hearted, and solemn all voice degrees of *sad.*

SCALING FEELINGS

Since feelings were likely modeled in extremes during childhood, clients often have no concept of mid-range feelings. They have experience with neutral and enraged, or neutral and bereft, or neutral and euphoric, or neutral and terrified, but they may have seen little or nothing of frustrated or sorrowful or contented or apprehensive. They need to learn to scale and titrate feelings as they explore the full range of emotional expression. Scaling and titrating feelings also renders those feelings less frightening.

DRAWING FEELINGS

Because emotion is the world of the Child, words are sometimes not enough to fully capture a feeling. Feelings were present long before the Child had spoken language to describe them. Imagery is the true emotional vocabulary of the Child.

Client exercise: Write down all the words you can think of that
fit under each category. Then scale them from 0 to 10 in the order
you think they increase for you. For example, is "inconvenienced" a 1 on the anger thermometer for you, or is "irritated"
your first mad feeling? Is "enraged" the worst anger you experience, or is "furious" the highest you get?

Mad	Sad	Glad	Afraid
10	10	10	10
9	9	9	9
8	8	8	8
7	7	7	7
6	6	6	6
5	5	5	5
4	4	4	4
3	3	3	3
2	2	2	2
1	1	1	1
0 neutral	0	0	0

Then begin to listen to your body. When you sense some
tension or discomfort, when you detect a shift in your internal
landscape, first put that sensation into one of the four feeling
groups. You may have to use the conditional tense to do that.
Look around you at the situation. What do you guess you could
be feeling? What do you think someone else might feel in your
place?

Next, gauge the level of tension or discomfort in your body
from 1 to 10 and label it with the matching word from your
feeling scale. Say your feeling out loud or in your head to make it
real: "I am upset . . ."

Feeling imagery works exactly opposite from the imagery that
enabled reconnection with the Child. In the last chapter, clients used
body clues to identify the symbols that led to the Child. In this
instance, the image of the feeling will lead them back to the place in

the body that particular feeling most frequently occupies. Their familiarity with imagery work will make the process easier.

Is anger shiny red static or smoldering yellow coals? Is sadness a gentle gray rain shower or a gaping black hole?

> *Client exercise:* Draw your feeling as you imagine it might look in the flesh. Where in your body do you experience that sensation most often?

John discovered his anger was the center of what he had always excused as shyness. A scarlet mass of rage blocked his throat and kept him from speaking (see Figure 12.1).

Sadie pictured her fear as a forest keeping her whole body immobile and isolated (see Figure 12.2).

> *Client exercise:* Go back to your feeling scale. Use the image you have just drawn to label the way you experience each level of feeling in your body. Decide how the image changes as the feeling intensifies. If anger is a volcano, how does it shift as anger increases? Does it get bigger, hotter, redder, more explosive? Draw the image as it happens for you on each level of the feeling scale, right next to the word you have chosen for that number on the scale.

DISGUISED AND HIDDEN FEELINGS

Feelings also occur in layers, with cover feelings hiding the emotional core. Anger sometimes masks hurt or fear. When Helena described her confusion as a long black cape that hung heavily from her shoulders, she discovered that her confusion, like a cape, kept all the other feelings covered up underneath it. Craig insisted he was crazy until he recognized his family used that word to condemn any display of emotion. He realized that every time he had a feeling he told himself he was crazy.

Deb's bottle showed the layers of feelings. Core pain was overlaid with shame, anger, sorrow, guilt, and crazy. Even the surface feelings

FIGURE 12.1. John's Scarlet Rage

FIGURE 12.2. Sadie's Forest of Fear

in the stopper—happiness, love, and hate—were separated from the world outside by a transparent membrane (see Figure 12.3).

EXPRESSING FEELINGS

Naming feelings takes time and practice. Clients are going against years of emotional denial and numbing. Learning to express those feelings appropriately also takes time and practice. Clients can use other people as models. They can watch how others look and act when they are mad, sad, glad, and afraid. They can ask themselves if such expressions would work for them.

Sculpturing connects feeling words to the body. Clients can experiment with using their own bodies like clay to sculpture each feeling. They can be coached to imagine what a body that is angry looks like and mold their own bodies to that image. With clenched jaw, tightened facial muscles, hunched shoulders, knotted fists, and raised voice, they can physically experience each level of anger. This may feel silly to them at first, and they may have to be encouraged to deliberately exaggerate to connect with the feelings.

The guilt they have been carrying can also be sculptured. If they are asked to pick up a heavy sack and walk around with it slung over their shoulders for a few minutes, they quickly realize what a weight they have been supporting and how much it restricts their movements. When they put it down, they are surprised to find their shoulders feel empty. When they consider leaving the family burden of blame behind, they can expect to feel a loss—even good losses leave a hole. Sculpturing provides a model for change. It may be more comfortable to ease the sack slowly to the ground rather than drop it abruptly.

It is normal for survivors to fear that any expression of genuine emotion will mean loss of control. "If I cry, I'll cry forever"; "If I get mad, I'll kill someone or go crazy." They may feel safer first experimenting with feelings in the therapist's office, with a caring friend, or in a support group. Group therapy can be incredibly helpful at this point. Group allows creative avenues for expression and validation of feelings that are more difficult to engineer in individual sessions. However, it is more likely that clients' feelings, out of control as they seem to them, are really underreactions. Any

FIGURE 12.3. Deb's Bottled-Up Feelings

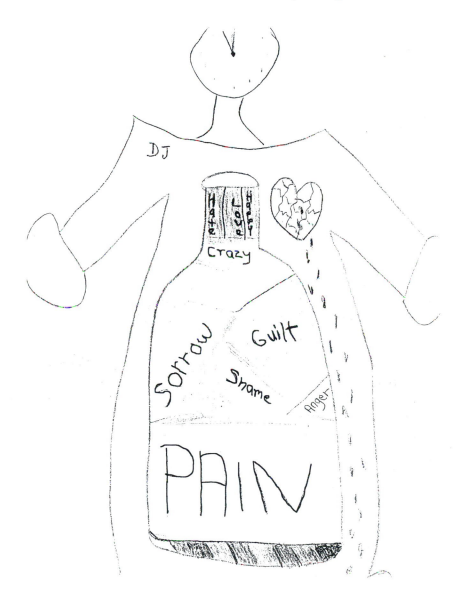

real feeling, no matter how tiny, is overwhelming after years of stuffing and pretending.

Mary's journaling reflected her fear of feelings:

> I feel like an accident waiting to happen. I feel tightly stretched in every nerve and sinew, so a faint vibration hums in me all the time and I am in danger of snapping, flying apart into little pieces with great force if anyone or anything twangs a string. Little bursts of adrenaline explode into my bloodstream and cause falling-elevator thuds in the pit of my stomach. I jolted out of sleep in terror somewhere after 3 a.m. this morning and thought someone was outside my window. It took several hours to calm my body, and I never did go back to sleep.

Deb pictured herself at the mercy of huge waves of pain (see Figure 12.4). As she learned to titrate her feelings, she found herself on top of the waves, protected from their power (see Figure 12.5).

THE IMPORTANCE OF ANGER

As the previous chapter emphasized, the Child holds the answers to healing. If the Child is the vehicle to recovery, then the Child's anger is the fuel. Anger gives survivors power to throw off the fog of depression and the net of craziness. Anger releases energy that drives the healing process.

However, anger at abusers and family is the one feeling outlawed in dysfunctional and abusive families. That kind of anger may be completely out of reach for clients at this point. Even thinking about it may trigger intense anxiety. Like Jessica, they may fear an explosion (see Figure 12.6).

The anger of an assaultive adult may have been life-threatening to clients when they were small. They may have feared the abuser would kill someone else in a rage. Any expression of anger would only increase the danger. If they learned to connect anger with fear of death when they were little, it is not surprising that they think their own anger is terrifying. Clients need to be taught to titrate all feelings, especially anger. Although an explosion of rage may provide a powerful and satisfying moment in session, it can leave the

FIGURE 12.4. Deb's Riding the Waves of Pain

FIGURE 12.5. Deb's Protection from the Waves

FIGURE 12.6. Jessica's Time Bomb

client terrified by loss of control. The therapy agenda should never risk the client's retraumatization. It will be safer for clients to experiment with fractions of anger at first. They can tear off a corner of their image of anger and verbalize just that much. When they do that and find no one dies, they will be able to express larger portions of their rage.

Client exercise: Draw or write just five percent of the anger you might be feeling.

Anger at abusers may also be difficult for survivors because it collides with the love and attachment they want to feel toward their parents. A child has a biological drive for attachment with parents (Bowlby, 1969). That biological drive for attachment is an instinctive, life-preserving force. Parents are the ones who keep a child safe in an unsafe world. Parents provide the food and shelter and nurturing necessary for survival. To deny that drive for attachment, even in adulthood, can feel devastating.

If clients are attending twelve-step recovery groups, they may insist the tenets of the program prohibit anger as a "luxury" they can't afford (Alcoholics Anonymous, 1976). On careful reading of the AA Big Book, they will find the program really warns more specifically against resentment, anger that is felt and refelt, anger that is carefully guarded and nourished in secret. The anger they are dealing with is anger that has never before been felt. It must be discharged in a healthy way so it does not turn into resentment.

Any anger will do to spark recovery. If direct anger at abusers or family feels too threatening, clients can be encouraged to grab on to whatever anger they can comfortably allow. Nora's recovery picked up speed when she became upset about the unpredictability in her current work situation. She recognized that the unpredictability reminded her of childhood chaos and redirected her anger. Carrie's first anger was generalized at stereotypes that discouraged higher education for women during her childhood. She was then able to let herself be angry at her parents' hypocritical use of those stereotypes to deny her a chance at the college scholarship she was offered. Julie initially expressed discomfort about being sent to her father for sexual information. That ultimately freed her to be furious that she was set up for the abuse that followed.

Anger at family and abusers has been forbidden throughout life, and it may not come easily now. Often survivors are able to be angry at an abuser who hurt someone else, perhaps a victim in a news report, before they can get angry at the people who abused them. Journaling and dialoging with the Child will help survivors give themselves permission to be angry.

Greta's journaling opened the floodgates to the Child's anger. The mix of singular and plural pronouns also hinted at the growing connection between the Adult and Child:

> Dear Little Greta,
>
> You were an innocent victim, just as your parents before you were. They had no idea how to take care of you. They did the best they could with what they had, but it was devastating to you! You can't just think it was okay because they were too sick to do any better. What they did to you, even though they didn't set out to do it, hurt you; it did, very much! It still affects our lives today. We need to realize we are not guilty for our past. It was not our responsibility. The fact that our parents were too sick to take their responsibility does not make us guilty! We, too, did the best we could with what we had. We have a right to feel what we need to about our childhood—anger at what happened to us, pain, grieving, rage. Whatever we feel is our God-given right. Please trust me. I love you. None of the past is your fault.
>
> Love,
> Greta

Mary's journaling illustrated the power in the Child's first release of anger and also set the stage for union between the Child and Adult:

> Congratulations! Today you did a really brave thing! You let me say out loud some of the anger we feel. You've never done that before.

After we yelled a little and said a few bad words, we stopped and talked calmly for a while. Then we drove carefully to the mall and bought beautiful earrings and a shirt of many colors and came safely home in the dark. We had dinner—so far, so good with the food—and now I am doing my homework.

Do you see how safe this whole day has been? You helped me find the anger last night in writing and to say it out loud today, and nothing bad happened! It's your very own anger and you have a right to say it, to yell it, to cuss and pound on pillows if you want to. I can keep us from hurting other people, or ourselves, and you can say "Go" and "Stop" anytime you want to.

Anger will unfold as clients write a series of no-send letters, one to every abuser in their lives, detailing what happened, how they felt about it then, and how it still affects them today. Writing is only half the process, however. To be released, the anger must be heard. The letters need to be read out loud—to the therapist, to the group, to a caring friend, to a picture of the abuser, to an empty chair in which the imaginary abuser is sitting, to the abuser's tombstone. Later, clients may choose to make one of their letters the foundation for a face-to-face confrontation with an abuser, or they may choose to modify a letter and send it through the mail. Right now the first rush of rage needs to be discharged in safety and support. Survivors need to get the anger outside them without risking being reassaulted or blamed.

Clients need to trust their own answers and their own pace. The support group's or the therapist's role is to guide, not lead. Being forced into anger before they are ready to experience it can be harmful to survivors.

Clients will likely be exhausted after their first experiments with expressing anger. Again, suppressing feelings is like holding a helium-filled beach ball under water. It takes a lot of energy, and the fatigue that follows release simply reflects the energy that has been used to stuff feelings throughout the years. All that energy is now free and available in the present.

Clients may find anger surfacing sideways at first—at work, with friends, in everyday situations. They may be inclined to judge themselves harshly if that happens. It is helpful for them to reassure the people close to them that they are working on some issues which may produce anger at times and that the anger is not really about that other person. When survivors are ready, the true anger will appear. It is there. It is the one feeling every abused child is entitled to, but it is also the one most abused children believe they have no right to feel.

Anger began to surface more directly as Jessica wrote no-send letters to her parents:

Dear Mom,

I'm writing this letter to tell you all the things I could be angry about. You never get angry at me for things you should be angry for. Instead you ignore those things and get furious at me over stupid stuff like getting a "B" instead of an "A," or cleaning the whole house and leaving out the furniture polish, or not moving fast enough. It's like I do things to get your attention and you don't notice, and when I'm not trying to get your attention you're all over me. That's frustrating and confusing. I'm angry that I wasn't and still am not good enough for you. I'm angry that you never respected me and what I wanted for myself. I'm angry that nothing I do ever pleases you and I've never been able to get you to love me. I'm angry that I even have to prove myself to you. I'm extremely angry that you never taught me about feelings or emotions. I'm angry that at twenty-four years old I sit in groups and need people to tell me what I'm feeling because I don't know. You never let me cry or be scared or be angry. You would do things to try to make me cry, and then you'd laugh and laugh—this awful creepy laugh—like it made you feel good to see me hurt. You'd make me do things that you knew I was afraid of. At least I know I have a right to be mad at you. It's taken a long time to get to that knowledge. I'm finding myself wanting to make excuses for you. This is really silly, but I'm scared of losing you. It's silly because you were never really there for me, so I wouldn't be losing you, only my fantasy of what you were and what I wanted you to be. I'm trying just this one time not to give you that power. This letter is to help me, not you.

I'm not going to let you turn it into something that hurts me. You've hurt me for twenty-four years.

Jessica

Dear Dad,

I need to tell you all the things I'm angry at you about. First of all, I'm angry that I even need to write this letter. If you hadn't done what you did, and if you had taught me that it was okay to be angry, then it wouldn't keep coming to me writing a letter like this.

I'm angry that not only did you take away my childhood, but you took away twenty-three years of my life. I'm angry that I still lose time and I still feel like I'm kind of floating sometimes. I'm angry that I'm terrified. The pieces I keep losing are the pieces you took. You have totally messed up my life and then waved good-bye and left me with the pieces. You have done nothing to help me. Not even an "I'm sorry, Jessica." That wouldn't change anything, except that it would say you have something to do with this mess. I hate you for taking away my father. I remember this man who was my dad. He was nice. He had a nice smile that would make me feel happy. I remember this man building a snowman with me once. He was real patient when I couldn't get the head on right. You took that from me. Mom always told me I had you on a pedestal and someday you would fall off. Well, you did, only I feel like the one who's been shattered into a million pieces.

Jessica

Jessica's anger finally exploded in poetry:

Dear Daddy

Dear Daddy,
It's me—your daughter.
Surprised to hear from me?
It's been a while—

I remember.
I remember what you did.
I remember your face, your hands, your body.
I remember your empty gaze, your force, your deaf ears.

Dear Daddy,
I feared you.
I feared your power.
I feared your anger.

I hurt now.
I hurt that you've been a fantasy.
I hurt that my Superman father never existed.
I hurt that I no longer trust you.

Dear Daddy,
I loved you.
I would have stopped the world for you.
I would have gathered all the stars.

I hate now.
I hate the pain I feel inside.
I hate myself and what I've become.
I hate what you did to me.

Dear Daddy,
It's me—your daughter.
Not the toy doll you once had.
She's gone—what's left?

- *Intervention:* Scaling and titrating feelings.
- *Rationale:* Decrease emotional polarization and resistance to feelings.
- *Result:* Access to broader range of congruent feelings.

Chapter 13

Continuing to Heal

Dear Little Girl,

How can I protect you if I don't know you? I do like you. It's me I don't like. It's me that's gross and disgusting—not you. You're only a baby.

Dear Jessica,

I'm not a baby! I take care of me. Daddy don't. Mommy don't. I do. If you don't like you, how can you like me? You're just like them—you just want to hurt me.

Dear Little Girl,

I do like you. I don't like what I've become. I don't like me. You're not me. I won't hurt you, I promise. I need to know what you know.

Dear Jessica,

I am you. I'm you twenty years ago. You are hurting me. You shove food in my mouth and it hurts. Please stop it. How can I tell you anything if you shove things in my mouth?

Dear Little Girl,

I don't want to hurt you. I try to stop—I try. I never thought that I was hurting you—only me. I don't care if I'm hurt. I don't care if I die. You need to live.

Dear Jessica,

> *If you die, I die. If you hurt, I hurt. I don't think you try. You still have that medicine stuff. You're the one who needs to stop it. You make me hurt.*

Healing does not happen magically with one journal entry, or with one moment of reunion with the Child, or with one flash of insight into the workings of the Destroyer. Survivors were taught to devalue themselves over a period of years. The Child was forced underground, and the Destroyer was shaped by a series of physical, mental, emotional, and spiritual assaults. Gradually, survivors retreated into the shell of self; they became chameleons; they had to surrender their right to think, to feel, and to be.

It will take time to resurrect that fallen self. It will take time to truly bond with the Child, to repair the damage, and to mount a defense against the Destroyer. If it took twenty years to destroy self-identity and self-esteem, it may take twenty weeks or even twenty months to rebuild.

Clients need to be encouraged to use the techniques they have already learned to nourish their healing. They are moving toward wholeness and true independence. Ongoing work will serve to measure the progress they have made and to propel further growth.

They will continue to define the truth of assault to the Child, and they will continue to celebrate the Child's brilliance in their journaling to the Child. They will continue to offer comfort and belief in their dialoging with the Child. They will continue to affirm the Child's feelings in unsent letters and drawings. The Child, in turn, will release more feelings to them, widening the ripples of healing to expand their understanding of their own worth and goodness.

Clients will likely find that one technique works better than others for them. Many survivors discover they can access the Child more quickly if they use a technique that is different from their usual communication pattern. If clients are highly visual, they can try writing. If they're fairly verbal, they can switch to drawing. Although it is helpful for them to experiment with many methods, they will undoubtedly find one they prefer. Since recovery work is building a framework for life, clients can use this opportunity to develop their own particular styles. Learning what works best for them lets them take charge of their own healing. As they follow their individual paths to recovery, they will find the work gets richer and more rewarding.

Hopefully clients have already made some discoveries as the result of their initial attempts at journaling, dialoging, and drawing. Putting words or pictures on paper makes history and feelings real. It gives thoughts and emotions substance; they can be held in the hand.

Jessica's dialogue with the Child at the beginning of this chapter confirmed the reality of assault and its legacy in her eating disorder. It also pointed the way to rebonding between the Adult and the Child.

Continued journaling solidifies the connection to the Child and the Child's feelings. It can also help clients recognize the Destroyer's manipulations. Jessica uncovered the Destroyer in disguise when she considered the rewards for her depression:

> I'm real depressed again. I've been thinking about that—what's the payoff for me? I think it has something to do with control. I've been looking at what I get depressed over—my parents, my sister, school, work. I have no control over changing those things. I can't make my parents love each other. I can't make my dad stop drinking. I can't make my sister look at what's happening. I can't make work supportive. I get depressed because then I won't be hurt anymore. I don't expect anything else. If I'm real, real depressed, how much lower can I get? If I already want to die, then no one can make me feel worse because no one can hurt me anymore. If I'm not depressed about these things, then I have to look at them realistically. I can't change them. I have no control over them. I'm not sure if this is right, but maybe my having choices means I can look at them differently. I think that's going to be harder for some things than others. I know that if I feel okay, then I'm open to being hurt. I'd rather not be open to that. That's real scary.

Journaling becomes a tool for affirming the brilliance of the Child. Greta's journal entries reflected her struggle to move from self-blame to self-acceptance by challenging the belief system learned by the Child. She had considered herself stupid for laughing at her parents' threats of abandonment. She began to see her laughter as a clever and lifesaving defense:

Somewhere between the ages of seven and eight my mother and father told me they were going to send me to the orphanage. I tried to cope by pretending it was a joke they were telling. I laughed to make myself think it was a joke. This infuriated my mother. She grabbed her yardstick and me and started beating me with the yardstick. My father said, "That's enough," but she kept right on beating, and he did nothing to stop her! I felt so alone, so abandoned, so guilty. It was all my fault. I felt I was making my parents do this to me. There had to be something wrong with me, or I would stop it. I must be insane! I must not have any brains at all.

I actually believed all this until a year or so ago when I started having flashbacks to the beatings and started working on this. I can see now that I was set up, by the way my parents treated me, to feel guilty and to take the blame for everything that made my parents feel bad.

Dear Little Greta,

Laughing at the threat of being sent to the orphanage kept you from being abandoned physically. Even though you got beaten and abandoned emotionally you did not get abandoned physically. Not being abandoned physically was an instinct of survival. You knew you had to have people to keep you alive. You couldn't do it yourself. If you stop and think about it, you weren't dumb. If you think of the human needs, survival has to come first. If you don't survive, none of your other needs can be met.

Love,
Greta

Greta also used her writing to encourage the Child:

Dear Little Greta,

It really hurt me that you still believe the old tapes. They started playing for us big time yesterday. Look how many years we felt this way. Mom has been dead for twenty years and Dad for eighteen years. The poison is still lasting! It's like we take over where they left off! Perpetuating the abuse and believing the old tapes. The only way we are going to change this is by working together! We've got to pull together. I will help you, love you, and keep you safe. We are no longer victims. We are survivors. We lived through all the abuse and survived. We could have killed ourselves or gone insane, but we didn't. We've come this far. There's no reason to stop and give up just because the old tapes keep haunting us. We can make it all the way to recovery. I know we can! Just think about what I've said and believe we can do it!

Love,
Greta

Mary's first dialogue with the Destroyer revealed how it belittled and patronized her:

Me: I've decided to call you the Tape Monster. I think of you as the old tapes I got my shoulds from (and my shouldn'ts). And you ARE a monster!

Destroyer: I resent that! Weren't you paying attention when Mary B. pointed out how important I am to your survival?

Me: Whoa! That's NOT what she said! She said you were important to Little Mary's survival way back when.

Destroyer: Right! You need me to keep you from saying something you shouldn't or doing something inappropriate. You'll be sorry if you don't listen to me. You never did have any good sense. You'll be in big trouble talking about these things.

Me: I'm in big trouble NOT talking! I'm in big trouble binge-ing and being lonely and scared and guilty if I open my mouth.

Destroyer: What makes you think anyone wants to hear any-thing you have to say? Except Mary B., of course, who is paid to listen.

Me: That was a good shot, you bastard! It took me a couple of minutes to go on after that one. You really are a monster!

Catherine used poetry to describe the struggle among the Adult, the Child, and the Destroyer. Her poem told her story and released feelings, and its ending signaled the shift that would lead to her final grieving and her rejection of her family's distorted belief system:

Discovery

You couldn't ask, you couldn't need,
For you were just a tiny seed,
One that grew among the pain,
Until you thought you were insane.

It was hard to breathe,
To be just right,
To be the one,
To end the fight.

You closed out the anger;
You shut off the pain.
After all, it is better,
Than going insane.

Where did you go?
What do you mean?
Why can't I know you?
You can't be seen.

You're there, yes, I know;
Only you will not breathe.
You remain in that closet,
Among all the seeds.

You remained in the shell;
You stayed in the cage.
And you are the one,
Who wants on the stage.

I want you to listen;
I want you to breathe.
I want all the anger,
To finally seethe.

Don't hold on to the terror;
Don't hold on anymore.
It's time that we opened,
The frightening door.

The one with the strength,
The one with the glue,
The one that you'll find,
Remains simply you.

I feel as though I have no parents,
No one to care for me.
But, then again, how could they care?
For me, they could not see.

It leaves one's life a little empty;
It leaves one feeling sad.
It leaves one wanting always something,
I guess—a Mom and Dad.

Don't be so close to all the suffering,
The pain, the strife, the rain.
And, oh my goodness, I can see,
They really are insane.

Drawing serves the same purpose as writing. Sadie found a suicidal threat from the Destroyer in the corner of almost every picture of a childhood memory that she drew. She identified the "pit of death" and "everyday numbness" as the Child's symbols for the *don't talk* rule that hung menacingly over her efforts at recovery (see Figure 13.1).

Clients can benefit from returning to earlier work and making revisions to reflect their advancing healing. When Patricia redrew her original tornado image, she discovered the Child locked in a cage beneath it (see Figure 13.2). As her recovery progressed, the cage opened, and the Child could move to join the Adult in freedom. The tight coils of the tornado, which Patricia associated with the Destroyer, were broken into gentle strands that surrounded the Adult like a protective halo (see Figure 13.3).

FIGURE 13.1. Sadie's Everyday Numbness and Pit of Death

FIGURE 13.2. Patricia's Trapped Child

FIGURE 13.3. Patricia's Child Freed from the Cage

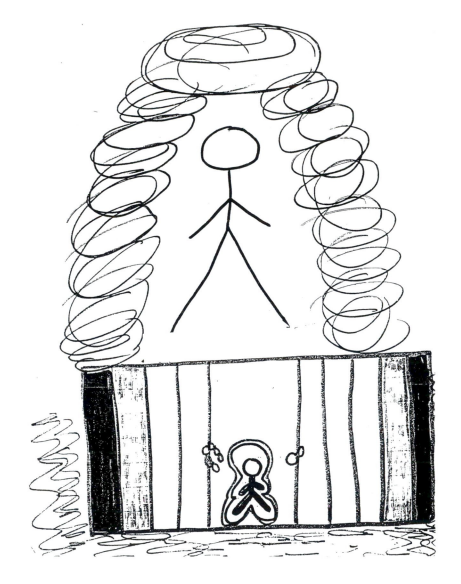

As Jessica stopped bingeing and purging, the Child's trust began to grow. Jessica's final dialogue with her four-year-old self set the stage for healthy reparenting:

Dear Little Girl,

It's me again. I got rid of the syrup of Ipecac and I haven't binged or purged. It's weird—since I've talked to you I haven't really wanted to, and the few times I have, I've thought of you. I won't let them hurt you anymore.

Dear Jessica,

I know you haven't hurt yourself. I thought you would from what I told you. I feel safe.

Chapter 14

Reparenting to Resolve Trauma

Dear Dad,

There's a part of me that wants you to hurt as much as I do. To survive I had to be depressed, and now it's killing me. I can't live and be depressed anymore. It doesn't work. I know that—so now I need to make that choice, and damned if dying doesn't sound good sometimes. But I know that gives you the power. I know I'm responsible for my life now. I'm responsible for everything I do or don't do. Sometimes that's hard to see. It's hard to see that I can change in spite of you. You will never again do to me what you did. I'm scared to death of you, but I have to keep telling myself that.

Jessica

When the events and emotions connect, when fact and feeling flashbacks combine, and when survivors begin to process the reality of each assault, they will be flooded with feelings long buried. To heal, they need to complete the emotional experience interrupted at the time of trauma. Completing feelings means they have to experience the feelings, let the feelings flow through them, and discharge those feelings. All the work that has been done so far has been leading to this moment.

Clients have defined what happened to them as assault. They have challenged the distorted beliefs they were taught. They have learned to use their bodies as barometers for feelings and to put accurate labels on those feelings. They have sourced the self-defeating patterns controlling the present in the brilliant and lifesaving survival defenses of the past. They have discovered the resourcefulness of the Child, and they are reclaiming and nurturing that abandoned piece of self. They have exposed the dark origins of the Destroyer and the ways it continues to sabotage their lives. The pieces of the puzzle are beginning to fit.

They have identified their own self-parenting skills. They have built a powerful base for the recovery work that follows. They are well prepared to complete the unfinished business of childhood that has blocked their full participation in adult life. They are well prepared to debrief from the trauma that has been frozen all these years.

DISCHARGING THE FEELINGS

To complete the interrupted trauma, survivors need to access the natural self-healing skills that were shut down in childhood. They have seen this spontaneous self-healing in other people all their adult lives. When a co-worker skids in the rain on the expressway coming to work and barely avoids a collision, that co-worker comes into the office overflowing with emotion, going from person to person describing the event, adding feelings and factual details as they are recalled. As the story is retold and reheard, it loses its intensity, and by the end of the day, it has become a blip on the screen of life, something that happened rather than the center of attention.

Finishing the emotional experience left uncompleted in childhood means both telling the story and discharging the feelings associated with assault that were not allowed to be felt at the time. Discharging emotions does not always have to be dramatic. Emotions can be discharged with a sigh or a shudder as well as with a scream. But for feelings to be truly freed, they must be heard and validated as they are being released. A tree that falls in the forest where no ear can hear makes no noise. Feelings emptied into a void echo endlessly.

It is not enough just to reexperience the pain and rage and fear and shock and humiliation. In fact, survivors have been reexperiencing these feelings all their lives, in the form of panic attacks, chronic pain, body flashbacks, and dreams and waking nightmares, and in the conviction that they are somehow flawed and doomed. Just because they now know how these are connected to the abuse will neither lessen nor take away those feelings.

Recovery should not be about getting stuck once again in the terror and helplessness of abuse. Discharging the feelings in therapy is sometimes done with a technique called regression, which consciously returns the survivor to the age, place, and time when the abuse was happening, the same age and place and time that panic attacks, chronic pain, body flashbacks, and dreams and waking nightmares were born. Survivors already know, without being told, that going back to age three or five or ten to reexperience the emotions they had to deny then, in the hope of completing the interrupted trauma, can instead leave them caught in feelings they have avoided for a lifetime. That keeps them victims. It also ignores the most important thing missing at the time of trauma—healthy parenting.

ADDING HEALTHY PARENTING

Being able to experience and discharge feelings was not all that was missed at the moment of assault. Survivors also missed appropriate, supportive parenting. If they could not tell anyone about the abuse, they had to pretend it didn't happen. If they were told the abuse was their fault or for their own good, they held themselves rather than the abusers responsible. If they were shamed for being bad or stupid or ugly, they believed they deserved the abuse. For whatever reason, they could not own the hurt and the outrage and the terror that are the natural emotional responses to assault. No one was there for them. No one affirmed their feelings or believed them or comforted them or protected them and told them it wasn't their fault.

In fact, it is the lack of affirmation, belief, comfort, and protection that causes more severe and longer-lasting damage than the assault itself. Not until reparenting is combined with emotional discharge can the trauma truly be resolved.

At the moment when the memories and feelings connected to each particular episode of assault finally surface, it is critical to provide the parenting that was also absent. Raw emotion may give temporary relief, but it also triggers a suffocating morass of helplessness that re-creates and repeats the original assault. Although it would be wonderful if the client could scream out in self-defense as the feelings start to flow, that rarely happens. When the client accesses the emotions of the three-year-old self, the powerlessness of that same three-year-old is also accessed. A child who was not defended against abuse at age three remains defenseless in the replay of that abuse at age thirty. A child who was not protected from abuse at age five remains unable to protect self in the replay of that abuse at age fifty. Deeper than fault or blame, this sense of worthlessness fills the entire being. The Child alone is unable to rescue self and stays locked in the tyranny of the assault.

Healthy reparenting, combined with emotional discharge, is the key to healing. A few survivors are finally able to talk about the assault with the abusers and receive from them the apologies missed at the time of trauma, for sometimes people do change and grow over the years. However, most survivors confronting abusers are faced with ongoing denial, defensiveness, and accusations. Going back for support to the same people who were unable to give that to them in the first place is usually destined to fail and may leave survivors open to another assault.

Even survivors who do receive a positive response from abusers discover it is too late to be meaningful. "I'm sorry," twenty or thirty years after the fact, is just that—after the fact and way too late. The only person who can really provide what is needed now is the survivor.

USING THE SPLIT PERSONAS

How can survivors carry the Child through and past the moment of impending death? How can they unfreeze that Child from frozen trauma? They will do that by rejoining the Child in that moment and then finishing the trauma with a different ending, an ending in which the Child finally gets what was needed twenty or thirty or forty years ago—to be listened to, believed, protected, and told, "It's not your fault."

The secret to recovery lies within the survivor. Survivors are the only ones who can truly reparent themselves through the feelings. They can protect better than anyone. They were there. They know what the Child missed and what the Child needs. The dissociation and fragmentation originally caused by the abuse now provides the perfect means for healing.

Reparenting and protection is best accomplished by using the split personas that already exist. The Adult who moved out into the world, leaving the frozen Child behind, is the best parent available. As feelings connected to specific incidents of abuse stir on the ends of their nerves, and as clients reenter the world of the Child to deal with those feelings, the disconnection that created the Child and the Adult will be present in their sense of detachment. Some part of them will be the Child, while some part of them will stay behind as the observer of the action, the face behind the camera, the watcher in the wings.

Forcing reintegration at that point, forcing the Adult to become the hurting Child, will diminish power and leave only a sobbing victim who has been hiding in terror for the last twenty or thirty or forty years. Tapping into emotion so long buried is not an end in itself. Instead, the emotion that some part of the client is still studying from afar can become the touchstone for finally meeting the Child's needs. Rather than encourage the Adult observer's retreat into the Child's powerlessness, the client can draw on the dissociated Adult's strength to parent the Child through the trauma.

The therapist's role is to lead the client through debriefing and resolution. As the abuse is being described, clean memory is ensured by the repetition of the forensic question, "What happened next?" The possibility for implanted memory is inherent in the simplest and most innocent variations of that question. "What did he or she do next?" suggests he or she did something.

When the memory gets stuck and the answers become vague—"He kept doing it" or "I don't know"—that probably signals the point of complete dissociation, the point at which the trauma became frozen and never ending. The client may never know the real ending because dissociation compromises perception and storage. However, the dissociative moment is the opening for resolution.

From the work they have already done, clients should have a clear concept of the Child frozen in the moment of trauma, whether it is a symbolic representation such as Shelley's in Chapter 4 or a more graphic image such as the illustrations in Chapter 7. They can envision the Child waiting there for twenty or thirty or forty years, as many years as it took the Adult to grow up and get big and strong enough to return and rescue that Child. They can imagine themselves reaching back into that encapsulated space and pulling the Child out and into the present. They will not go back and get lost in the assault.

Word pictures painted by the therapist prepare them for the process and create a sense of power and safety.

To initiate the resolution, clients need to be coached to concentrate all their awareness in the watching Adult so that the biggest part of them is the observer. Resolution is set in motion by a question: "What does the part of you that is watching want to do for that terrified Child?"

With that one question, sympathy for the Child's feelings flows into the watching Adult and a third person enters the script. The Adult as rescuer becomes part of the original scene. As the Adult responds to the Child's pain, power increases, and the dispassionate observer becomes the compassionate parent. The Child can finally be heard and defended and freed from guilt.

RESOLUTION FANTASY

Clients need to fully consider all the possibilities for rescue and resolution. They may feel a killing rage. Imagination is a safe place to vent that anger. They may want the Adult to lead the Child through a violent battle with the abuser. Jeff shoved his father to the ground, stomped on his chest, screaming "No!", and kicked him, whimpering and pleading, down the stairs and out the back door. Becky locked both parents in tiny rooms and made up a rigid schedule, allowing them out only when she wouldn't have to see them. Maureen dumped a truck load full of mud over her attacker in the town square, burying him up to his eyes so he couldn't move but would still be forced to see his shame.

They may want to carry the Child in fantasy to a safe place. Alice fled with the Child to a hidden clearing in a deep woods. Sally took the Child home with her to rock in her rocking chair and play with her dolls. Once in their refuge, clients can imagine holding the Child tightly to them until the Child fuses with them and becomes a part of them, the Child's presence a warm glow in the Adult's heart.

If clients cannot imagine rescuing the Child alone, the same questions that moved the imagery in Chapter 11 will move the resolution: "What do you want to have happen?" "How could that happen?" "Who or what could help?"

When the resolution fantasy is complete, it needs to be solidified. Clients can act out the resolution fantasy by physically pushing against the therapist palm to palm and feeling the therapist's hands give way in response to their power. They can say "No!" and "Stop!" and "Go away!" aloud for the first time. They can orchestrate a resolution psychodrama in group.

Resolution psychodrama does not have to be time consuming or complicated. The survivor picks someone to play the abuser, and that person stands on a chair to represent the abuser's size and power. Another person plays the survivor as a child, huddled beneath the abuser on the floor. The survivor remains the observer on the sidelines, who begins to tell the abuser, "Go away!" The person playing the abuser, who has been coached prior to the psychodrama, responds to the strength of each "Go away!" by first flinching, then crouching, then climbing down from the chair, and finally slinking out of the room. When the abuser is gone, the survivor enters the scene as comforter and rescuer, giving to the Child, in whatever manner seems right, the things that were needed and never received—belief, safety, and exoneration from blame.

Clients need to make the empowering new ending real and tangible. At the very least, they need to write or draw. Writing and drawing reinforce the resolution fantasy and pattern energy onto frozen nerve endings. The trauma was active, not passive, and it must be actively resolved.

Client exercise: Write down in detail or draw what you have just imagined.

In dialogue, Mary's Child outlined the course the resolution fantasy should take:

> I am seven again today and I remember yesterday. I wish you would stop overeating and get thinner. Then it would be easier to feel safer. You would feel safer if you could move better. No one in my house will ever help, so I have to cross the street. When I was three, I wasn't allowed to cross the street. I had to stay where they could get me. Now I can get away. And so can you. You have to take me with you. Then we will be safe.

Mary then described the rescue in the conditional tense:

> If I saw my two-year-old looking scared and running, I would hold out my arms to her and pick her up and hold her very close to me. I would urge her with my hand on the back of her head to hide her face in my shoulder. I would walk slowly in the direction she had been running or rock back and forth in place. I would make soothing "there, there" sounds and words to her until she was calmer, patting her back as I did.
>
> Then I would say, "Are you scared? What happened?" and let her tell me. I would try to sort out what she was saying, to clarify, to understand. I would thank her for telling me, and praise her, and keep telling her she's safe now. I would not put her down until she asked me to. I would carry her over to the rocking chair and rock her and sing to her. Then I would carry her outside into the garden to look at the flowers and tell her their names.
>
> When the little girl felt safe and calm again, I would have someone safe watch her, and I would go inside and take care of the situation. I would do whatever I needed to do to prevent that little girl from being hurt and frightened by abusers ever again.
>
> And, finally, I would tell her, "They're gone. They will not come back. They will never touch you again."

As a very young child, Greta repeatedly stood rooted to the kitchen floor watching her mother play out a suicide threat with knives. At first Greta could identify feeling only numb and frozen, but after she rediscovered the Child, she was able to acknowledge her childhood terror and to use that watching part of herself to parent the Child through the trauma. The Child's imagination provided the solution. The Adult's capabilities made the solution possible. Since her adult procrastination was sourced in the suicide scene, it was important for Greta to discover her ability to achieve safety and serenity as an adult. Greta wrote her fantasy resolution:

> I'm going back to the house where I remember most of the abuse. I drive down the street, past the ice cream factory. There it is, the second house on the left. I am afraid to go in! It's really Little Greta who is afraid to go in. "Come on, I'll keep you safe."

"No, I'm scared!"

"I will protect you. I won't let anyone hurt you! They can't if I don't let them!"

Little Greta reluctantly trudges forward. I pause to gather my courage. I go up the walk slowly, open the front door, go through the porch and into the dining room and on into the kitchen. At the cupboard stands Mother sharpening a knife! I feel the old horror! Little Greta stands watching, transfixed, unable to move or speak! My God! She's suffering again!

I grab the knife, fling the sharpener, scoop out all the knives, clench them tightly, and pick up Little Greta with the other arm and say to Mother, "This is it! You're not going to touch this child again! You have a choice—get help to get better or kill yourself! I don't care what you do! You're on your own! Do or die! You'll never hurt this child again!"

I carry sobbing Little Greta from the room, out the kitchen door through the porch. I put her down and open the car door for Little Greta, who climbs into the car. I open the trunk and fling the knives in. I jump into the car and drive off. We stop at the river, get all the knives out of the trunk and, as Little Greta watches, I throw them all into the river at once! They drift, then sink down, down into oblivion! I tell Little Greta, "They are gone forever. We have helped Mother all we can. Now it's up to her!"

I take Little Greta in my arms, hug her, and take her to the car. We drive off. I have detached! I have turned Mother over. What a relief! What a feeling of peace. So much has been lifted from me! I can let her go! I can acknowledge my powerlessness over her actions.

Greta also recognized she was carrying guilt and shame for her father's sexual assaults on her. Drawing a resolution fantasy of the Child hurling guilt and shame at the offender finally allowed Greta to put those feelings back where they really belonged (see Figure 14.1).

The strength and simplicity and sheer rightness of the Adult's solution for the Child cannot be duplicated. Clients can trust their own intuition and their own imagination as they become the healthy parent. Never again do they have to remain frozen in that unending assault. They can move themselves through and past the moment of

FIGURE 14.1. Greta's Resolution Fantasy

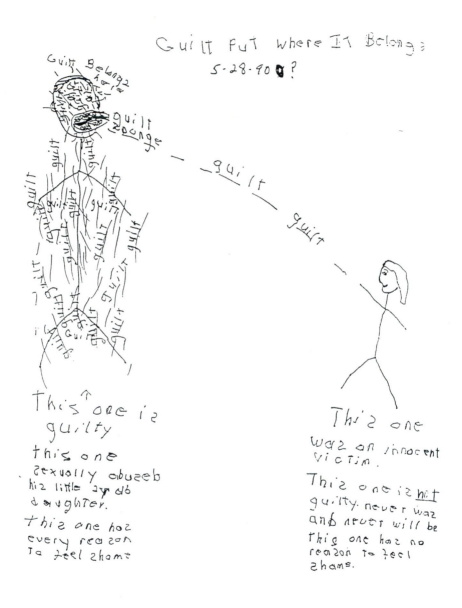

trauma. They now have a way to finish the trauma differently. They have become their own self-healers.

Clients will need to work with one particular scene at a time. Parenting isn't like the preventive maintenance done to a car in the fall so it can ride out the winter snows and ice. Children don't get parented in broad brush strokes. They get parented by being lifted over and led around each pothole or obstacle in the road. Clients will need to reparent the Child through separate episodes of abuse.

However, clients will likely find several core incidents that speak to the whole of childhood or represent major losses for the Child, times that crystallized feelings of shame and craziness, times that speeded and hardened the Child's withdrawal. It is on these core incidents that they will focus their greatest reparenting efforts. Resolving these core incidents will produce the cascade of healing described in Chapter 1.

Bonnie found herself returning again and again to the first beating she received at her father's hands, an attack she made unforgettable by carving the date into her bedroom woodwork. Carol worked repeatedly with one incident of teasing, which represented the shift into subtle sexualized abuse by her father. Jill realized that the vaguely recalled sound of a door closing represented her mother's refusal to protect her from the abuse.

As the survivor proves to be a compassionate and caring parent to the Child, the Child will entrust more feelings to the survivor. Resolution fantasy gives clients a powerful tool to process new feelings, as well as an effective way to deal with abreaction and flashbacks and dreams. It works just as well upon awakening from an unexpected nightmare as it does when it is deliberately initiated. Clients can use the anchoring techniques discovered earlier to calm the fear. They can turn on a light, stand up to affirm their size and strength, move to a safer room. Resolution fantasy itself is the ultimate anchor for abreaction.

Again, writing or drawing the resolution fantasy after a nightmare or flashback makes the new ending more real. Writing or drawing consolidates power and lets healing energy flow onto frozen nerve pathways. Resolution fantasy begins with one simple question: "What does the Adult part of you want to do for that Child?"

THE DAWNING OF INTEGRATION

The act of parenting the Child is a bridge to wholeness the Child will cross over to become a part of the Adult. A piece of self that has been sleeping is awakening, and as the Child yawns and blinks and comes to life, that rebirth may spill into present life. Clients may find their adult control cracked by unexpected outbursts of anger like the temper tantrums of a two-year-old. Like a three-year-old who is just learning to trust, they may feel afraid to leave home or walk into a roomful of strangers. They may suddenly find themselves shy in simple social situations. Like an eight-year-old, they may be distracted and bored by the tasks they have always found stimulating, and they may have difficulty concentrating at work. If they understand that these are just temporary aberrations, they can be amused, rather than impatient, when they surface.

Clients need to be encouraged to find creative ways to make the vulnerable Child feel safe. They can offer themselves physical comfort, rocking and hugging themselves to acknowledge the Child's presence and the Child's feelings. They can buy that little self a stuffed animal to cuddle. They can mentally take the Child by the hand for reassurance as they face familiar situations with unnumbed and unfamiliar emotions.

DECLARING INDEPENDENCE

The culmination of reparenting and resolving trauma comes with a full-fledged declaration of independence from abuse, directed to the abuser but delivered by the Adult to the audience of the Child. The declaration does not ask for permission to heal or demand apologies from the abuser because that still puts the abuser in charge of healing. The survivor hasn't come this far just to let the abuser win. The declaration states the survivor's right to heal and puts responsibility for the abuse on the offender, regardless of the offender's willingness to accept it. The declaration's only purpose is to protect the Child and to free the Child from blame. The survivor must establish self as champion of the Child with a defense meant for the Child to hear. Direct confrontation with the abuser has no part in this.

Some survivors balk at a formal declaration of independence. Holding abusive parents fully accountable breaks any remaining connection, however fragile or twisted. Even a connection based in abuse and fantasy satisfies attachment needs. If the bond is severed completely, survivors may fear disappearance or death. They will again need to be reassured that speaking the truth about the abuse is not betrayal.

Catherine's declaration of independence took the form of poetry:

My Choice

I won't let them win;
I won't heed their call.
It's my life, it's my life,
You can't have it all.

Go away with your thunder,
Your threats and your pain.
It's my chance for once,
To do it again.

This time I'll live different,
This time without sin.
This time I'm contented;
This time I can win!

You want me a loser;
You want me to sweat.
You want me to toil,
To pine and regret.

Oh, no, Mom,
That was your thing.
I have a chance,
To do it again.

This is my life,
To live as I choose.
I owe you nothing.
Both of us lose.

You lose my laughter;
I lose your pain.
We both made a choice.
I choose to be sane.

Heather reclaimed her physical being and her right to protect herself in her declaration:

My Body Is Mine

My body is mine.
It is mine.
I will defend it.
I am a survivor,
    not a victim anymore.
I reclaim my power.
My body is mine.
My life is mine.
I will fight for it
    every day.

Client exercise: Write your own declaration of independence.

The declaration needs to be spoken aloud. Studied silently, it is only thoughts on paper. Saying the words gives them life and meaning; they must not be expressed in a vacuum. The declaration can be shared with the therapist or with a support group. It can be read to a trusted friend or even to the survivor's own image in the mirror. The Child needs to hear the Adult's voice raised in protest and protection.

Some survivors compose imaginary responses from abusers to put closure on healing. This technique allows them to hear now what they needed to hear then: "I'm sorry; I was the one who was bad." However, that the reply comes from the abuser still implies that survivors require someone else's consent to heal. A response that comes only from the Adult seizes power directly.

Jessica's first journaled declaration of independence to her mother was brief but powerful:

> I'm Jessica—a separate person with my own thoughts and dreams and even feelings.

Jessica's first unsent letter to her father at the beginning of this chapter offered both belief and protection to the Child, and it contained the outline for a declaration of independence. Jessica's final no-send letter to her father at the end of this chapter reclaimed power confidently and absolutely.

THE POWER OF RESOLUTION FANTASY

When the Adult reaches back to rescue the Child from the never-ending moment of trauma, the Child learns for the first time that both the Adult and the Child survived. Once the new ending is introduced, the memory loses its power and panic, and clients never again have to be trapped in the terror of the abuse.

The elegance of resolution fantasy lies in its simplicity, in its use of the dissociation forged in the moment of assault as the vehicle for healing. Completion of trauma with resolution fantasy, accomplished by the only person truly equipped to do that—the self—provides a solution guided by the wounded Child and carried out by the competent Adult. It appoints the Adult part of self that split away at the exact moment of abuse as savior of the Child left behind in that same moment. It allows integration of those two personas. It unites the power and strength of the Adult with the creativity and spontaneity of the Child. It releases and resolves long-suppressed feelings. Reparenting the Child through trauma, using resolution fantasy, puts closure on the trauma and empowers the client. Reparenting will continue as clients work to repair the developmental damage caused by the abuse.

> Dad,
>
> I'm writing this letter because there are some things I need to say to you—not because you need to hear them, but because

I need to say them. First of all, it really bothered me when you told me you thought I'd come a long way since last June. It bothers me, no actually it angers me, because in the last year and a half, almost two years, I've worked very hard to change, and with that one statement you attempted to wipe it all away. I say that because your idea of me coming a long way is that I go back to keeping your damn secret. Well, I refuse to keep it a secret anymore.

I've learned some things. First, I've learned that I have choices now. Maybe I didn't then, but I do now. And I choose not to live in that black pit anymore. I've learned that I'm not that helpless child anymore. I'm still fearful, and I still have terror, but that doesn't make me helpless. It makes me a survivor. See, Dad, I'm not a victim anymore. I'm a survivor, and I'm getting better, not because of you, but in spite of you.

I've also learned the most important piece. You are that monster. You are the one who hid in my closet. You are the one who tried to destroy me. For so long I've tried to separate you from the monster, believing the two couldn't exist together. But when I saw you last Thursday, for the first time I also saw the monster, and it was in the light—it wasn't dark. I believe that it was then that I realized you're not only coming in the night, but now you invade my days and you always have.

I don't want apologies or anything like that because it's too late. You're about twenty-two years too late for that. Besides, I wouldn't believe you. I also would not accept your apologies. Forgiveness is the farthest thought from me right now. I know you're sick, but you're still responsible for everything you do and have done.

I keep telling myself you and these feelings can't hurt me. I'm in control of me. I refuse to give you any more power over me. I want you out of my life. I feel like I've been carrying you for twenty-five years, and I've just realized how heavy you are. I don't want that weight anymore. I want you gone.

I pity you because you live in a fantasy world and, as yet, have been unable to see reality. I used to live there, but now I have real friends, and I get real hugs and real smiles, and I hear real laughter, and I see real tears, and I feel that I have people who care about me—not care for me, but care about me. I pity you because I don't think you know the difference. I pity you because you say I'm your life, and you would die without me. I'm telling you today that you no longer have any rights or control in my life. I am not your life and I am not your special little girl. I am a survivor, and in spite of you, I will have a healthy life, which includes telling the secret you so desperately want me to forget.

Jessica

- *Intervention:* Resolution fantasy.
- *Rationale:* Orchestrate an imaginary ending to the interrupted trauma that provides closure by combining the needs and feelings of the Child with the power and perspective of the Adult.
- *Result:* Decrease in intrusive flashbacks and mastery over traumatic material.

Chapter 15

Repairing Developmental Damage

As healing solidifies, clients will move to deeper levels of understanding and awareness. They will grow beyond their primary focus on the facts of assault to recognize the umbrella of dysfunction that hung over the abuse and prevented rescue or revenge.

This is a time when clients may have to take a complete break from their families of origin. It may be too difficult for them to maintain independence against the family's efforts to reentangle them in the web of dysfunction and denial. They may be too furious to have contact with the family. They not only deserve their anger, but they need it to fuel recovery.

Clients don't have to confront their families to take this break. They're adults now. They can protect themselves without being mean. They can scale and titrate just enough anger to step back gently and without rancor. Explanations and accusations don't give them any more power than their recovery already does. No amount of blaming takes away their responsibility to heal and to keep themselves safe. They can protect themselves from ongoing abuse because they have reclaimed the right to say "No!" or "Don't!" or "Stop!" They can be with their families and not get caught up in triangling, caretaking, or guilt. They can be with their families and not have to surrender their own reality.

CONSIDERING DIRECT CONFRONTATION

Any decision to confront abusers should be very carefully examined. Direct confrontation may be impossible or inadvisable. Abusers may be dead or unavailable, or they still may be locked in their own denial and sickness.

Confrontation should be based on always-retained, uncontested memories to avoid any debate about false memory. If any retrieved memories are used in a confrontation, they should be verified by independent sources.

There is a difference between power fueled by reasoned anger and that fueled by blind rage. Carrying out a confrontation just to vent rage can make the survivor feel immature and out of control. In some ways, the survivor descends to the level of the abuser. A major goal of recovery is empowerment. Anger expressed in an adult fashion augments power; childish rage diminishes power. Any confrontation meant to cause only more pain or damage is questionable. Particularly when the abuser is a family member, such a confrontation can isolate the survivor from the whole family, and the survivor may not want that to happen. The survivor gets hurt, and innocent family members get hurt. The abuse continues, and that is abusive to everyone. When anger is still the driving force, it is better to discharge that in no-send letters and role-plays. Survivors are never ready to confront until they can deal with anger responsibly: "During the past year I have been very angry with you at times. I haven't been around you because it was up to me to deal with that anger."

The primary agenda of any direct confrontation should be protection and healing. The goal is a relationship based on truth. Although clients may choose to have no further contact with an abuser who is not a family member, they may not really want to cut themselves off from the entire family. They cannot ask the nonoffending members of the family to choose them over the abuser, tempting though that may be. If they were still three or five or ten, family members would have to make that choice. But it's up to clients to protect themselves now. If having no further relationship with the abuser would also keep them away from the rest of the family, they may want to reestablish some kind of a relationship with a familial abuser for their own reasons: "I have a right to be part of my family." It's possible that they see some redeeming qualities: "I hated the violence, but I have good memories, too, and I want you to be a part of my life." They can explain how the abuse affected them, even as they take responsibility for their own healing: "It's my job to change and to deal with my depression, and I'm doing that very well." They can claim freedom from the labels and the scapegoating: "I wasn't a 'stuck-up snob'; I had to hide because I was scared and I couldn't get you to stop fighting." They can set boundaries with a family member who is still violating: "I won't let you touch me," or "I will leave the room if you start to ridicule or criticize me," or "You can't shout or scream when we're together at family gatherings." They can also reclaim control by establishing limits around any future discussion of the abuse: "We'll talk about this again when or if I want to."

Clients' decisions about the direction of any future relationship with their families or the abusers must be their own. The abuse didn't happen in a vacuum. It was woven into the complex dynamics of the family, one of the defining contexts of identity. Few clients are willing to voluntarily orphan themselves. The therapist's opinions and biases should not interfere as clients determine what will be right for them.

Even the most well-planned confrontation may result in a stalemate. Again, clients' anger is theirs to process, and distance may be required. Backing off from the family at any point in healing allows them to buy time. Then they can decide if or how they want to reconnect. Backing off avoids more damage to a relationship that they may find they don't want to end completely as they move further into recovery.

Jessica stated her purpose for confronting her parents in terms that spoke to her own needs, not her expectations of them:

> I'm doing this because I don't want to keep the secrets anymore, because I don't want to be blamed for what is wrong in the family. I need to do this for me, not for their reaction.

When her parents denied and blamed, Jessica still knew she had met her own goals:

> I showed up. I said what I wanted to say. I told my dad I wasn't crazy. I didn't stop breathing. Even though he got angry, I didn't back down. I confronted my mom about physical abuse and suicide, and I didn't accept her excuses. I kept my feet on the floor. I didn't kill myself. Now I need time—not a permanent cutoff, but space to work this through. I will contact them when I'm ready.

SETTING LIMITS

At the very least, the declaration of independence sets the stage for establishing ground rules for communication with family of origin.

Clients can take control of the three Ts—time, turf, and topic. They can set limits on how long they will talk to family members or be with them on any given occasion. They can decide where encounters will occur—their home, the family's house, or on neutral territory. They can determine what topics are unacceptable and how they will state those boundaries: "I won't talk about _____ with you" or "I don't think it will be helpful for us to discuss _____." Clients need to prepare themselves before walking into the lion's den by rehearsing their declaration of independence. That rehearsal can be enhanced by sculpturing. Clients can stoop down and mentally take the helpless Child into their arms. Then they can stand up and square their shoulders and concentrate on the breath moving through their grown-up bodies to affirm their maturity and competence. They can brainstorm ahead of time ways they will nurture themselves and parent the Child during visits—walks, journaling, calling friends. They need to have a plan ready if crisis erupts. They always have the right to leave danger or abuse. They can allow themselves to do whatever they must to hold on to their power.

As clients begin to do things differently they will likely feel guilty. The therapist can warn them to expect to feel guilty and encourage them to do things differently anyway. It helps to identify the overriding rule that guarantees, "You can't do anything right." Even if they sacrifice themselves to please the family, clients will likely still be criticized. They might as well choose what they're not going to do right. If they're going to be made to feel guilty no matter what, they might as well feel guilty about doing what they want to do and what is good for them.

As clients withdraw from playing their part in the family game, the family may create crises and try to reengage them. At this point, the rigidity and inflexibility of the dysfunctional family works in their favor. Clients will probably be able to predict the ways the family will try to pressure them. Even if they know exactly what the family will do, they may still be frightened to leave the playing field. They may feel they will or should die if they don't give in. They may fear something terrible will happen to someone else if they don't apologize. They will need help to identify that this is the Destroyer talking. They will need to be reassured that their refusal to be a victim again won't kill anyone. Their anger won't cause a catastrophe. Their disagreement won't make the world come to an end.

Because many survivors don't enter therapy until their parents are aging, the possibility for a change in health or a death is very real. If something bad does happen to a family member during the recovery process, it may be difficult for survivors to believe that it is a coincidence. The magical thinking and distorted reality from childhood argue that the survivor's betrayal is to blame. Clients will need help to remember that their thoughts and feelings are simply their thoughts and feelings. They can't destroy others. No one has that kind of power.

ANGER AT THE COLLUDERS

Dear Mom,

I know I should be angry about how you never protected me from Daddy. You never stopped him. Your silence told him he could get away with it and told me to keep quiet.

I know it sounds like whining, but where was everyone? Where were the police and the teachers and the neighbors? Didn't they hear the screams in my head? Couldn't they see? I thought adults protected children.

Jessica

Clients may find themselves suddenly angry at the nonabusive parent for going along with the abuse. The parent they believed was good, the parent who did not actively participate in the hitting or the slapping or the teasing or the ridicule or the sexual assault now seems at least as guilty, if not more guilty, than the actual aggressor. The nonabusive parent is the person who should have protected them from attack, but that parent turned away and couldn't or wouldn't see what was happening. This is the parent truly responsible for offering the client as a sacrifice to keep the family peace.

Will finally realized that he was used as a buffer between his mother and his father. He took the abuse that would have been directed at his mother if he had not responded to her pleas for rescue. Janice recalled her mother sending her to her drunken father's bed to calm him down. She was furious when she finally saw that her mother set her up to be her father's surrogate spouse.

Clients may feel rage at the other adults who were in a position to protect them but who chose to ignore—teachers, ministers, police, neighbors, relatives. Although they may believe to this day that they never gave away the family secret or never asked for help, there were many clues to tell the world that something was wrong. Perhaps outside adults overlooked bruises or cuts or illnesses that fairly shouted assault. Perhaps relatives or neighbors witnessed or heard the sounds of abuse but choose to look away and turn a deaf ear to avoid getting involved. Even if clients were abused by a stranger, even if they now recognize there was no way anyone could have known they were being abused, even if they are now convinced that anger at the other adults in their lives is totally irrational, in children's minds, adults are supposed to protect, and those adults didn't.

If clients went to an adult and risked telling and instead were dismissed or blamed, they have a right to their rage. Eleven-year-old Candy fled to a priest for protection from incest and was told, "Pray and God will forgive you." When Cal tried to tell his aunt about the beatings, she became angry: "Don't you dare say such horrible things! My brother wouldn't do anything like that." Try as they may to excuse past collusion as the result of ignorance and fear, the fact remains that survivors were assaulted not once, but twice—once by the actual abuser and again by all those people who could have helped but didn't.

LAYERS OF ABUSE

Clients may also begin to identify layers of abuse that occurred under the umbrella of family dysfunction. They may define as sexual abuse what they have always believed was only physical or emotional abuse—violent spankings, intrusions on privacy, sexual name-calling. They may recall abuse by brothers or sisters, ignored or even encouraged as sibling rivalry or teasing.

PUNISHED FOR BEING NORMAL

Dear Mom,

I'm angry that you always took those damn pills. I remember crying and begging you not to take them, and you'd get angry and hit me. I remember cleaning out the cupboards and throwing them out, but you had an endless supply. I couldn't keep up with it. I tried and tried but never could. I'm angry that you used to say, "Say good-bye to Mommy because she won't be alive when you get home." What the hell was I supposed to do—I was only nine years old! I felt like your life was my responsibility. I'm angry that you lied to me and told me Daddy was dying and I couldn't upset him. I couldn't make any noise because Daddy might get upset. I was a child. Children make noise. I'm angry that you never let me be a child. I had to be a grown-up all the time.

Jessica

Clients may also become aware of more subtle kinds of abuse that happened when they were little, abuse that left them just as confused and stripped of self-identity and self-esteem as the open assaults. In the altered and two-faced reality of the abusive and dysfunctional family—where black is white, up is down, shadow is substance, child is parent, and victim is offender—normal childhood development and normal childhood feelings are not allowed. Clients may now understand that they were often punished for being normal children. They may recognize that they were often punished for having normal feelings.

Children lack coordination because they have not yet developed fine motor skills. They spill things and bump into things and fall down and knock things over. If clients were labeled "clumsy" and hit or yelled at consistently for that, then they were abused for being normal children. Children are exuberant and noisy. Their feelings bubble to the surface, and they haven't yet learned to control or express emotions appropriately. If clients were humiliated or ignored consistently for being "overexcited," then they were abused for being normal children. Children are impatient. They don't understand "later." "Later" means "never" to them. If clients were punished consistently for being "selfish," then they were abused for being normal children.

Deb's poem recalled a beating she got for licking cake batter from the bowl when she was three:

Chocolate Face

A little love and a lot of hate,
I got chocolate on my face.

You skipped love and showed me hate,
When I got chocolate on my face.

I missed love and learned to hate,
When once I got a chocolate face.

I loved you, it's me I hate,
Just because of a chocolate face.

I was bad, that's why you hate,
Because of chocolate on my face.

When kids are normal, do they hate,
Because of chocolate on their face?

You taught me about love and hate,
For being normal, with a chocolate face.

PROJECTION

Clients need to consider how self-esteem and self-image were affected by projection. The name-calling that went on and the labels that were used reflected the reversed reality of dysfunction. Not only was responsibility for the abuse projected onto the victim, but there was also projection at a much deeper level. Parts of personalities and behaviors were reassigned to other members of the family, causing boundaries to blur and overlap.

Client exercise: Go back to your list of the labels that were used to describe you and your behavior (from Chapter 8). Were you called "dumb," "stupid," "selfish," "spoiled," or "lazy"? Were you scolded for being "a daydreamer," "melodramatic," "an obnoxious brat," "a troublemaker," or "a know-it-all"? Look carefully at those labels. Which ones more accurately describe the behavior and the personality of the abuser?

Clients will recognize they were accused of doing things and being things that really belonged to the abuser. The abuser's behavior and personality were blamed on them.

FAULTY BELIEF SYSTEM

As the result of abuse and dysfunction, clients fell heir to a belief system about themselves and the world that is inherently false. That false belief system has been the source of their guilt and shame.

Guilt about some act or behavior signals a disagreement between behavior and belief system. When guilt arises in someone raised in a healthy family with flexible and adaptive rules, that guilt usually indicates a violation of some well-established moral code, from a thoughtless word to a more serious offense causing harm to people or property. This kind of rational guilt is a demand for a change in behavior. Rational guilt is based in behavior, and rational guilt can be relieved by a change in behavior, from a simple "I'm sorry" to more serious financial or legal restitution.

If clients were made to feel guilty about normal behavior and feelings, then their guilt may be irrational. It may not point to something wrong in them or their actions. It may point to something wrong in their belief system. If reality was altered and normal development and feelings were forbidden, the disagreement between behavior and belief system that triggers guilt may signal a need for change not in behavior but in the belief system.

If clients were labeled and ridiculed and humiliated as children, then they were also shamed about who they were as people. Guilt is related to what someone does. Shame attacks who someone is. Shame allows neither remedy nor redemption. Clients could not question those labels and that ridicule and that humiliation in the clouded mirror of family dysfunction, but they can disagree now.

CHALLENGING THE BELIEF SYSTEM

At work someone was talking about Scott Peck's book, People of the Lie, *and how he writes that people are evil. I was so upset. I felt panic, and I was shaking, and I finally realized why—because what my dad did is evil, not me. He told me I was evil, but he is.*

Jessica

Clients had to challenge the most blatant distortions in the belief system they were taught to begin recovery. Those earlier challenges now need to be solidified and expanded to alter the self-defeating patterns that may still be compromising their lives. Clients have a right to challenge those false labels and to change that faulty belief system to allow normal behavior and feelings for both the Adult and the Child. They have the right to discard the bill of goods sold to them in childhood and to build a healthy foundation for the present and the future. Most of all, they have an obligation to finally grant the Child permission to exist.

If the messages clients routinely heard were negative, they made decisions about their place in the universe which reflected that negativity. It required only a small step to move from "I can't do anything right," "Everything is always my fault," and "I'll never be good enough" to "I shouldn't be here at all."

If clients had to absorb brutality to survive or to shelter siblings even tinier than they from assault, they came to believe that verbal or physical violence is what they deserve. They may still tolerate abusive relationships. If clients were the target of silence and rejection, they came to believe that they have no rights or needs. They may still frantically try to please others at the expense of self. If their developing sexuality was violated, they came to believe that all relationships are sexualized. They may find themselves being intimate without desire or choice. Since saying "yes" in any meaningful way is not possible until the right to say "no" has been established, some clients may realize they have never really had consensual sex. If clients learned to use sexuality to gain some control over the abusers, they came to believe that power equals sex. They may still use sex as a means to shift the scales in a relationship. Those beliefs and behaviors are the outgrowths of the confusing lessons taught in the dysfunctional family classroom, and clients no longer have to live their lives by those rules.

Greta outlined the changes she was making in her belief system in a letter to the Child:

> Dear Little Greta,
>
> Now that I've grown up, I can take care of you and keep you safe. Together we can beat the old tapes and make new and realistic tapes. We can learn to love and take care of ourselves. We have every right to do this. All the abusers are gone. We

don't have to abuse ourselves. We can be good to ourselves and make choices in our own best interests. We can love and nurture ourselves. We are worth it! We are just as good as anyone else. We always have been, and we always will be! There is no reason for us to feel ashamed of ourselves. Absolutely none! We can get rid of those old tapes.

Love,
Greta

Clients can use the declaration of independence and journaling and dialoging and unsent letters and resolution fantasy and art to further the Child's trust, the Child's self-worth, and the Child's right to be and to grow. They can help the Child decide what is true about self and the world, based on observation and experimentation, not on myths and rigid rules and projection and secrecy and shame. They need to construct a belief system of fact and reality that challenges the denial and delusion of the past.

That new belief system will help clients label the abuse more accurately. They were not seductive children. Someone else was a seducer. They were not bad seeds. Someone else was a criminal assaulter. They were not clumsy or stupid or lazy or selfish. They were normal children in a sick family system.

IDENTIFYING AND GRIEVING WHAT WAS MISSED

Revising the belief system requires clients to identify the developmental steps they were denied and to grieve what was lost. Their own recollections give them the information they need to begin that process.

Although children pass through many developmental phases on their way to maturity, a child's needs can be summarized in four basic stages: trust and autonomy from ages birth through five; purpose and competence from ages five through ten; identity and independence from ages ten through fifteen; and interdependence and intimacy from ages fifteen through twenty (Erikson, 1963). Jenny's poem, "Why Did You Abuse Me?," at the end of Chapter 11, speaks eloquently about the many losses caused by abuse during every developmental stage from infancy through young adulthood.

Client exercise: How were you taught to count on others and trust the world? Children learn to trust when their caregivers are positive and predictable. Were your needs met consistently? Did your infant cries bring food and comfort, or were you often ignored? How was your drive to become a separate self met? Infants can't distinguish between themselves and others. They have to learn where their skin ends and others' skin begins. They do that by expressing their own ideas and their own desires. Could you indulge your toddler's delight in saying "No!," or was such disagreement punished? Write your observations.

How was your sense of purpose nurtured? Children need to know they make a difference in the world. Were you taught that you were important, or did you feel your existence didn't matter at all? How did your sense of competence about activities and chores and schoolwork develop? Children gain confidence in their abilities by having their accomplishments recognized. Were you praised for childish efforts, or was what you did never good enough? Were your drawings and school papers admired and displayed, or were they criticized and discarded? Were you encouraged to succeed, or was failure predicted? Write your observations.

How was your struggle for self-identity dealt with? Teens need stability to balance their own inner turbulence. Did you know your emotional peaks and valleys would not destroy your family, or did your ups and downs threaten to swamp the family boat? How was your drive for independence treated? Teens need to be prepared to move away from dependence on the family and assume responsibility for themselves. Were you gradually taught the skills you needed to function as an adult, or were you suddenly thrust out into the world unprepared? Did you know you could separate from your family and not lose their approval and support? Write your observations.

How was your need to connect with peers handled? Were your teenage friendships encouraged while safe limits were enforced, or were your friends criticized? How was your search for a life partner viewed? Were you given information about sex in the context of a loving, committed relationship, or was sex a forbidden subject you were left to discover on your own? Were your dates welcomed in your home, or were they ridiculed? Did your parents communicate their hopes that you would find a partner and their confidence that you would have much to offer your future mate, or were you told, "You'll be lucky to find anybody who wants you!"? What did your parents model for you in their own relationship? Were mutual respect and enrichment obvious, or did you see marriage as violence and abuse or stony silence? Write your observations.

Jenny's poem outlined the birthright she was denied and needed to mourn:

Grieving

I grieve for the baby,
So pretty at birth,
Who grew up too quickly,
And lost her self-worth.

I grieve for the freedom,
Most children possess,
For all I remember,
Is fear and distress.

I grieve for the friendships,
I never enjoyed.
My virtue was shattered;
My joy was destroyed.

I grieve for the attention,
I needed to see,
For no one acknowledged,
My presence, but me.

I grieve for the boyfriends,
That most young girls date;
The ones I selected,
Were all full of hate.

I grieve for the house rules,
That should have been laid;
I did what I wanted,
And dearly I paid.

I grieve for the parents,
That couldn't be there,
For they were too busy,
To hear or to care.

I grieve for the grieving,
I've done all these years,
For I was too busy,
To shed any tears.

LETTING GO OF THE FANTASY

The part of the fantasy about my family that I need to let go of is that someday soon they will see that I'm telling the truth—that all of them will see and admit what happened and stop saying that I'm crazy. I keep thinking that I'll find the right words or do the right thing to make them care about me—that, somehow, I can make them love me. I need to let go of the fantasy that they are the only ones who can make me better—that until they believe me I'll always be sick. I have to give up the fantasy that this time they're going to believe me, or this time they're going to care, or this time they're going to be happy for me, or this time they're going to be supportive. I have to stop thinking and hoping that they'll change tomorrow.

Jessica

Identifying and grieving the developmental losses leads clients to relinquish the fantasy of the perfect and happy family they have clung to for so long. Although there is sadness in recognizing that it was never the way they wanted it to be, there is also power in finally accepting the truth. They will no longer be driven by delusion. They will no longer be exhausted by denial. And that will free energy to heal further.

> *Client exercise:* Write a letter to the fantasy of the family you have been clinging to, expressing your willingness to let go.

REPARENTING THROUGH GRIEF

Finally acknowledging all the losses gives rise to deep, overwhelming sadness. This part of healing takes time and patience. That clients were assaulted and not protected is incredibly sad. Recognizing what was not there produces profound and wrenching and inconsolable pain. It is much more difficult to grieve and let go of something that was deserved and never experienced than it is to grieve and let go of something that once was there.

This grief is not linear; it is messy. It does not move neatly through the stages of denial, anger, bargaining, and depression to acceptance (Kübler-Ross, 1969). Clients may return to denial or to bargaining. They may recant their disclosures or minimize the impact of them. They may go back to pretending the family is fine, or they may fixate on finding a way to make it so.

Catherine summarized this void in poetry:

I Did Not Count

It's rather like a well,
Only it's deeper and it's dark,
And that's what this feeling,
Is truly about.

It's full of such terror,
For no one is there,
And if they were,
They would not care.

They'd walk right on past me;
They would pay no attention,
For I was so lowly,
Not worth a mention.

So, what I am saying is,
I did not count,

And that's what this feeling,
Is really about.

The object of grieving is not to leave clients stuck in depression; it is to help them chart a course to follow as they continue reparenting themselves. The process is already well underway. The Child they have reparented through frozen trauma is the same Child they are now reparenting through the developmental stages that were absent or fouled during childhood. The parenting skills they have mastered are the skills they are using to accomplish that task.

Their belief and unconditional love are already allowing the Child to view the world for the first time as a trustworthy place. Their repeated affirmation of the Child's brilliance is helping the Child to feel competent. Their willingness to learn new skills and refine old ones provides a sense of independence. Their acceptance of both the wounded Child and the wonder Child frees the Child to be real. Their declaration of independence from abuse has given the Child permission to grow toward wholeness.

Clients will need to imagine resolution for the specific childhood incidents of abuse that robbed them of safety, importance, individuality, and integrity. However, simply by accepting and nurturing the Child, they are repairing the developmental damage they identified in the exercise outlined a few pages earlier. They are replacing distrust with trust, worthlessness with purpose, inadequacy with self-sufficiency, and isolation with connection.

However, unless survivors go back to the developmental stage where the loss occurred, no amount of present tense affirmations about trust, competence, self-respect, and lovability will be truly meaningful. They first have to direct their reparenting to the exact places in their lives where parenting was missing or inadequate.

Although survivors needed and deserved healthy parenting in childhood, they didn't get it. Ideally, children get what they need from others—mostly parents—internalize that, and learn to give it to themselves. Ideally, children learn self-care by being cared for first by others. It's too late for survivors to go back and get what they missed from their parents. Those parents couldn't give it to them in the first place, and they have now grown past the developmental window for getting what they need from outside of self. They now must give themselves what they needed then and didn't get. It's not fair that they have to do it all, but they are the only ones who can do it now, and they can be sure that they will do it right this time.

This is a time when the unsuspecting therapist can be lured into becoming parent to the client. The therapist must remain the model for the process, not become part of the process. Although it is understandable for the client to seek what was missed from outside of self in the natural order of development, giving in to that pressure disempowers the client and delays healing.

Because introjection is an active process, reparenting to repair developmental damage must also be active. Clients can't just think about how that damage could be repaired; they have to take steps to repair it.

Client exercise: Write your infant and toddler self a "welcome to the world" letter containing all the love and acceptance with which you deserved to be greeted. Describe what hopes and dreams you have for your own self as a unique and special gift to the world.

Write your elementary school self a letter of congratulations celebrating all the accomplishments that were not recognized— learning to skip, ride a bike, add, subtract, multiply, and divide, print your name, write. Even if you don't remember how or when you learned those skills, you have them now, and you have a right to be praised.

Take a mental walk around your house and through your life and see what they reflect about the person you are—creative, organized, caring. Go back and recognize in writing all the qualities and talents from your adolescent self that contribute to your success and your identity today.

Write your young adult self permission to claim growth from your early relationships. Identify the positive things you gave and the positive things you received in each, with understanding that each relationship also taught you something about who you could be with others. Allow yourself to discover how every relationship molded you and provided you with gifts to give yourself and your partners in the future.

Clients can also reparent themselves in the adult world. It's not too late for them to rock and hold themselves when they are frightened. It's not too late for them to kiss a cut and put on a cartoon Band-Aid to make it better. It's not too late for them to tack a memo of congratulations from the boss or a note of thanks from a friend on the refrigerator. It's not too late for them to pat themselves on the back or give themselves a reward for a job well done.

Identifying losses to grieve leads only to sadness and depression and still leaves the Child without direction and meaning. Combining grieving with reparenting leads to self-acceptance and growth. Unless clients understand what they lost in childhood and retrace that path with the Child, all the present tense urging to trust, all the present tense praise of ability and accomplishment, all the present tense insistence on self-esteem and self-worth will remain hollow words. The Child, who has no footing in healthy self-concept, will stay stuck in the childhood quicksand of self-hate and self-rejection.

FILLING IN THE GAPS

Most survivors berate themselves for their lack of life skills, but they can't know what they didn't learn. If they didn't study French in school, they wouldn't expect themselves to speak French fluently if they suddenly found themselves in Paris.

If they lost chunks of childhood to abuse and dysfunction, it is equally unfair for survivors to blame themselves for lacking the life skills they never had a chance to learn. It's unfair for them to blame themselves for being financially irresponsible if they never learned how to manage money. It was impossible to learn manners if the family dinner table was a battleground; social skills took a backseat to survival skills. They couldn't learn to grieve if a family pet suddenly disappeared and was never spoken of again or if talking about death and suicide was taboo. They couldn't learn to play and relax if they had to be sure Mom was in bed before the younger children got home. They missed learning the art of casual conversation if they couldn't bring friends home for fear of embarrassment. Moreover, overpracticing the limited defenses they needed kept them from expanding their range of coping skills.

Now is the time to strengthen the weak links in that chain of skills. Understanding that upsetting and puzzling behavior patterns are the legacy of abuse and neglect increases self-acceptance. Changing those patterns leads to improved self-esteem. This part of reparenting is when recovery goes public.

It is not too late for clients to teach themselves to cook or sew or balance a checkbook. It is not too late for them to read a book or take a course to fill in any of the other gaps in training the family failed to provide. They have already identified the developmental losses they suffered as a result of abuse and neglect. Their responsibility now is to teach themselves what they did not learn. It will take study and practice, but it can be done. They may want to find a model, someone who seems to be good at the skill they want to learn, and imitate that person. This is when support group meetings can be especially helpful. Not only is it freeing and validating to tell the story of abuse to people who can relate and listen and believe, but a support group provides a safe place to experiment with new behaviors.

Clients need to bear in mind that it is more difficult to acquire a skill if they are not learning it at the natural developmental age. Young children absorb language effortlessly, but if a second language is learned later in life, it takes study and practice and many mistakes. However, any skill acquired deliberately is mastered better than one learned haphazardly.

Deb journaled both her grief and her pride about the task of reparenting herself in therapy:

> Try to imagine yourself as a child growing up in an adult body. Try to imagine being thirty or forty or fifty years behind on an emotional level. There are days when you fight for your life, just to survive the pain. And, yes, there are days that you actually take steps forward, actually internalize some things, and actually feel like you are doing some growing. But it is a horrendously and deeply painful gut-level process that feels like your heart is being torn out of your chest. It is shattered because it has been broken, over and over and over again. It is shattered even more when you take a look at why you are so far behind. Your therapist looks at you and says, "Nobody can fix it except you." That is what they call healing.
>
> I started internalizing a child's needs, and I learned what was okay and what wasn't. I had to learn to trust first, which took a very long time. Then I had to be vulnerable and take risks. Eventually I learned to connect feelings to events and then take risks in expressing them. It was okay to cry, and it

was okay to be angry. Once I learned how to connect and express feelings, then I had to learn to express them appropriately. I had to strip myself and rebuild, piece by piece.

That is what it is like to miss out on normal growth and development. I grew up long ago, only to find out that I had to do it all over again. That is what it is like to grow up, with your therapist, in a little blue office, instead of with a set of capable and loving parents.

BUILDING BRIDGES AND FENCES

As clients begin to see themselves as deserving and worthwhile people and as they work to surround the Child with safety and protection, they will have to decide where they end and other people begin. The most common response to childhood abuse is indistinct personal boundaries or no personal boundaries at all. No matter how many self-help books they have read on the subject, no matter how many assertiveness tapes they have listened to, no matter how many "How to Have a Healthy Relationship" seminars they have attended, their best attempts at setting boundaries may have failed in the past. Those failures do not mean that the books and the tapes and the seminars were not good, nor do they mean that the efforts were not genuine. Instead, those failures reflect the deadly contract between the Destroyer who victimized and the Child who had to be a victim. Now that clients have begun to challenge the Destroyer and empower the Child, that subconscious dialogue will no longer sabotage their attempts to establish healthy boundaries.

Clients need to be taught that the clues to boundary violation are their own feelings of guilt, shame, anger, and fear. If they find themselves freezing and going numb, that is also a clue that their boundaries are being violated. The techniques they have learned to define feelings and connect feelings with body sensations have made them better at listening to their own bodies. They can recognize and respond to the guilt, shame, anger, and fear that are warnings of boundary violation.

Guilt suggests that someone is asking them to do something inappropriate or something they don't want to do. Shame implies that someone is condemning them for who they are or what they feel. Both are attacks on them and their personal rights. Anger points to demands that they enable or caretake in ways that are no longer acceptable to them. Clients can watch for words such as "should" or "must" or "ought" or "always" or "never" to identify boundary violations. Those words indicate that someone is trying to leap into their minds and change their thinking, feelings, and behavior. Fear is the cue to life-threatening boundary violations that was stolen from them in childhood. They were left with only *freeze—go numb—forget*. As they begin to identify the triggers for freezing and going numb, as they begin to feel rather than deny fear, they will finally be able to protect themselves from attack and abuse.

Clients also need to clarify their often diffuse emotional boundaries, which lead them to feel other people's feelings and apologize for other people's faults. They can learn to say "I'm sorry" only when they have done something for which they need to take responsibility. They can learn to say "I'm sad" when whatever is happening has nothing to do with them or their behavior or when the other person's feelings are not their own.

The reverse of highly unclear or nonexistent boundaries can also result from childhood abuse. Clients may have built thick walls between themselves and the rest of the world, determined that no one will ever get close enough to hurt them again. Building bridges to the outside world requires them to risk being vulnerable. They may be tempted to tear down all their fences impulsively: "If I'm going to do this intimacy thing, I'm going to do it now." A better and saner way is to learn to take the walls down one brick at a time, sharing a bit of self, then considering what the other person shares in return. If it is at the same or a slightly increased level of closeness, they can follow suit or even increase a notch. If the other person spills and dumps everything or retreats defensively, they can reevaluate the health and safety of the relationship. They may choose to leave it at the acquaintance stage, or they may reach again for deeper connection. They can give themselves permission to end or renegotiate a relationship at any time.

To address boundary issues, clients also need to recognize their all-or-nothing approach to people and relationships. If they lived with a parent who both loved and assaulted them, if they lived with those two personalities in one body, they learned to react to people in a vacuum. The father who kissed them good-bye in the morning could return that evening on a rampage. They could not expect the people in their lives to remain constant. They could not construct a stable image of people from their ongoing interactions with them. Instead, self-preservation meant they had to see only what was in front of them at the moment. They had to deal with what was happening now. They couldn't waste any energy remembering what is was like yesterday. Reducing people into isolated encounters leads to rubber band relationships—close one minute and distant the next. If a friend does something caring or nice, that person becomes the most wonderful person who ever walked the face of the earth, and the friendship is going to last forever. If a friend does something unkind or disagrees about something, the friendship is over, and the client never wants to see that person again.

Abuse and dysfunction seem to interfere with the development of object constancy (Piaget, 1952). Their extreme responses may be why many survivors are labeled borderline personalities. They tend to react intensely to the present and seem unable to call on past experience to temper their judgments. The exercises and suggestions in this section target Axis II symptoms.

Since healthy relationships grow from accumulating mutual experiences, clients need to adjust their observations and responses. They need to learn to integrate past and present to form more reasoned assessments of reality.

Client exercise: Make a note of each time you use a superlative—"best," "most," "worst"—to describe people or their behavior. Challenge your black-and-white thinking by mentally rewriting your judgment in more moderate terms, using plain adjectives, such as "pleasant" or "unpleasant," rather than words ending in "-est." Try to recall other things that same person has done or said in similar situations to help yourself build a more balanced picture of the relationship.

Boundary issues are also reflected in impulsive behavior. Clients engaged in self-parenting need to learn that healthy parents both affirm and set limits. Letting themselves off the hook for irresponsible behavior is not healthy parenting.

> *Client exercise:* Identify the impulsive behavior you want to stop. Imagine how a healthy parent would handle the situation. Draw up a plan for change, with rewards for compliance and consequences for lapses, and keep a record of the results.

Group also teaches love with limits. It mediates the one or ten zone reactivity and the polarized shift between withdrawal and spilling. The group member who repeatedly waits until the last few minutes to drop the bombshell can be told, "You'll be first next week." Group can also begin with "doorknob" therapy: "Imagine group is ending. Now what do you need to say?"

As clients begin to honor their own feelings and their own perceptions, they will begin to trust themselves to keep themselves safe in relationships. They will no longer have to look outside themselves and helplessly count on others to be trustworthy.

Even if past boundary exploration has been unsuccessful, clients now have a new base from which to pursue this part of recovery. Knowing that they are protecting and nurturing the innocent Child is a powerful motivation for assertion or risk.

THE SURVIVOR AS PARENT

Many survivors also condemn themselves for their lack of parenting skills, never considering what was modeled for them. They may lack parenting skills because the people who taught them were sadly lacking those skills themselves. There were also times when they could not experience what it was like to be a child. If they had to be little adults and take care of a parent or younger siblings, they can't have any realistic sense of what it's like to be a normal child. If, at age four, they had to watch a drunken mother asleep on the couch to make sure she was breathing, that took tremendous concentration. They may get impatient if a four-year-old loses interest in a game after fifteen minutes because they have no idea what a normal attention span for a four-year-old is. If messing up the house or screaming brought swift retribution at age six, they may expect a six-year-old to clean up toys and play quietly, and that is unrealistic for a normal six-year-old. If they had to get up for school and make breakfast at age eight, the level of responsibility they demand of a normal eight-year-old may be way beyond that child's capabilities.

Again, what clients didn't learn, they can learn now. There are lots of books and classes available. And their own children can be their best teachers; they can become students of their children. They can identify their children's interests and abilities. They can talk to other parents to discover what is normal to expect for each developmental stage.

RECOGNIZING ONGOING ABUSE

I talked to Mom tonight. I told her it was okay to call me. I may live to regret that. But I can't isolate myself forever. They are my family. She did her usual crazy stuff—asking me questions, then cutting me off mid-sentence, listing all the reasons I shouldn't move, not understanding that I want to, blaming me for not visiting. Her "Oh, well, I thought so" response to finding out I didn't get the job I applied for was typical.

Why is it so damn important to me that she'll care? She won't. No matter what I do it will never be good enough. When I do what she wants, she changes it, so I'm not doing what she wants. Why go through this? Why change? She's never going to see that I've changed.

Jessica

Clients may realize that abuse from the family has never really ended; it has just gone underground. As an adult, Taylor was written out of her parents' will whenever she did something that displeased them. Her family refused to allow her to become an independent adult. She recognized she was punished for marrying, for having children, and for pursuing a career. She was forced to choose between functional adulthood or slavery to family sickness. Meredith recognized she was still being forced to encounter her father in various stages of undress. Chelsea saw that her mother's criticism and verbal brutality were substitutes for childhood battering.

Clients may also become aware that many of their adult relationships have been abusive. They have a right to be angry that they were set up to be the victims of repeated violation. If they were stripped of boundaries, if they were robbed of their inborn fear reflexes, if they were taught that physical and emotional violence were normal and deserved, then violence and abuse became routine. They may have been victimized again, not because they are sick or attracted to violence, but because it is a familiar pattern for which they have well-established skills and defenses. They find themselves caught up in violence again not because they are comfortable with it but because it feels acceptable and fits into their coping mechanisms.

Similar to so many survivors, Jessica recognized that abuse was not isolated to parents and to childhood. An unsent letter helped Jessica free herself from the shadow of a violent boyfriend.

W——

> This letter should have been written a long time ago, but I never had the nerve to say what I need to say to you. You harassed me and scared me for four years, and then you haunted me for the next eight years. It's time to end this now. You were so sick. You used to get wasted and drive on the wrong side of the road and dodge cars. If anyone looked at me, you chased them with your knife. I wasn't allowed to talk to any of my male friends. Then I wasn't allowed to see my girlfriends, either. I had to go directly home from school because if you called and I wasn't there you would come over and be furious and yell and hit. I felt like a prisoner, and I was too scared to leave you. You had lots of threats. I didn't tell you where I was moving, and I figured you wouldn't find me. I haven't heard from you since, but I feel like you're still screwing up my life, and I'm still letting you. I think you're a bastard for what you did, and you should be locked up so you don't hurt anyone else. You're a monster and I hate you. I am not willing to have you mess with my head anymore. I am sorry I ever let you in my life and let you do what you did to me. I won't ever let you near me again—so get lost.
>
> Jessica

Just because survivors are healing, there is no guarantee that someone will not try to harm them again. It may be deliberate cruelty or unintentional carelessness, or they may be victims of a criminal who robs or physically injures them. They need to believe that they do not wear a sign that says, "Hurt Me." An attack does not mean something is flawed in them or their recovery. It does not mean they invited the attack or that all they are good for is to be used and discarded. It simply means there are always going to be abusive, wicked people out there, and one of them may stumble into a survivor's life from time to time. Recovery means survivors won't blame themselves if something bad happens, nor will they stay around and try to "fix" the abuser.

BLOCKS TO RECOVERY

Dear Mom,

I'm finding myself wanting to make excuses for you. This is really silly, but I'm scared of losing you. It's silly because you were never really there for me, so I wouldn't be losing you— only my fantasy of what you were and what I wanted you to be.

Jessica

Healing means challenging the beliefs of a lifetime, and that is not an easy task. It means convincing self that the guilt and shame are irrational and mistaken. It means revising the view of reality that has ruled existence for so long. It means assigning all the guilt and all the shame where they really belong—to the abuser.

Revising the entire belief system causes a profound shift that shakes the survivor and the survivor's world to its foundations. When survivors begin to entertain this new and more accurate view of reality, when they begin to consider this changed belief system, it feels to them like the sky has suddenly turned green and the trees have become blue. It will take time to adjust and to truly alter deeply learned beliefs. Patience is required as they move through this stage, questioning and requestioning their opinions, their thoughts, their feelings, and their very beings.

There seems to be a final surge of resistance before clients can break out into the light. Framing this as yet one more struggle among the personas makes it less intimidating and easier to overcome.

THE CHILD RESISTS HEALING

The devalued Child balks and returns to core shame: "Don't you understand? This is deeper than fault or blame. I'm flawed and evil and I don't have a right to exist." Survivors' belief that they have no right to be is perhaps the highest wall to climb.

Defining the abuse as assault helps the Child to believe that defense-less does not equal not worth defending. Celebrating the Child's brilliance convinces the Child that unprotected does not equal dumb or bad. Believing and telling the Child's story says that assault and denial do not mean there is no right to exist. And reparenting through trauma assures the Child that feelings once forbidden do not forever deny emotional life.

Greta's Child showed both her reluctance and her trust in alternate hand journaling.

Dear Greta,

I'm feeling tired and scared. We are moving too fast. I can't keep up with you. I'm scared the good feeling will go away. Then I'll feel bad again. I don't get enough sleep. I need more. You can help me by slowing down and putting me to bed earlier. Keep up the nurturing. It makes me feel safe.

Love,
Little Greta

THE DESTROYER FIGHTS HEALING

The Destroyer also combats healing. Its role was to defend the family against exposure and to keep survivors from even thinking about telling the truth. Healing may still hold terror of death. Clients may fear that they or the family will perish if they get well. Surrounded by his group and miles away from his family, Luke could only whisper a challenge to the abuser. Raising his voice was too scary to try.

The Destroyer may get more devious as survivors become able to challenge its messages. As it begins to lose its power to control their thoughts and their lives, it may try a final life-or-death struggle for supremacy. When Ellen discovered the voice of the Destroyer, it shifted to hide itself deeper. The words in her head changed from *"You should kill yourself"* to *"I should kill myself."*

Mimi drew the Destroyer as violent orange-yellow flames that engulfed the Child. She recognized she had internalized the abuser's anger as self-hatred, which still tortured the Child and kept the Child out of reach of the Adult trying to rescue her. Mimi needed to see that escape would be possible when she directed that anger back to the abuser (see Figure 15.1).

Client exercise: Figure out how the Destroyer still speaks to you or acts in your life. Does depression exhaust you and rob you of the energy you need to talk and to heal? Does overeating shut your mouth? Do you criticize and judge yourself or feel hopeless about recovery? Once you identify those behaviors and thoughts as part of the Destroyer, you can challenge them just as you did previously.

CYCLES OF HEALING

Nothing seems to need to be said anymore. I'm tired of going to therapy. I'm tired of talking. I'm tired of trying to become something I'm never going to be. I'm tired of looking for something I'm never going to find. I lie in bed, and sometimes I don't even know where I am. I'm just sort of floating. I'm never really anywhere—just floating in space. Maybe the nightmares aren't dreams—maybe they're real. Maybe what I think is real is the nightmares. Maybe I really don't exist. Maybe there is no world—only space and floating. Maybe the times when I'm floating are the only times I'm real.

I'm real worried that if I get healthy and they don't, then I'll fall back into my old patterns. I'm also worried that I won't be able to stay undepressed. I'm tired of flying and dropping and flying and dropping.

Jessica

FIGURE 15.1. Mimi's Child and Destroyer

Recovery goes in loops or cycles. It is predictable that clients will revisit old behaviors as they strive to change and grow. A return to childhood defenses does not mean that recovery is going backward. It just means they are testing the strength of those childhood patterns, maybe for the last time. When a foreigner can't understand them, most people's first instinct is to talk louder. When something doesn't work, people usually try harder to make it work the old way before they are ready to try a new approach.

It is natural for deeply instilled behaviors to come back under stress, and no one can claim that changing core survival beliefs and behaviors is not stressful. When people move to England, they soon learn to drive on the left side of the road, and after some practice they get good at it, and it becomes almost second nature. But if they leave for work late one morning after burning the toast, misplacing the car keys, and having an argument with the person they live with, they swing out of the driveway onto the right side of the street, the side they originally learned to drive on, heading for a rude awakening somewhere down the road.

Rather than condemn the temporary return of old patterns, clients can begin to use their reemergence to celebrate progress. Every time they catch themselves in an old defense, they will struggle harder to shake it off. Each cycle back into an old pattern leads them one loop higher in the upward spiral of recovery.

Clients can also begin to use the return of the Destroyer to celebrate recovery. Its bullying means that they are struggling against the Destroyer's messages. Why would they need to feel depressed or suicidal if they hadn't defied the Destroyer and broken the old rules? Why would they need to feel wrong if they weren't right? It is the Destroyer that is doomed, not them.

The cycle of recovery is just that—a cycle of ever-increasing levels of healing. Clients will take and retake the same steps many times. That should not be discouraging, but energizing. The difficulty of the path they have chosen to travel should not be underestimated, but clients can learn to take credit for each step along the way. They are approaching the bend around which lies journey's end—integration and transformation.

Melanie's poem spoke to both the repetition and the rewards of the cycles of healing:

Healing

And I struggle, and I fight,
And I journal and I write.

And I think, and I fight,
And I journal and I write.

And I feel, and I fight,
And I journal and I write.

And I remember, and I fight,
And I journal and I write.

And I doubt, and I fight,
And I journal and I write.

And I rage, and I fight,
And I journal and I write.

And I grieve, and I fight,
And I journal and I write.

And I fear, and I fight,
And I journal and I write.

And I believe, and I fight,
And I journal and I write.

And I give up, and I fight,
And I journal and I write.

And I struggle, and I fight,
And I journal and I write.

And I scream, and I fight,
And I journal and I write.

And I sob, and I fight,
And I journal and I write.

And I shake, and I fight,
And I journal and I write.

And I trust,
'Cause I must.

And I know,
And let go.

And I care,
And she's there.

And I'm real,
And I heal.

And I'm me,
And I'm free.

And I love . . .

- *Intervention:* Repairing developmental damage.
- *Rationale:* Expand repertoire of coping skills.
- *Result:* Alteration in self-defeating behavior patterns.

Chapter 16

The End of Healing

Fully integrating the Child and the Adult and achieving a healthy accommodation to the trauma are the ongoing and final tasks of healing. As that happens, the client's beliefs about self and the world undergo a gradual transformation. The client begins to consistently define self as worthwhile rather than worthless—a person to be valued and protected, a person who deserves to thrive. The client discovers at the center of self a real identity rather than an empty shell or a bottomless pit. Stage II recovery is characterized by an acceptance of self and an acceptance of history that anticipates further growth and enhancement. Life becomes an adventure to be enjoyed rather than a sentence to be served.

Recovery is not about becoming a whole new person with all new skills. Clients are working to fill the developmental gaps they have identified. However, recovery is also about learning to use the skills they mastered in childhood, by choice, not by compulsion. Just because skills were overpracticed does not make them bad. Recovery is about understanding how brilliant those skills are, fine-tuning some of them, and making them deliberate options. Rather than having defenses take over unconsciously, clients can purposely choose to use them when they can be helpful. For example, if they have always suppressed feelings, they can learn to identify and express feelings, but numbing out when a crisis needs to be handled will always be a strategy available to them. They now know how to add debriefing from trauma after the crisis has passed.

The wonderful talents clients bring from childhood are an ample foundation for recovery. Although the ways they had to learn those skills were awful, they learned them nonetheless. Nothing or no one can take those skills away.

The skills clients used in childhood were helpful and necessary for survival then. Transferred into adulthood unaltered, they may be less helpful, and even interfering, with fulfillment now, but their core value remains.

IDENTIFYING SKILLS AND STRENGTHS

Strengths I've developed due to abuse:

Numbing and splitting—I can disconnect in an emergency situation; I can hold conversations and not really be there.

Independence—I can take care of myself; I don't need anyone to protect me.

High tolerance to pain—I can take physical pain without it hurting much.

Awareness—I am really aware of my surroundings unless I have split.

Perseverance—I usually keep at something until it's done correctly; I don't quit.

Jessica

The easiest way for clients to identify the particular skills they possess is to examine the roles they played in childhood. Each role demands special strengths, and each role develops special talents. The following is a summary of brainstorming done by workshop participants over a number of years:

Hero

Accomplished
Dependable
Good caregiver
Innovative
Highly motivated
High achiever
Good time manager
Not easily bored
Verbally skillful

Intuitive
Observant
Courageous
Puts up a good front
Able to manage crisis
Reliable
Careful
Good leader
Deliberate

Scapegoat

Assertive
Honest
Direct
Loyal
Good communicator
Risk taker
Persistent
Persevering

Lost Child

Good listener
Creative
Intuitive
Independent
Accepting
Not overreactive
Perceptive
Introspective
Sensitive
Empathetic

Mascot

High-impact person
Flexible

Good public speaker
Icebreaker
Energizer
Hangs in there
Motivates others
Good with children
Doesn't take life seriously
Optimistic
Relieves tension
Extroverted
Spontaneous

Client exercise: Identify the skills and strengths that are yours as the result of the roles you played in childhood.

Clients had to play the roles assigned to them in childhood all the time, no matter what was going on, so sometimes the skills and strengths didn't fit and caused problems. Now they have choices. They can begin to use their skills and strengths intentionally to move toward the goal of healthy adulthood.

The very defenses clients have condemned as defects need to be redefined as positive and powerful pluses. They may have ordered the chaos of childhood with ritual, and they may have had to become superresponsible, but as they modify the compulsive quality of those skills, they will find there is no employer who does not favor the organized and competent worker. They may have had to be aggressive to attract attention and to take abuse that would otherwise have fallen on someone weaker, but translated into assertiveness, this toughness empowers adult boundary setting. Disappearing into the woodwork and becoming invisible may have been necessary to avoid injury, but there are many occasions when quiet observation balances the noisy demands of more impulsive people. Distracting and entertaining may have been a childhood career, but there is no task that does not benefit from a leavening of laughter.

All the skills survivors learned in childhood shared the hidden agenda of caretaking and enabling others to be dysfunctional and abusive. The unhealthy purpose they served then does not change their healthy potential. Recovery allows survivors to free themselves from the resentment of caretaking—doing for others what they should be doing for themselves. They can now choose the rewards of caregiving—supporting both themselves and others as they meet their own needs.

INTEGRATING AND TRANSFORMING CHILDHOOD DEFENSES

Rather than continue to use skills blindly to caretake others, take the blame, retreat, or distract, clients can now reject the less helpful and less useful parts of childhood defenses and mobilize their more helpful and more useful qualities to enrich life. Drawing on the strengths from the various roles, the client can become responsible to self rather than responsible for others, a protector rather than a blamer, an initiator rather than an avoider, an actor rather than a reactor.

As they protect and parent the Child, survivors forge a new and deserved place in the universe and bring to full circle the devastation of childhood. The coping skills they had to learn become the Child's gifts that allow them to reclaim self-esteem and self-identity. That desolate childhood wasteland becomes a fertile garden of talents that other people, raised in less violent surroundings, never had the need nor the opportunity to develop. Consciously using these skills gives survivors an edge on human interaction and growth that others simply do not posses.

> *Client exercise:* Write a plan outlining to the Child the ways you will use your skills to parent yourself.

Now, verbal affirmations will work because the affirmations can be anchored in the client's own history. Clients can praise brilliant skills sourced in childhood instead of reading affirmation lists from a book. Even so, countering a lifetime of labels requires a real effort. It may take more than ten "brilliants" to undo 10,000 "stupids." A five-step process solidifies the affirmation. Clients think the affirmation to themselves; they write it down; they say it out loud; they say it out loud to someone else; they look in a mirror and say it out loud. Eye contact locks the affirmation in place. What clients didn't see reflected in the eyes around them when they were little, they will now see reflected in their own eyes. Looking at themselves while saying the affirmation comes last because they need to truly believe the message before they can mirror it back to themselves.

The stage is set for gratitude. As survivors let go of the less helpful and less useful parts of defenses from childhood, their skills are transformed into healthy adult behavior. Some defenses need to be eliminated completely because they were necessary only for surviving abuse, such as self-harm and self-punishment. Survivors don't deserve to be abused ever again by anyone, least of all themselves. However, hurting themselves gave them some sense of control and hope when they were too little to stop the abuse. It is important for survivors not to rudely discard the very things that kept them alive as children.

Client exercise: Write a letter thanking your childhood defenses for the ways they helped, even as you assign them to their rightful place in the past.

Greta wrote a final farewell to the eyebrow and eyelash pulling that she had long considered a horrible defect:

Dear Eyebrow and Eyelash Pulling,

I'm supposed to write you and tell you why I'm grateful I found you and to thank you. I thought about that. At the time it was happening, I felt you were a bad thing I was doing. I suffered all kinds of abuse for pulling my eyebrows and eyelashes. So it is a new idea for me to think about the positive aspects of you.

I didn't do any of this consciously. I am grateful to you that you came to me without my having to think of you consciously. I am grateful I found you that way. I am grateful to you for getting my father to talk to me for five years. He probably wouldn't have if I hadn't been pulling my eyebrows and eyelashes. Thanks to you I got touched and noticed and less abandonment. If I had had more abandonment, I might have been a lot sicker or died. Even though the touching and attention were negative, I needed them to survive. Thank you for helping me to survive.

Greta

RELEASING THE ANGER

Integration and transformation do not need to include forgiveness if clients are unable or unwilling to forgive. On the other hand, forgiving may now be the only logical conclusion. Clients must not confuse forgiveness with absolution, however. The act of forgiving acknowledges wrongdoing. Absolution means an absence of guilt. Only the Child is worthy of absolution.

If survivors find themselves unable to forgive, it is time at least to release the anger. Survivors needed every ounce of their anger to ignite and power healing. Now that anger has served its purpose. Its residue can smolder into bitterness and resentment that will suffocate joy and block the path to wholeness. Releasing the anger does not mean that survivors will return to pretending the abuse didn't happen, nor does it mean that they have to let abusers back into their lives and leave themselves open to further assault. It simply means that they are ready to walk free and unburdened into the world, leaving the ashes of the abuse behind.

Clients who have been driven by anger may fear that if they let it go there will be nothing left and they will be empty. However, they are no longer numb; they can now choose the feelings they want to replace the anger.

Deb's bottle cracked open and the anger spewed out, releasing all the buried feelings and making way for a healed and whole self that could finally be real (see Figures 16.1 and 16.2).

Clients can create rituals for letting go of the anger. Ceremonies catalyze and reinforce healing because they are active and because they create visual images that become landmarks in the journey.

Client exercise: Write about your anger or draw a picture of it. Then tear it up, or burn it, or bury it, or scatter it on the abuser's grave or into a river or a lake.

FIGURE 16.1. Deb's Bottle Cracking Open

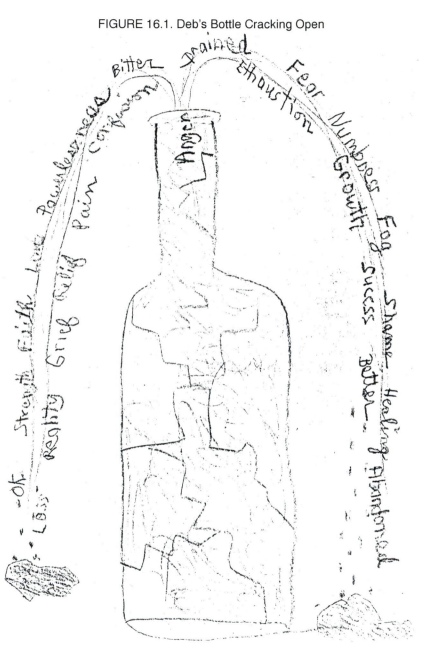

FIGURE 16.2. Deb's Healed and Whole Self

If an abuser does remain part of the client's life, that person may accidentally or deliberately manage to hurt the client again. The client will be angry all over again. That does not mean that healing has been flawed or that the anger about the past has not been released. It means that there is new abuse, and there is fresh anger to address.

INTEGRATING AND TRANSFORMING HISTORY

Dear Daddy,

I believe this is the hardest letter I've ever tried to write—hard because in writing this I'm finally acknowledging on paper something I believe I finally accepted in me not too long ago. I finally accept, not just acknowledge, that you were the Night Monster in my closet and you are the man who abused me and hit me. You are also the man who told me funny stories to make me laugh and built snowmen with me in the winter. You hugged me when I cried, and you were the one who told me to believe in myself and I could become whatever I dreamed. Well, Daddy, I do believe in me now. I believe that I am sane, not crazy as you would like others to think I am, and, most important, I believe that you are human. You are not the super-god I built you up to be as a child—the all-perfect, all-wonderful, do-no-wrong father that every girl should be so lucky to have. You are also not the all-terrible, all-horrible, cruel and vicious monster that I have come to think of you as in the past two years.

Jessica

Clients' perceptions of the past will become more balanced. Out of the denial of childhood to the all-consuming rage of the early healing stages will grow a tempered view of childhood for what it really was—part good and part bad. No childhood, like no family, is altogether miserable. Similar to Jessica, survivors may come to see that there was happiness in the midst of horror.

INTEGRATING AND TRANSFORMING FEELINGS

Now the Child will push to complete the cycles of emotion frozen during childhood. The discharge may be at first sideways. Clients may simply be aware that their reactions to daily life events are exaggerated. It's easy for them to judge themselves crazy or out of control at such moments. Instead, they need to look at the circumstances to which they are responding. Are there any reminders in the present of something they were forbidden to have feelings about when they were growing up? Is someone blaming them, invalidating their feelings, or threatening them in some way? Is another child being hurt or criticized for normal childhood behavior?

Rather than condemning themselves for overreacting, clients can use these times as opportunities to further healing. Using the self-parenting techniques they have learned, they can find healthy ways to validate and vent the feelings. The promise for outlet, even if it can't happen immediately, will stop the old tendency to numb out, and it will also allow them to approach the current situation more calmly.

Client exercise: Do some focused journaling to the Child, defining the similarities between past and present and then separating the two: "That was then; this is now." Hear and respond to the Child's rage or terror or pain: "You had a right to feel angry then, and you can feel angry now." Outline a plan for venting past feelings that is both safe and healthy: "When I'm alone tonight I'll let you shout, or pound pillows, or run around the block really fast to let the anger out."

INTEGRATING AND TRANSFORMING THE DESTROYER

It is time for clients to finally let go of the harmful pieces of the Destroyer they have been challenging all along. Because introjecting is a normal stage of childhood development, and because no family is completely bad or dysfunctional, they will find some internalized family rules and beliefs that deserve to be salvaged. They can separate and reject the hurtful parts of the Destroyer but keep the useful parts that ensure safety, guarantee survival, and provide wisdom. They can merge the parts of the Destroyer that speak to health and protection into their self-parenting plan. They can claim a positive legacy from their families of origin.

The Destroyer, damaging as it has become, really was formed to allow survival in an otherwise unsurvivable environment. The Destroyer's denial of self and independence and its demand for silence really had the client's best interests at heart. At a bare minimum, it kept the client alive.

> *Client exercise:* Write a declaration of independence to the parts of the Destroyer you now want to unlearn, including in your declaration words of thanks for that childhood help and rescue.

Greta called the Destroyer the Phantom Tapes. Her final farewell to the messages of childhood combined both gratitude and angry rejection:

Dear Phantom Tapes,

Thank you for helping me to survive as a child. I needed your help then to survive. I don't need your help anymore! I no longer am buying into "something is wrong with me." I don't need to anymore! You have put in over forty years of service. It is time for you to retire. I don't have to live like that anymore. I can be my own person now. I don't plan to spend the rest of my life like that. I know there is a much better way to live than to blame myself and take on everyone else's blame. It is no longer necessary for me to mutilate myself. I no longer have to feel inferior to everyone else. I know I'm not, and I need to stop feeling that I am. I need to stop being mean to me. I can't do that if I let you keep playing over and over. So stop playing now! You are no longer needed or wanted! Out you go and don't come back! You are a part of the past but not the present or the future. I will no longer put up with you! Get out and don't come back! I won't let you! You will just be wasting your time if you start playing again! You're going whether you want to or not!

Greta

INTEGRATING AND TRANSFORMING
THE CHILD

As clients come to the end of the active part of the recovery process, they will discover that healing is really a lifelong celebration of the Child and the Adult as they move closer and closer to oneness. As they continue to use self-parenting skills to protect and nurture the Child, they will journal evidence of that nurturing and protection to the Child. The Child, in turn, will be freed to drop the defenses of silence and seclusion, becoming gradually the sum of all those creative, joyful, and precious pieces. Clients will use imagery and dialoging and drawing to braid the slender threads of reconnection into a strong, unbreakable cord that bonds the Child to the Adult. The lines between the Child and the Adult will blur and disappear, giving way to a wonderful whole.

Catherine's poem validated her history of self-parenting from her unknowing tries in childhood through her deliberate efforts in therapy:

To Me

You waited until I was stronger;
You held off until I could stand.
You knew I would be the winner,
When you took me by the hand.

When you took me far from Walker Street,
When you taught me how to play,
When you held me tight all by ourselves,
When we knelt together to pray.

When you loved me so each time I cried,
When you never laughed at me,
When you let me tell you everything,
When you smiled to me with glee.

When you believed the unbelievable,
When you took me every week,
To someone who would listen,
Each time that I would speak.

When you bought me the yellow teddy bear,
When you permed my hair in curls,
When you bought me pretty clothes and then,
Told me you were glad I was a girl.

When you kept me far away from drugs,
When you refused to become fat,
When you read and read and never gave up,
When you held me where we sat.

When you let me know that I was real,
When you touched me with your smile,
When you knew that very deep inside,
I was living all the while.

Kevin's dialogue showed a lifetime of cooperation between the Adult and the Child:

Dear Child,

I am learning that I have always been your loving parent. Even when we were little and felt so isolated and invisible, I hoped that somewhere there would be a better, safer place and knew that it was worth it to hang on. The nights I spent alone in my room listening to the radio, I was really taking care of you, although I didn't know it then. And yesterday, when I stood up for myself and wouldn't take the blame for someone else's mistake, I hope you heard that I will never let you or me be guilted or blamed unjustly again. I am teaching people how to treat us. No one can make me a doormat unless I lie down!

Love,
Kevin

Dear Kevin,

Well, you're finally catching on! I always knew that about the doormat. Yesterday my part was scared when your part was brave, but my part was brave when your part was scared.

We both heard the mean voice (the Destroyer), but we didn't listen. I like being you.

Love,
The Child

Dennis promised that same lifelong partnership in poetry:

Pledge to the Little Boy

I have rescued you from past destruction,
And now will protect you from harm and pain.

I will love you as you deserved to be,
And will teach you all you can gain.

The innocence lost cannot be brought back,
But I will show you the good in men, and teach you to be one
   of the pack.

A career as a doctor, of handing out pills,
Instead I'll help you to heal with your heart and good will.

You will live with my family as we work and we play,
Loving and respecting each other a lot very day.

I'll protect you and keep you from the sharp teeth of guilt,
I'll show you that life is for growing, that you just shouldn't wilt.

You see, it was never your fault; you were never to blame;
And I'll tell you this over, 'til I'm old and lame.

You'll grow to be confident that you're a normal old guy,
And that's the kind of happiness that money can't buy.

SPIRITUALITY

Spirituality is not a comfortable part of the therapeutic agenda for all clinicians, but it looms large for many survivors and can silently disrupt the integrative process if it is not addressed. Just as cognitive and emotional development are circumscribed by abuse, spirituality is also underdeveloped (Ganje-Fling and McCarthy, 1996). The question of God's role in the abuse leads to self-abrogating conclusions: "God didn't care about me"; "God willed the abuse"; "God hates me." God's indifference or condemnation wreaks havoc on self-worth and self-esteem (Sargent, 1989). Development of a mature spirituality is difficult when the phase of critical questioning, which leads to a self-determined and internally synthesized spiritual life, is not allowed. Many survivors remain stuck in a faith that is literal and external, loyal to family and childhood precepts (Kasl, 1992). Some survivors abandon spirituality, as they believe God abandoned them.

Although the spiritual journey is uniquely individual, the therapist can at least suggest it as worthy of exploration. It often begins as survivors recognize the brilliance of their childhood defenses and find them sourced in a higher power who could not lift them magically out of the abuse but did give them strategies to survive. The idea that dissociation kept the spirit from being touched by the abuse allows survivors to finally imagine a God who did care and who did not blame.

BECOMING WHOLE

Healing involves accepting that the abuse was real. History cannot be rewritten. The past cannot be changed. However, the abuse will become "something that happened to me," a far cry from "The abuse *is* me; the abuse was my fault." Clients will move beyond the identity of survivor to realize themselves as full persons. They are, after all, the sum of all their parts, the blend of all their life experiences. Abuse and violation are but a piece and not the whole.

Healing also means clients will understand what responses are normal for them, given their histories. When Gwen took a college course on domestic violence, she saw her anxiety and anger as evidence of her lack of recovery. She needed to realize that what looked like overreactivity was really just a natural reaction for a survivor of childhood battering. Other students were reacting differently based on their own backgrounds of nonviolence and safety.

Survivors may always respond more intensely to situations involving abuse of children or to sights, smells, and sounds that are reminders of abuse, and those responses will be normal for them. Identifying their personal triggers gives them a sense of control over such reactions. Defining their reactions as normal for them affirms recovery.

The goal of healing is a healthy accommodation to trauma. There is understanding and compassion for the ways the trauma influenced development, coupled with a responsible and realistic determination to change patterns from the past that are no longer useful. The trauma is no longer denied or minimized, nor does it dominate identity and functioning. If triggers provoke reactions, or if situational or seasonal reminders provoke grief, that does not mean healing is incomplete. It simply means survivors are responding normally, given their histories.

LETTING GO OF THE SURVIVOR IDENTITY

Clients will ultimately need to shed the survivor identity that has been their rock during the intense phases of healing. Surrendering this may not be an easy or even welcome task. After all, discovering what is normal for survivors and accepting that identity for themselves finally gave meaning to their lives. Matt described that stage as wanting to run up and down the street shouting, "I'm a survivor! I finally have an explanation for it all!"

The identity of survivor has allowed clients to make sense of behavior that previously seemed senseless. It has empowered them to move away from being victims to find their own brilliance and strength. It has been the hinge upon which the door to a new worldview and a new self-view swung open. It has given them the right to tell truth and feelings blocked by denial and dissociation. It has opened the gates to reparenting and resolution. As they have healed, they have transformed the damage that was done to them into a source of power. Scar tissue is the strongest tissue in the body.

Moreover, being a survivor has been the focus of much of their conscious and unconscious thought over the months or years of healing. It has periodically consumed their energy and dominated their awareness. Letting go of what they have just learned to be may leave them feeling empty and sad. Remember, even good losses leave a hole.

However, at some point, clients will be ready to embrace life on life's terms as complete human beings, not as victims with no right to exist, and not just as survivors whose right to exist derives only from understanding the impact of their childhood experiences and fighting to undo the damage. Clients will be ready to accept a secure place in the world and to contribute to the ebb and flow of life that surges around them. They will be ready to thrive. And if they choose to reach out and help other survivors, they may find that gives even deeper richness and meaning to their lives (Gravitz and Bowden, 1985).

Clients need to hold on to the identity of survivor until they no longer need to do so. They will know when the time has come to let go. They may find some grief surfacing as they think about taking this step. That does not mean they are not ready. Grieving is simply a natural part of change and leave-taking.

Client exercise: First, write a description of who you are and where you come from that includes all of your qualities, both positive and negative, and all of your history, both joyful and sad. Then write a farewell letter to your identity as a survivor, thanking it for all the ways it helped you to heal.

As clients reach the end of healing, they will come to a different place with their families of origin. They may choose to limit contact, but that will be based on gentle caring for themselves rather than consuming anger at the family. Or they may choose to reenter the family sphere. They can be with the family and not give up their own reality. They will be able to see the family both for what it was and for what it is. They can separate the past from the present. They can maintain their own adult identity in the here and now. If the client is the only one engaged in recovery or if the family has not changed at all, there may be sadness in any renewed relationship, but there will never again be destruction. The circle of protection the Adult has built around the Child will see to that.

THRIVING

This is the point in recovery that most clients become independent and autonomous, taking total control of the process. They intuitively and spontaneously know what they need next. They come to session having done the assignment the therapist planned to give the following week. They cease to depend on the therapist for direction. Instead, they report what they have already done. They set their own course for ongoing healing.

This can be a bittersweet time for both client and therapist, a time of mixed grief and celebration as the therapeutic partnership comes to an end. The therapist who has invested in the process knows that a little part of self goes with the client; the client knows a little part of self will always remain connected to the therapist's office. A ceremony devised by the client to mark the end of therapy can put closure on the therapeutic alliance.

Healing is a process, not an event. It is a never-ending cycle that draws life from the Child and gives it back again. The Child will become a steadfast, glowing presence in adult consciousness, a wellspring of feelings and a beacon for self-care and self-nurture. The survivor will draw from the wisdom and wonder of the Child to replenish the soul.

In harnessing the energy of the Child, survivors are really reaching inward to allow the Child to gift them with their own talents. Just as the Wizard of Oz gave the Cowardly Lion and the Tin Man and the Scarecrow qualities they already possessed, the Child will grant to survivors only that which has been theirs all along.

Sometimes the shift that underlies healing is realized in a moment of inspiration, as in Catherine's poem:

My Song

So now everything is okay;
The pain has finally gone.
And though I waited quite a while,
I can finally sing my song.

The song that's happy and content,
To see beyond the stars.

And now that way down deep inside,
I have healed all the scars.

Even though I am my mother's child,
Now I speak with power.
And though the days, they challenge still,
It finally is my hour.

My time to recollect the past,
To wonder how it was.
And sometimes I am very thankful,
To the One above.

I'm growing now in leaps and bounds;
It's only natural to catch up.
I have only now relief and sighs,
For filling up my cup.

Sometimes healing steals up silently:

I wonder if mom is worried. Is she being found out? Is the facade crumbling? I feel as if she knows I know the secret, that things were not as they seemed. I feel she is fighting to hold on but doesn't fully understand why or what. The cord has been cut. I feel so different inside. The constant hollow feeling is not there. The need to fill up that hole seems to have left me. What an incredible relief!

Marie

Marie wrote a final letter to her abuser:

T——

It has been a long and arduous journey to overcome the damage you have inflicted upon me. I am determined to no longer be a victim. Through talking to whomever would listen, reading numerous books on surviving incest, and finally, through years of counseling, I have begun to travel down the long road of recovery. I've come to realize there is no justification for what you did to me. Your actions will no longer serve as the cement in my wall. I will tear it down, brick by brick, until the wall is gone. As my mind heals, so will my body. Your power over me is no more. I WILL SURVIVE! I just thought you ought to know.

Marie

The words and pictures of those who have traveled the path are more eloquent than any words I can write:

Enough

I don't wish to be anywhere else,
But here with me and mine.
Here inside where all is calm,
Truly is divine.

To reconnect with who I am,
To once again be sane,
To finally know that I am free,
Not to feel the pain.

There is no shame, no horror or fear;
There only is what is.
And I have tools to build the bridge,
Because I have my kid.

I listen softly when she speaks;
I trust her when I do.
For she knows all and life's complete,
Because I am not you.

I'm me, I'm me, I'm only me,
And now I can so clearly see,
That all the secrets weren't so bad,
And now I am so very glad.

The searching has passed; the looking is done.
I'm learning to fill my cup.
And though the process isn't quite over,
I REALLY AM ENOUGH.

Kathy drew the stages of healing and the freedom she found in recovery (see Figure 16.3).

Recovery allowed Heather to flourish and thrive. Her self-image changed from a tiny seedling being struck down by a merciless, knife-edged pendulum to a lush, flowering plant with the scythe forever stilled (see Figures 16.4 and 16.5).

> *When I begin to doubt myself or feel that I am making no progress, I reread my journal and am again amazed at the strength and will to live of my inner child. I owe my biggest debt of gratitude to the little girl who lay sleeping inside me and who now walks beside me. It was she who survived the Night Monster, she who allowed me to remember and to grow, and she is the reason that today I am alive to tell my story.*
>
> Jessica

- *Intervention:* Integration of recovery process and techniques.
- *Rationale:* Achieve healthy accommodation to history of trauma. Solidify positive and realistic self-concept.
- *Result:* Increased self-esteem; increased life satisfaction and engagement.

FIGURE 16.3. Kathy's Picture of Healing

FIGURE 16.4. Heather's First Self-Image

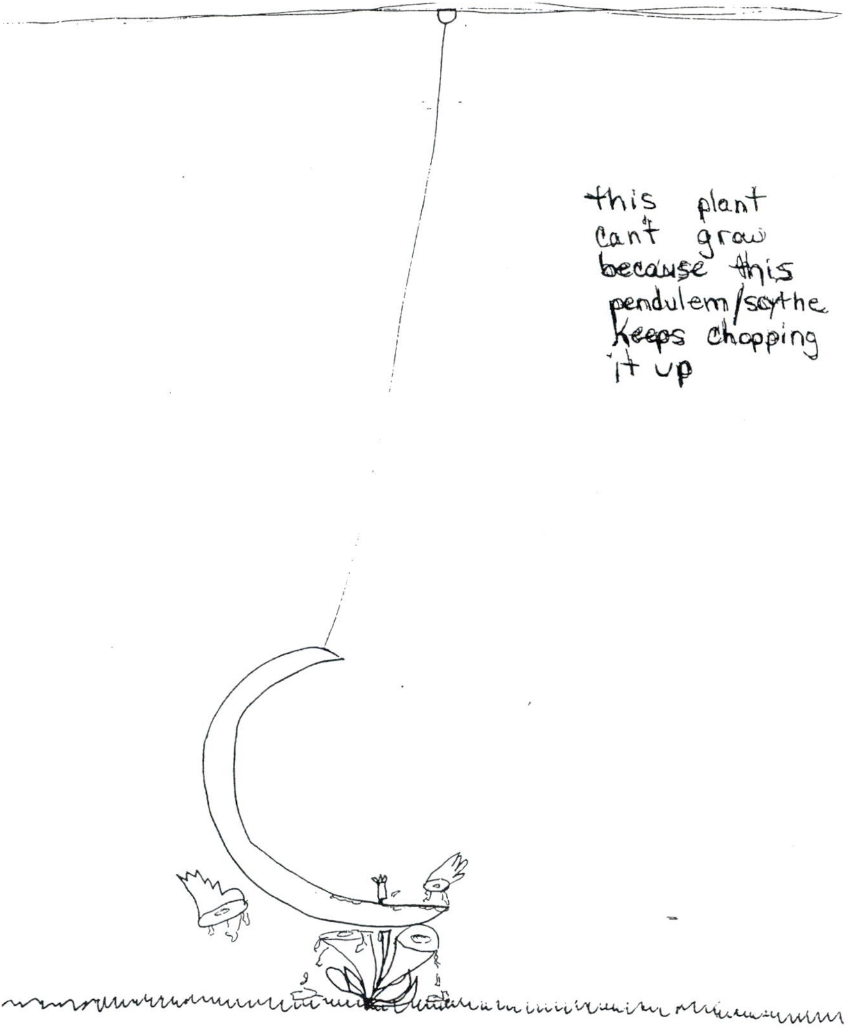

this plant
can't grow
because this
pendulem/scythe
keeps chopping
it up

FIGURE 16.5. Heather's Freedom to Grow

This pendulum, with a scythe at the bottom, has stopped swinging, and the plant can grow now, not being chopped off anymore.

References

Alcoholics Anonymous (1976). *The big book of Alcoholics Anonymous* (Third Edition). New York: Alcoholics Anonymous World Services, Inc.

Alpert, J. (1995). *Sexual abuse recalled: Treating trauma in the era of the recovered memory debate.* Northvale, NJ: Jason Aronson, Inc.

American Psychiatric Association (1987). *Diagnostic and statistical manual of mental disorders* (Third Edition, Revised). Washington, DC: American Psychiatric Association.

American Psychiatric Association (1994). *Diagnostic and statistical manual of mental disorders* (Fourth Edition). Washington, DC: American Psychiatric Association.

American Psychological Association (1996). *Working group on investigation of memories of childhood abuse. Final report.* Washington, DC: American Psychological Association.

Bandler, R. (1985). *Using your brain—For a change.* Moab, UT: Real People Press.

Bandler, R. and Grinder, T. (1979). *Frogs into princes.* Moab, UT: Real People Press.

Bandura, A. (1977). *Social learning theory.* Englewood Cliffs, NJ: Prentice-Hall.

Black, C. (1981). *It will never happen to me.* New York: Ballantine Books.

Bowlby, J. (1969). *Attachment and loss, Volume One: Attachment.* New York: Basic Books.

Bradshaw, J. (1988). *Healing the shame that binds you.* Deerfield Beach, FL: Health Communications, Inc.

Bradshaw, J. (1990). *Homecoming.* New York: Bantam Books.

Braun, B. (1988). The BASK (behavior, affect, sensation, knowledge) model of dissociation. *Dissociation,* 1(2):16-23.

Briere, J. (1989). *Therapy for adults molested as children: Beyond survival.* New York: Springer.

Briere, J. (1992). *Child abuse trauma: Theory and treatment of the lasting effects.* Newbury Park, CA: Sage Publications.

Brown, D. (1998). *Memory, trauma treatment, and the law.* New York: Norton.

Brown, L. and Pope, K. (1996). *Recovered memories of abuse: Assessment, therapy, forensics.* Washington, DC: American Psychological Association.

Carlson, E. (1996). *Trauma research methodology.* Lutherville, MD: Sidran Press.

Denton, L. (1994). Interim report issued on memories of abuse. *American Psychological Association Monitor,* December:8-9.

Erikson, E. (1963). *Childhood and society* (Second Edition). New York: Norton.

Everly, G. (1989). *A clinical guide to the treatment of the human stress response.* New York: Plenum.

Everly, G. (1990). Post-traumatic stress disorder as a "disorder of arousal." *Psychology and Health: An International Journal*, 4:135-145.

Everly, G. (1993). Psychotraumatology: A two-factor formulation of post-traumatic stress. *Integrative Physiological and Behavioral Science*, 28(3):270-278.

Everly, G. and Lating, P. (1994). *Psychotraumatology.* New York: Plenum.

Foa, E. (1997). *Treating the trauma of rape: Cognitive-behavioral therapy.* New York: Guilford Press.

Ganje-Fling, M. and McCarthy, P. (1996). Impact of childhood sexual abuse on client spiritual development: Counseling implications. *Journal of Counseling and Development*, 74:253-258.

Gravitz, H. and Bowden, J. (1985). *Recovery: A guide for adult children of alcoholics.* New York: Fireside.

Grove, D. (1988). Presentation: Healing the wounded child within. Dayton, OH: David Grove Seminars.

Harrison, M. and Kellogg, T. (1992). Echoes of trauma: Counseling and PTSD. *Professional Counselo,* 6(4):25-28.

Herman, J. (1992). *Trauma and recovery.* New York: Basic Books.

Herman, J., Perry, J., and Van der Kolk, B. (1989). Childhood trauma in borderline personality disorder. *American Journal of Psychiatry*, 146:490-495.

Kasl, C. (1992). *Many roads, one journey.* New York: HarperPerennial.

Kramer, P. (1993). *Listening to Prozac.* New York: Viking.

Kritsberg, W. (1985). *The ACOA syndrome.* Deerfield Beach, FL: Health Communications, Inc.

Kritsberg, W. (1993). *The invisible wound.* Deerfield Beach, FL: Health Communications, Inc.

Kübler-Ross, E. (1969). *On death and dying.* New York: Macmillan.

Larsen, E. (1988). *Old patterns, new truths.* New York: Harper/Hazelden.

Marshall, W. and Eccles, A. (1991). Issues in clinical practice with sex offenders. *Journal of Interpersonal Violence,* 6(1):68-93

Marshall, W., Laws, D., and Barbaree, H. (Eds.) (1990). *Handbook of sexual assault: Issues, theories, and treatment of the offender.* New York: Plenum.

Maslow, A. (1970). *Motivation and personality.* New York: Harper and Row.

McCann, L. and Pearlman, L. (1990). Vicarious traumatization: A framework for understanding the psychological effects of working with victims. *Journal of Traumatic Stress*, 3(1):131-149.

Miller, A. (1981). *The drama of the gifted child.* New York: Basic Books.

Miller, D. (1994). *Women who hurt themselves.* New York: Basic Books.

Ochberg, F. and Soskis, D. (Eds.) (1982). *Victims of terrorism.* Boulder, CO: Westview.

Parkside Publishing Corporation (1989). *Help for helpers.* Parkridge, IL: Parkside Publishing Corporation.

Piaget, J. (1952). *The origins of intelligence in children.* New York: International Universities Press.

Piaget, J. (1954). *The construction of reality in the child*. New York: Basic Books.

Piaget, J. (1967). *The child's conception of the world*. Towota, NJ: Littlefield, Adams.

Pope, H. and Hudson, J. (1995). Can memories of childhood sexual abuse be repressed? *Psychological Medicine*, 25:121-26.

Post, R. (1985). Stress, sensitization, kindling, and conditioning. *Behavioral and Brain Sciences*, 8:372-373.

Post, R. (1992). Transduction of psychosocial stress into the neurobiology of recurrent affective disorder. *American Journal of Psychiatry*, 149:999-1010.

Post, R. and Ballenger, J. (Eds.) (1984). *Neurobiology of mood disorders*. Baltimore, MD: Williams and Wilkins.

Post, R., Rubinow, D., and Ballenger, J. (1986). Conditioning and sensitization in the longitudinal course of affective illness. *British Journal of Psychiatry*, 149:191-201.

Sanford, L. (1990). *Strong at the broken places*. New York: Random House, Inc.

Sargent, N. (1989). Spirituality and adult survivors of child sexual abuse: Some treatment issues. In Sgroi, S. (Ed.), *Vulnerable populations: Treatment of sexually abused children, adult survivors, and mentally retarded adults, Volume Two*. Lexington, MA: Lexington Books.

Sgroi, S. and Bunk, B. (1988). A clinical approach to adult survivors of child sexual abuse. In Sgroi, S. (Ed.), *Vulnerable Populations: Evaluation and treatment of sexually abused children and adult survivors, Volume One*. Lexington, MA: Lexington Books.

Shengold, L. (1989). *Soul murder: The effects of childhood abuse and deprivation*. New Haven, CT: Yale University Press.

Terr, L. (1988). What happens to early memories of trauma? *Journal of the American Academy of Child and Adolescent Psychology*, 27(1):96-104.

Terr, L. (1991). Childhood trauma: An outline and overview. *American Journal of Psychiatry*, 148(1):10-20.

Terr, L. (1994). *Unchained memories: True stories of traumatic memories, lost and found*. New York: Basic Books.

Van der Kolk, B. (1985). Inescapable shock, neurotransmitters, and addiction to trauma: Toward a psychobiology of post-traumatic stress. *Biological Psychology*, 20:314-325.

Van der Kolk, B. and Fisler, R. (1995). Dissociation and the fragmentary nature of traumatic memories. *Journal of Traumatic Stress*, 8(4).

Wegscheider, S. (1981). *Another chance: Hope and health for alcoholic families*. Palo Alto, CA: Science and Behavior Books.

Whitfield, C. (1987). *Healing the child within*. Deerfield Beach, FL: Health Communications, Inc.

Whitfield, C. (1995). *Memory and abuse*. Deerfield Beach, FL: Health Communications, Inc.

Williams, L. (1992). Adult memories of child sexual abuse: Preliminary findings from a longitudinal study. *American Society for Prevention of Child Abuse Advisor*, 5:19-20.

Williams, M. (1994). *Handbook of post-traumatic therapy.* Westport, CT: Green-
    wood Publishing Group, Inc.
Woititz, J. (1990). *Adult Children of Alcoholics.* Deerfield Beach, FL: Health
    Communications, Inc.

Index

Page numbers followed by the letter "f" indicate figures.